"A RICHLY ATMOSPHERIC JOURNEY ...
The writing is as muscular and lean as its
canine hero, conjuring up dawn mist or
giant catfish in prose haiku before moving
on to the next killer one-liner."
—*Daily Telegraph* (UK)

TERRY DARLINGTON was brought up in Pembroke Dock, Wales, during the war, between a flying-boat base and an oil terminal. He survived and moved to Staffordshire, where he founded Research Associates, an international market research firm, and Stone Master Marathoners, a running club. Like many Welshmen, he is talkative and confiding, ill at ease with practical matters, and liable to linger in pubs. He likes boating but knows nothing about it.

MONICA DARLINGTON comes from Radnorshire, Wales. Her father was a gardener and her mother was a housemaid—or perhaps it was the other way around. She has a first-class degree in French, has run thirty marathons, and can leap tall buildings in a single bound. Her three children have all reproduced themselves, removing doubts about whether she and Terry are the same species. She quite likes boating but knows nothing about it.

Brynula Great Expectations (JIM) is sprung from a long line of dogs with ridiculous names. Jim can run at forty miles an hour. He is cowardly, thieving, and disrespectful, and he hates boating.

Visit their website at www.narrowdog.com.

NARROW DOG TO CARCASSONNE

Terry Darlington

DELTA TRADE PAPERBACKS

NARROW DOG TO CARCASSONNE
A Delta Trade Paperback / April 2008

*Originally published in Great Britain by Bantam Press,
a division of Transworld Publishers*

Published by
Bantam Dell
A Division of Random House, Inc.
New York, New York

Book design by Steve Kennedy

Library of Congress Cataloging-in-Publication Data

Darlington, Terry.
Narrow dog to Carcassonne / Terry Darlington.
p.   cm.
"Originally published in Great Britain by Bantam Press"–T.p. verso.
Includes bibliographical references.
ISBN 978-0-385-34208-7 (trade pbk.)
1. Boats and boating–France. 2. France–Description and travel. 3. Canals–France.
4. Rivers–France. 5. Canal boats–France. 6. Carcassonne (France)–
Description and travel. I. Title.
GV835.3.F8D37 2008
797.10944–dc22
2007030295

Printed in the United States of America
Published simultaneously in Canada

www.bantamdell.com

BVG   10 9 8 7 6 5 4 3 2 1

To Monica
with love

I am I: thou art she: Jim is him.
T.D.

Contents

NARROW DOG TO CARCASSONNE

One

MOON RIVER

Stone to Westminster

On the floor of the Star Inn Jim was fighting to push his entire body inside a bag of pork scratchings. I could have had a dog that ate its dinner, a dog that barked and wagged its tail, a normal dog, a dog with fur. But the book said a whippet was the easiest dog and I had trouble enough already.

Whippets are hounds—miners' dogs, racers, rabbiters. They are very thin. On top they are velvet and underneath they are bald. They are warm and smell of buttered toast. They love every living creature to a rapture unless you are small and furry and trying to get the hell out of here. They like running the towpaths and thieving off fishermen; but fire up the engine, cast off the ropes, and it's the eyes, the betrayed eyes. So the narrowboat *Phyllis May* has a dog that hates boating.

We'll call him Gonzales, I had said, because he's fast, or Leroy because he's golden brown, or we'll have a dog called Bony Moronie. Good thinking, said Monica, and named him Jim. He's your dog, she said—you look after him. I read *Your Dog Is Watching You*, and *Your Dog Will Get You in the End*, and *How to Stop Your Dog Behaving Like a Bloody Animal.* Jim and I went to school on many dark evenings, but neither of us learned very much.

The door from the canal opened and it was Clive. Like most inland boaters, Clive looks like a pregnant bear. Got you, he shouted—greedy greedy, early drinkies, surprise surprise, make mine a pint. He sat down and slapped his pipe and his Breton sailor's hat on the table. Jim was ecstatic. Jim sees Clive and Beryl as part of our pack, who sometimes make their escape owing to my lack of leadership and poor attention to detail. But through his tracking skills we get them back, and How about some scratchings?

Are you nervous? asked Clive, pulling Jim out of his trouser pocket. Yes, I said. I'm worried about getting away from Stone. I might crash or fall in. People will be watching.

Clive has a Dudley accent, and a deep voice, as if he is saying something important. Beryl and I should never have encouraged you, he said. You are old, you've only got one eye, you are a coward and you can't jump. You're no good at anything useful. Monica ran your business while you wandered around being nasty to your customers.

By the end of the summer I'll be fine, I said. I can handle the fear—running a market research agency scared me stiff too. We had another pint, to handle the fear.

• • •

TWO HUNDRED AND FIFTY YEARS AGO A bunch of engineers met in a public house by a canal. They decided the size of the locks on the English canal system and then they had another round and started talking about girls. In the morning the secretary could not remember what had been decided, or indeed where he was, so to be on the safe side he chose the narrowest gauge mentioned in his notes, which was seven feet. That is how the English narrow lock was born, and the English narrowboat–the cigarette, the pencil, the eel, the strangest craft ever to slither down a waterway.

The five windows of the *Phyllis May* lit the towpath for the length of a cricket pitch. With her flat roof, fairground lettering, brasses and flowers, a traditional narrowboat has a louche charm, though sixty feet by seven is a preposterous shape. Clive and I stepped into the front deck and down to the narrow saloon. Panelling, armchairs, lamps and pictures–second class on the Orient Express. You live in comfort, and you live sideways.

Monica was curled on the sofa. Beryl folded her hands in her lap, in a cornflower stare. Clive stood in the middle of the saloon. We have news, he said–we are forsaking earthly things. We are selling our house and our possessions, giving what is left to the poor, and having a narrowboat built, on which we will live out our days. Ah the poor earthbound rabble, tramping their warren streets–for me the silver highway, the gypsy life: my companion the heron, lone sentinel of the waterways, my constituency the ducks, my gardens the broad valleys, my drawing room the public bar of the inn called Navigation. I've been trying to persuade the bugger for years, said Beryl.

But first we are going up the Bristol Channel with you on the *Phyllis May*, said Clive. But I am not going up the Bristol

Channel on the *Phyllis May*, I protested. The *Phyllis May* is a canal boat. There are fifty-foot tides and the Severn Bore. We will finish up dashed through the window of Woolworths in Bewdley. I don't think there is a Woolworths in Bewdley, said Clive, but if there is I can pick up a CD of Felix Mendelssohn and his Hawaiian Serenaders. And next year when you go to France we will all put out to sea together, and sail across the Channel side by side.

I could feel my palpitations coming on. Clive, I said, narrowboats don't sail across the Channel. I was brought up by the sea. I remember the empty seats in school when boys drowned themselves. I might sail the *Phyllis May* to France if there were thirty Tommies to take back and it would tip the balance in the struggle for Europe. Otherwise it's the lorry, and a crane into Calais.

Let's have a drop more of that Banks's, said Clive—you know I have blue water experience. You mean we went out once from Padstow, said Beryl, in a cruiser, and nearly drowned. That was a trick of the tide, said Clive. But they warned you, said Beryl, they begged you, they called it the Maelstrom and you went straight into it. But we got back in, said Clive. Yes, said Beryl, we got back in.

Is this Old Speckled Hen a strong one? asked Clive—it tastes so smooth. The thing is you rope them up together side by side, so if one breaks a belt on the engine the other tows it out of the way of the tankers and car ferries. Piece of piss really. Clive, I said, you come from Dudley, you have been to sea once and you nearly didn't come back, and now you want to put at hazard the December years I could spend in the Star or watching Kylie Minogue on the box.

But narrowboats are like those toys, said Clive. The bottom is full of bricks so they roll back. What about that chap, I said, who built a narrowboat in Liverpool and set out across the Irish Sea? How did he do? asked Clive. No one ever found out, I said. Must have run into a maelstrom, said Clive. Is that single malt as good as you say it is? He sat back and smiled. Jim looked at him with eyes full of love. He had found a leader at last.

When I woke up the next morning, and I wished I had not woken up the next morning, I realized that I had agreed to sail an inland boat across the English Channel, roped up to a madman.

A CANAL LOCK IS A SIMPLE IDEA. YOU CLOSE the gate behind you and empty the water out at the other end and you sink down, and then you open the gates in front of you and sail away. Going up you fill the lock instead of emptying it. In real life locks are dark and slimy and foaming. They flood you and hang you by the stern. Often they don't work. But today I wound up the paddles in the lock gate with my new aluminium key without spraining my wrist, and when the lock was empty heaved on the beams and opened the gates without shouting for help. The *Phyllis May* mumbled out of the Star lock into the sunshine, Jim riding shotgun on the roof.

Friends and family waved. Pints were brandished in the sunshine and granddaughters wept. The swans that nest below the Star dipped their beaks and raised them in perfect time. Past the tower of St. Michael's, to drinking, and dancing, and waving, and tears, and coarse encouraging shouts. A Cunarder leaving New York, country style.

Under Aston lock the Trent valley falls away in spires and farms. It's like Ulysses, I said, whom I so closely resemble.

Come, my friends,
'Tis not too late to seek a newer world . . .

It may be that the gulfs will wash us down:
It may be we shall touch the Happy Isles,
And see the great Achilles, whom we knew.

Your dog has jumped ship, said Monica, and is probably in Rugeley. And there is a corpse under the prop, so you'll have to go down the weed-hatch again.

WHEN MONICA AND I BOUGHT THE *PHYLLIS May* she was worn out, and we had her refurbished. We had not had a boat before and sometimes we would go down to the cut and lick her all over. We loved the gangling shape and the long windows, we loved the curve of the bow and the front deck where you could sit, and the teak and oak saloon running on and on into the galley. We loved the iron stove, the shower that worked, the little bedroom cabin, the warm engine-room. We held the grab-rail along the roof and walked the gunwale, trying not to fall in. I would stand on the back counter, leaning on the tiller, musing upon our boatyard manager's sins and on the follies of the yard before him.

But one day we found a boatyard we could trust and soon we sailed away, in shining grey and white and crimson, with primroses on the roof and a brass tunnel light at the bow, and our names on the engine-room in fairground lettering a foot high, and ran into the first bridge.

The *Phyllis May* is not right yet—no narrowboat is right yet. Lumps of metal drop into her bilges, or she leaks from the rear. Then I strip naked, grease myself all over, and hang upside down among the ironmongery, grunting and cursing. It is dark, it is wet, I freeze and I burn and I get stuck and we call out the boatyard anyway. I have gone all sweaty in my hair so let's talk about something else.

Jim lets me use his kennel as my office. I put my laptop on it and sit on the coal-box with my feet on Jim. The coal-box has *Phyllis May* painted on the front side and *Kiss Me Again* on the backside. Jim lies quietly under my feet, which is more than my secretary ever did, and sometimes he licks me behind the knees, and in forty years in business there was no chance of that. In pubs he is the cause of much wise country talk about lamping for rabbits, and is seen as the next best thing to a lurcher. The trouble is he camps everything up.

In Stone I fastened him outside the supermarket. When I returned he was in the arms of an old man in a cloth cap. Both were crying softly. I crept away. I came back and a crowd had gathered. In the middle lay Jim, pretending to be dead. Was this your dog? asked a lady.

On the boat I opened a bag of pork scratchings. Jim manifested himself at my knee. He sat down—Can I have a scratching? Then he lay down—Please can I have a scratching? Then he rolled on his back and waved his legs in the air—Please please can I have a scratching? Then he sat up and looked straight at me—What do you want me to do—sing 'Moon Fucking River'?

A cathedral of oaks to Fradley, and we moored at the end of the nave.

CALL ME MOZZA, SAID OUR NEW FRIEND IN THE cowboy boots, settling into my chair. Some people call me Mad Mozza, he added proudly. He was a sturdy young chap, maybe forty, with sandy hair and blue staring eyes. Cheers Mozza, I said, I'm Terry and this is Monica and you've met

Jim. We're really grateful Mozza, said Monica—Terry loves that dog.

He stole Captain's bone, said Mozza, and ran away—Captain didn't stand a chance. Jim looked out of his kennel, his eyes wide—He begged me Your Honour, Steal my bone; he went down on his hands and knees. He was on the road, said Mozza, but he came to me. They come to me because I have The Power. Would you like a cup of tea? asked Monica. Er yes, said Mozza. I poured him half a tumbler of rum.

I know this boat, said Mozza—*Starbuck.* Billy Ishmael had her built—lived on her for ten years. Knows his boats, Billy. Very artistic. Carried him home twice from the Plum Pudding in Armitage. Goodness, said Monica—but we are really pleased with her shape, Mozza: the low line, the big windows, and we've kept the grey. The lettering on the engine-room is not bad, said Mozza—why *Phyllis May*? My mother, I said, rest her soul—she still comes back. They come back all right, agreed Mozza. We had another rum, to stop them coming back.

We just retired, I said, and we bought a little house and we bought the boat and we bought Jim. We keep crashing into things and running out of fuel and falling in and people shout at us and stick notes on the door. Maybe we started too late. It's a way of life, agreed Mozza. You've got to be born to it. To tell you the truth, at your age you would probably be better off in a home—you must be a menace to the navigations. You're right Mozza, I said, but you can't get the beer.

Click click, said Mozza. Pardon? I said. Click click, said Mozza, let the water in click by click. Oh yes, I said, that poor chap last summer, two locks behind us. The lock filled too fast, knocked overboard by the tiller, engine in reverse, cut to pieces. Wife, two kids. Click click, said Mozza. What's the hurry?

We want to go south to see if we can handle the big rivers, explained Monica. This year we want to go down to London and past the Houses of Parliament and up the Thames and along the Kennet and Avon Canal to Bristol. Next summer we want to go to Paris, and the summer after to Carcassonne. Never heard of it, said Mozza. It's in France, I said, right down the other end. It's sort of an adventure before it's too late. They say at our age you are at the end of vigour.

Yes, said Mozza, of course you are, just look at you, but what can you do? What do you want to go south for at your age? Why don't you drink yourself to death in the Star like a normal person? Narrowboats belong in the Midlands, in the narrow cuts. They don't work in the big locks; they bang about, they get caught up. They don't work on the rivers; they are too long, too slow, the currents turn them over. Don't you like it here? He had started to wave his arms. We do, Mozza, said Monica, we do like it here.

Staffordshire is good enough for some, Mozza persisted— you can get oatcakes and pork scratchings and people talk to you and you can understand what they are saying. You don't get the southerners here. You can go line-dancing. I go line-dancing all the time and do you know how many legs I've got? He rapped on his knee. And do you know how many legs my dog has got—my poor old Captain Ahab?

Next morning we passed an untidy white cruiser, and Mozza grinned through the window. Click click, he shouted, and threw out a black Labrador cross with three legs, which staggered about and fell sleepily back on board. Click click, cried Mozza, click click.

I'm glad you didn't tell Mozza we are sailing across the Channel, said Monica, he gets upset. Who said we're sailing across the Channel? I asked—we can't even steer yet. We'd miss. We are not boaters, we are civilians. And the sea is not all limpet shells and sandcastles. Have you ever watched a spring tide go by at ten miles an hour? Christ Mon, enough is enough—we are supposed to be retired. You told Clive we were doing it, said Monica. He was drunk, I said, he won't remember.

THE CANALS ARE THE OLD WORK OF GIANTS, and fifty years ago they lay desolate. It took heroes to save them and now the cuts seethe with fish and birds, and flow for thousands of country miles up slopes, down valleys, along mountains, through hills, and across the flats of the East Midlands. We muttered east down the Trent and Mersey Canal, on to the river Trent at Shardlow. It was April and every week they changed the flowers for something more seasonal madam.

At Trent Junction the Soar joins the Trent and you turn right for Leicester and London. On the ampler current you sway and go faster and you feel you are on a real boat. The new engine, *ma petite folie*, my pride, left the mornings as quiet and clean as we found them. Even the fishermen smiled. The engine was built in Bordeaux for the fishing boats that go out into the Bay of Biscay, and the people that make them don't mess about. A great deal was going to depend on the engineers of Bordeaux.

We locked and drifted to Loughborough, without impatience, periscoped by grebes, and crowds of Queen Anne's lace waved from the banks.

WHEN A BOAT ARRIVES MOST TOWNS SAY OH my God, you're here already, I'll just get a few things out of the children's room. Others throw a stone or a curse, and some redecorate and wait for you in the parlour. Loughborough shows you to the garden shed, throws in a bun and locks the door.

Jim and I picked our way through a brickyard and on to the main road. The first pub turned us away without apology, and at the second there was no room for us in the inn. At the third I paused at the door and pointed down at Jim. A couple of people at the bar nodded furiously so we went in.

What is it? asked one of the nodders. A whippet, I said. The nodder was a small man, illustrated with tattoos and covered in white powder. I'm Ken, he said, and this is Mario–I'm a plasterer. What's his name? Jim, I said. Gin? asked Ken. No, Jim, I said. My mother had a dog called Gin, said Ken, it's a small world–why do you call him Gin? My wife likes a drop of Gordon's, I said, giving up. I was a mercenary in Africa, said Ken, I saw terrible things.

Mario broke in. Why your dogga so thin? It's a whippet, I said, it's the breed. They don't like food except pork scratchings–they live on them in the wild. I am waiter, said Mario. You not believe the food goes out the back. I will give you some every day for your dog and then he will not be such a small thinna dog. Jim looked up at him with starved and grateful eyes. I am sixty-five, said Mario. I was in the war in Italy. I saw terrible things. Can I have bagga scratchings? he called over the bar.

Clive rang when you were out, said Monica–he wanted to tell us about their new boat. He's having portholes. Portholes? I said–portholes? For cheap good looks he gives away the world. Each of our windows can hold a full cloud. Is it for this that the canal hero Robert Aickman cruised the dying waterways comforted only by his beautiful secretary Elizabeth Jane Howard? Was it so generations to come could sail the silver highway in blind portholed poncing boats, full of washing machines and televisions, never to see the sunset canal incarnadine, and the fish rising like rain?

Clive says portholes are a good thing, said Monica, they are more secure. Let them steal all I have, I said. I wish them well–I shall not care if I can see the sky. That isn't what he meant, said Monica. He said that when we are going across the Channel a wave would smash our big windows like an egg, and what are we going to do about it?

I'VE FOUND THE WHIPPET CLUB BREED STAN-dard, said Monica. *Balanced combination of muscular power and strength, with elegance and grace of outline.* Goodness, Jim, who's a pretty boy?

All forms of exaggeration should be avoided. I never knew a living thing that exaggerated more, I said. He is a screamer. He can't say hello without going for the Oscar. If he wants something he pretends he has broken his wrist.

Highly adaptable, said Monica. Not on boats he isn't, I said.

Free gait, hind legs coming well under body for propulsion. Forelegs thrown well forward low over the ground, true coming and going. True at going, I said–he is no good at coming back.

Jim was by the door. It was time to go to the pub and he had broken his wrist.

LEICESTER IS FAMOUS FOR ITS VANDALS, SO IT'S a case of dive at dawn and keep going until you drop dead or get to Kilby Bridge. But Monica and I have been less worried about vandals since we visited the mouth of hell.

The mouth of hell is in Manchester, where hardly flows the filthy Rochdale through a waste of concrete. The address of the mouth is 111 Piccadilly–Rodwell Tower, which gropes the clouds and broods over its terrible secret. Under it the fire, the pit. This is the fault line, where the newly dead meet those soon to die, and trade in drugs and sodomy. As the boat slips under the tower they stand in the darkness and watch. If you are not currently in the drugs or sodomy business they let you pass.

One wraith, a boy in a white singlet, stepped forward to help Monica close the lock. He was frail, dying or dead already—his weight on the beam made no difference. Why don't we go back, said Monica, and save him and bring him up as one of us? I know, I know, I said, but I have got enough on my hands with you and a sixteen-ton boat, not to mention a dog that knows no respect, without getting mixed up with the walking dead.

So we were not afeared when we moored at Leicester, by Abbey Park, gathering our strength for the six-hour leg the next day. Until there came a knocking and a huge figure in rainbow leathers sprang aboard, a spaceman helmet under his arm. Good gracious, said Monica, he's come to kill us all. Showing no fear Jim leaped on the giant as he advanced down the boat, ready to bear him to the ground, lick him into submission, and take him to the pub to buy scratchings.

I am your ranger, said the giant. In fact I am your lone ranger—the other one is off today. I understand you have had your boat let loose. Yes, I said, we had to fetch it back from under the bridge. We have never had boats loosed before, said the Lone Ranger. Yes you have, I said, the security man opposite said it happened on Friday. Ah, said the Lone Ranger, there was Friday. And on Saturday, I said, they let a big barge loose and blocked the whole navigation. There is some truth in that, said the Lone Ranger, but you should not think badly of our city—look how secure this mooring is. But they stepped over the fence, I said. Yes, I suppose you can step over the fence, admitted the masked rider of the plains, but this vandal reputation is not fair. People expect trouble and the kids see the fear in their eyes and take advantage. It's only fun, with a bit of theft and intimidation thrown in. You must take a positive attitude—ours is a peaceful and beautiful city. What time are you leaving tomorrow? Six o'clock, I said.

The sun rises at five, said the Lone Ranger, you don't want to leave it too long.

TO STEER A NARROWBOAT YOU STAND ON THE back, look forward along the roof, and grip between your buttocks a brass broom-handle which is bolted to the rudder. Every ripple strikes to the roots of your teeth. A moment's inattention and sixteen tons of steel and crockery smash into the scenery. If you hit another narrowboat you bounce off, and if you hit a fibreglass cruiser you pass through it, making practically no noise at all.

But boat-owners don't go boating—they leave their craft where moth and rust do corrupt, and mink break through and steal, and sit at home watching *Star Trek*. So we laboured alone down the wide locks of the Grand Union. For days we hit no bridges nor knocked anything off the roof. Then we met the most fearful danger.

I was filling a lock and a gongoozler leaned over the side— Is this your boat, have you come far? A gongoozler is some- one who stares at boaters. Monica answered from the tiller, trying to be polite, holding the boat steady with a rope through a ladder in the wall. But the rope had jammed and as the lock filled the stern of the boat was being pulled under. In seconds water would flood through the engine-room and the *Phyllis May* would sink. Jim was shut inside; Monica had no life jacket and she can't swim. Last year four people drowned like this.

Time stopped and I seemed to watch myself from the outside. I engaged the lock key and dropped the paddle in the lock gate to stop water flowing in. Then I hurled to the other end to let water out. I was barefoot and there were stones and nettles but in my own dimension I was safe from harm. Returning to Greenwich Mean Time and working on my oxygen debt I watched the lock empty and the *Phyllis May* come level. The rope slackened and Monica pulled it free. The gongoozler had fled.

We hung a knife under the throttle so next time we can cut the rope, then I will take the knife and Jim and I will go and find the gongoozler.

NEAR DAVENTRY OUR SECTION OF THE GRAND Union Canal meets the main branch from Birmingham, and together they head south for Milton Keynes and London. The centre of Milton Keynes is black glass and concrete and does not allow dogs or people. Under the flyover the stalls of an outdoor market had sprung, like flowers between the tiles of a urinal.

We moored for a sunny fortnight among the parks and lakes. In the mornings the swans woke us, tapping politely as they cleaned the waterline. In the afternoons we dozed as the ceiling swarmed with light, and in the evenings the radio played the songs we used to know.

Before breakfast Jim would come into the cabin and fix us with his burnt gold eyes–Lazy buggers, what about the run? Your dog is taking over, said Monica, he's gaining control, like it says in the books. No he isn't, I said, he's a whippet, they like to run, that's what they're for. I don't like the way he stares at me while he does his stretching exercises, said Monica, and I don't like the way he sits by the door, lacing up his running shoes and looking at his watch.

As we jogged Jim did fast interval work, then long slow distance, drifting an inch above the ground. He drifted straight, not sideways like a wolf. If we met other dogs he always raced them and he always won. When he met an obstacle he would take to the air, pausing in mid-flight like a dancer.

A DAY DOWN THE GRAND UNION TO LEIGHTON Buzzard. What a nice old-fashioned name, said Monica, and a supermarket right by the towpath. As Jim and I sat on a bench a girl in a leather miniskirt lowered herself alongside. Jim began to lick her blubbery knees lasciviously. Suddenly she rose and struck through the window of a passing car, punching and screaming as her victim fishtailed away. Then she swaggered by with a friend—a young man who had been thrown out of Hell's Angels because of dress sense and body-fat ratio. Jim made a final pass at the knees, but his heart was not in it.

Later we set out through streets paved with chewing gum and kebabs, to look for a launderette. We found one, but there were people fighting inside.

Jim added to the sorrow in this strife-torn community by seizing a teddy bear from a gift-shop shelf and jumping on it. I mean, what do you say? What would you say in France? *Madame*, I am desolated, my small dog has ravished your bear of plush. But *madame*, I insist, I am going to buy it, because my small dog will amuse himself with it well—oh my God let's get out of here.

· · ·

RANKS OF HIPPIE CRAFT ROTTING PEACEFULLY under the hedges—we were near the capital. At Bulls Bridge we turned left on to the Paddington Arm of the Grand Union. We have reached an historic junction, I said to Monica—it is time to pull out the big one. *Faire sortir le grand jeu?* asked Monica. Yes indeed, I said, the hour has come.

We went forward and opened the gas locker, which is the bit you sit on in the front of the boat. It held gas bottles, dead fenders, rusty saws, and the remains of creatures that had crawled in out of the cut, planning to set up home. There was also a bundle that looked like the construction kit for a light aircraft.

When the lavatory tank on the *Phyllis May* is full we call at a marina, which attaches a hose to the boat and pumps the tank out into a green lorry, which drives off and empties itself over the head of the man who runs Railtrack. But in France everything has to go into the cut. So we had bought our own pump-out kit, which we laid out on the bank next to the sanitary station. It looked like a sixty-foot brown snake that had died in congress with a lawnmower, gathering up in its final convulsions other gear and tackle and trim, including a stout hose.

An hour and a half later we had fitted most of the parts into each other. We laid the brown snake down the towpath and put the stout hose in the cut. There was a pump handle and I started pulling on it. The hose reared up out of the canal and stared at us, spitting and hissing. We wrestled it back and started pumping again but once more it appeared, coughing and farting and thrashing, until we twisted it down and it drowned. It was strong and it died hard. Sixty feet away water started coming out of the end of the snake.

Now we wound open the hole on the gunwale and screwed in the hose. Monica went into the sanitary station with the end of the snake and I threw myself into pumping. The little platform on which I stood was flexible, and I was losing my power. When I had lost all my power there was an old man with a face like a doughnut, looking at me with concern. I have been thinking of getting one of those, he said—do they work? I'm from Leighton Buzzard, he added. I'm sure it's a nice town, I said, but personally we found it a bit violent. Violent? he said, well I suppose it is a bit violent. To be honest when I was there I was a bit violent myself.

He stood on the other end of the platform and held on to me. We rocked back and forth, while the snake bulged and Monica's cries of encouragement and success echoed from the sanitary station. I do hope no one was watching.

THE NEXT NIGHT I RANG OWEN IN FRANCE. Owen was once a sergeant major in the South Wales Borderers—we had met on the cut and exchanged visits. Hiya, yelled Owen, as one consummating a bayonet charge upon a terrible enemy.

We're under way, I said. You can steer it can you? shouted Owen. Not quite, I said. But next year we could be over—how are things down there in the Midi? Fine, cried Owen. I had a disagreement with Valmai, so me and Ianto are down the café.

Ianto is a three-year-old white and brown Jack Russell terrier, who shares the inside pocket of Owen's combat jacket with a couple of hand grenades. The love between Owen and Ianto is wonderful, passing the love of women.

When are you coming over, boyo? cried Owen. Next year about this time, I said. How are you going to do it? he asked. The lorry, the crane, I said. There has been talk of sailing, I added with a laugh. Sailing? Owen shouted. You beast, you beast, sailing! He spoke off-mike and there were shouts and cheering. I could hear a table fall over.

You know, said Owen, when I met you I thought you were the biggest wally I had ever seen. I mean you are old and a coward and no good at doing anything. We only put up with you because of Monica. Thanks Owen, I said. In Montgiscard a dog-fight had broken out. Sorry, said Owen, Ianto bit someone. He seemed to think this was very funny. Deep down you are OK, he gasped, go for it, go for it I say, and Terry I shall be there, standing by your side at the tiller, breathing the fresh sea air with you my old boyo, riding the Channel swells my old darling, because Terry you are OK, I have made up my mind about you; you are not a fucking wally after all.

Next morning the phone rang. Terry, last night–did I say you should sail the Channel? Yes, I said. Look, said Owen, I want you to be quite clear about what I actually said. Men have died because they misunderstood my orders. I am not surprised, I said. Now listen, said Owen–I had a word with my friends Gérard and Benny who are *matelots* and we talked it over and I may have misspoke myself. You mean all previous statements are inoperative? I suggested.

Exactly, said Owen–do you know how long you have got before a narrowboat goes down?–two minutes. Do you know the temperature of the Channel in May? No, I said. Fucking freezing, said Owen. Twenty-five minutes and your core temperature has gone and you are dead. Look, I'll be straight with you, I was pissed last night. Really? I said. Yes, said Owen, got carried away. Don't do it Terry, I beg you– take the advice of one who has stared death in the face a thousand times.

You mean you don't want to crew for us then? I asked.
You don't want to stand by my side at the tiller, riding the
Channel swells with your old mate? The trouble with you,
said Owen, is you are a smart-ass.

HOW GRAND LONDON WILL BE—WHAT WATER-
side boulevards, what rich craft, what shining people trip-
ping along the towpaths, pursued by yelling paparazzi! We
drifted under the M40, and then over the North Circular like
Mary Poppins at rooftop height. Harlesden smelt of Lamb
Rogan Josh, with ladies' fingers and two poppadoms.

But the London canal world is a poor shrivelled thing.
There are more canal pubs in Stone than in all London
town, more chandlery, more boat-builders. Little Venice is a
token, a publess wonder, a fraud.

We stole away on the Regent's Canal in the dull heat of
the afternoon, leaving rows of boats looking at each other
and wondering where you could get a pint round here, or a
bottle of gas or a piece of rope to hang yourself. As we slid
through the Zoo, a scream arose from a vulture in its abol-
ished tower—widowed, unconsoled.

In Camden thousands of gongoozlers from the Sunday
markets leaned over the walls, overflowing on to the grass,
staring as we sweated through the locks. Many were drunk
or worse. I had to brush them off the lock beams like flies—
we were on the run. There was only one place on the
Regent's Canal where the boat would be safe from attack by
vandals, and that was Islington, and there were only six
moorings in Islington.

Through a tunnel and into a dark cutting, overhung with
trees. Plenty of room—there were not six boats on the move

in London. A gentleman calling from the bank asked Monica to marry him. Perhaps I should reply on her behalf.

. . . slowly answered Arthur from the barge:

I am going a long way
With these thou seëst—if indeed I go
(For all my mind is clouded with a doubt)
To the island-valley of Avillion . . .

So clear off, wino.

It was four in the afternoon when we climbed out of the cutting. Empty side streets, roadworks, grey houses, grey heat. A café bar with stained shutters. Tin cans, litter. Graffiti: hopeless, inarticulate—*Fuck off*. City Road raged with traffic. Most of the pavements had been dug up. A line of faded trees had lost its way among hoardings and gaps. By my troth, quoth Lancelot, this is a dreadful place.

Going back we pushed at the door of the café, which was cool and spacious and sold thirty-eight Belgian beers. A barmaid with skin like Guinevere brought a bowl of water for Jim. He began to work the tables, beginning with the couple next door, who were dressed for the Tour de France. Then he vaporized and I pulled him by the loins out of a bin in the lane outside. This raised some laughter among the few couples present. They were friendly in their cautious southern way—not much was going on in Islington that afternoon. Look at his little face, someone said, and his big ears, like a mouse. He's a very *narrow* dog, said someone else.

A young man with a guitar began to sing about how his love was making him suffer, but as he was only about seventeen I imagine everything will sort itself out in the end.

Scattered applause—he had a nice voice. He sang another song to make it clear he had suffered even more than he had told us the first time. We paid our bill. It gets very busy later on, said Guinevere, and we believed her.

Back at the boat the cutting was darker than before. Monica's suitor had departed. Good evening sir, madam—a man in green rushed by with a set of keys to lock the iron gates that protected us from the loyal citizens of Islington.

NEXT MORNING THE GRANDEUR OF LIME-house Marina, once Regent's Canal Basin. Tall apartments full of bankers shaving before they shuffle on to the Docklands Light Railway. Here we go, here we go—a million desks, all in a row. The tower and clock of St. Anne's standing back a step, the castle walls of the old basin, a great pool, yachts, cruisers. A few narrowboats in the corner, their roofs piled with herbs, flowers, and bicycles.

From his tower of glass, momentous in his British Waterways overalls, Joe the lock-keeper, God's green deputy, watched over us all. He kept the gateway between the quiet inland waters and the Thames Tideway—turn right for Westminster, Hammersmith, Reading and Oxford, and left for the vasty deep. For a Midlands canal-boat skipper the Thames Tideway is vasty enough, and deep enough too.

Joe said practically all his inland boaters who went out of Limehouse lock on to the Thames lived through the day. I wondered if they were all as frightened as we were and Joe promised they were. Run at normal speed, he said, let the tide do the work, don't push your luck, don't hammer the engine just because you've got some water under you. It's not used to the vibration and something could break.

What's the water quality like in the Thames now? I asked.

Last year we had a dolphin in the Tideway, said Joe. He was frolicking. He was happy with the water then? I asked. I don't know if he was happy or if he was not happy, said Joe, but he was frolicking.

Did you know the man who cleaned up the Thames was called Sir Huge Fish? I asked. Joe thought I was joking. There were funnel clouds in the Channel last night, he said, and it may be rough tomorrow.

Back to the boat to fight with our life jackets and brace ourselves to steer through fleets of thundering craft captained by bearded men all born afloat, all with large and disrespect-ful vocabularies and all drunk.

We did not sleep well.

AT LAST WE HEARD BOATS MOVING INTO THE lock in the darkness. Terrified we followed them, our ropes held by Joe and his Jolly Green Giants. They were cross be-cause we didn't have navigation lights—and surprised we had never heard of them. At first light they let us creep into the throat of the lock and waved good luck. A grey dawn, short jostling waves.

From the bow Monica shouted All clear and I revved on to the great tide and swung right, and we were carried to-wards central London. Full fathom five for a boat that had rarely known a foot of water under her flat bottom. The wa-ter was looser than the muddy element we knew, and there was a lot of it in all directions, some of it in the air. The prop faltered and thrashed but the *Phyllis May* was steady because the waves ran along the hull and held it up.

What had they done with the drunken sailors? There were no drunken sailors; there were no sober sailors. We were alone, except far behind where two more narrowboats out of

Limehouse drew white chalk marks in the grey. No docks, no ships, no wharves, no cranes—it's all over—though you can still see places where things used to happen, some of them quite recently.

I leaned on the tiller round a forgotten brood of lighters and we passed the Tower of London on the right, which sailors call the starboard side. I fancied forty beefeaters lining the walls blowing bugles into the wild wind. They didn't raise Tower Bridge but I felt as if they had.

Then bridge after bridge, all known from memories and books. I was standing inches above the water and could feel the strength of the supports as the tide heaved us through, and see the massive mouldings, the colours.

Under Blackfriars Bridge, past the offices where I had for so long worked for a soap company, coming into the City by train. Save me Lord, in my tower of glass. Monica and I quit, and we made it in our own place, in our own time, and we were free, and now we are back, and sod the lot of you.

The London Eye on the port side, and on the starboard the Houses of Parliament. We had dreamed that one day we would sail the *Phyllis May* past the Houses of Parliament, and now we were doing it. All the MPs came out—we could not see them for the dim light and the spray but we could hear their thin cheers on the wind. They were clapping each other on the back and saying By Jove, if these *Phyllis May* people can do this with the aid of a half-starved dog, heaven knows where they might land!

The bridges swept over us and we were the still centre— the engine roaring, the prop shuddering and gargling, Monica and I at the tiller, Jim brooding below. The *Phyllis May* drove on into the wind, foaming at the neck, most like to a swan.

. . .

THE TIDEWAY ABOVE PUTNEY WAS KNOWN TO me from fifty years ago and had not changed much. Monica says she fell in love with me as I came off the river one afternoon. I wasn't very pretty and I wasn't very nice, but the sun was in my hair and there was a twelve-foot oar on my shoulder.

When respectable people were beginning their day's work, we reached Teddington, moored up and went to sleep. Jim licked us awake in time for lunch and I felt guilty because this was not his day. I still feel sad but as I write he lies half asleep under my feet, and when I move he sighs happily and from time to time he farts.

Two

THE FLIES, THE FLIES

The Thames to the Severn

*Y*ou had a girl in Oxford, didn't you? said Monica. Is that why you want us to go out of our way? In her green eyes flickered a wintry fire. She was older than me, I said, she's dead by now—you know it's always been you since we met. It was the night before my finals, said Monica. I was nervous and you took advantage of me.

The *Phyllis May* picked up her skirts and ran—from Teddington through Richmond, Kingston, Windsor. Easy on the throttle because of Joe's warning, but the sweet Thames ran softly and we made five miles an hour, leaving a tunnel of white prop wash under the water.

The main craft on the Thames are white cruisers. These

are all the same shape but come in different sizes like Russian dolls. Some are twenty feet high, and announce on the stern that they have two engines, each with a power that passeth all understanding. The cruisers are all driven by the same bloke, in a white captain's cap, at his side a fat woman in a plum sun-top, with burned shoulders. In the eyes of God all men are equal, but a narrowboat skipper does not believe this includes stiffs in Tupperware boats. The cruiser captain feels the same about gypsies in sewer tubes, and we all wave cheerfully as we pass.

The other craft on the Thames include boys in rubber rings, sculling shells like long-legged flies upon the stream, drunken Aussies in canoes trying to impress a British sheila, families in rowing boats who have decided to drown some of the children, and slipper launches you want to take home, leaving all else to decay as you varnish them in the garden shed. The outcome is misrule bordering on a shambles. In the Midlands these people would be shouted off the cut. The canals are a precious amenity, for which Elizabeth Jane Howard and many others gave their all. The Thames, with its bounty of green water, is a playground.

AS THE MIST BURNED OFF THE WATER AT Cookham we ran together through the linear parks and by the corn and heaven was nothing to look forward to.

That evening a riot of whippets romped alongside the boat. There was a brown one, a brindled one, one nearly blue, and a white one with a black mask called the Lone Ranger. They are so beautiful, so delicate, said Monica, as they climbed inside her singlet, grinning—are they all yours?

The gentleman on the end of the lead said Yes, they are all mine. I am the chairman of the Thames Valley Whippet

Racing Club. He had a brush-cut and a sour face. We race them, he explained, so they can fulfil themselves without killing anything. They run at forty miles an hour. Over a fifty-yard dash they can beat a greyhound. Did you know that for its weight the whippet is the fastest animal in the world? We knew Jim was fast, said Monica, but no, we didn't know he was the fastest in the world.

It would be all right to kill something if you ate it afterwards, said Monica, I mean that's sort of fair play isn't it? Would they catch rabbits? My dad was a gardener—I can skin a rabbit. I think Jim would like to catch rabbits.

No, said the gentleman. First they have to learn to run after a lure, then they have to run in a muzzle, then they run in lanes, then they race, grouped by how much they weigh. It's a matter of discipline. It takes years. But if they catch a rabbit and taste blood they are finished.

He had with him a little terrible boy. The boy hung on him as he spoke, talking over him. I had to stop myself clipping the boy round the ear. The gentleman explained his dogs had won a lot of trophies and he told us about them. He told us the name of Jim's colour, which is fawn. He asked to see Jim's pedigree and said that Jim had good racers in his line and was his own grandpa. He talked without drawing breath, inching backwards, sure to fall in the river. Meanwhile Jim was working his way round the back of the whippets, trying to shag them.

By the mercy of time passing I was back in my chair on the *Phyllis May* with a large whisky in my shaking hand and they had gone away. Why don't you try a bit of rabbiting with Jim? Monica asked. On the hearthrug Jim yawned, showing four rows of mother-of-pearl teeth.

• • •

I COULDN'T SLEEP LAST NIGHT, I SAID. I WAS worrying about what I said to Clive. I think I promised him we were sailing across the Channel. Yes, said Monica, you promised and shook hands and drank to it and then you hugged each other and Clive said you were a brave man and a true friend and started to cry. Oh dear, I said, I taught our kids to make as few promises as you can and if it is in your power, keep them. Yes, said Monica, it was enough to turn them to crime. But it's crazy, I said. Hardly anybody has sailed across the Channel in a narrowboat. We are not heroes, we are not even boaters, we are pensioners. You didn't see the sea until you were twenty. I can't keep track of a spanner for fifteen seconds, much less the North Star or Cap Gris Nez and if we go more than six feet from the bank the dog goes into convulsions.

We can afford to lose the boat, said Monica. Oh that's all right then, I said. And we're old anyway, she said. We have had our share—the grandchildren will carry on our chromosomes. I want to carry on my chromosomes myself, I said. Look, said Monica, why don't you e-mail that nice man with a beard. All boaters are nice men with beards, I said. No, said Monica, the one who is big in the Dutch Barge Association. They sometimes sail those big barges across and he lives in France and he would know. And the gentleman from the St. Pancras Boat Club—the nice man with a beard.

It took the nice man from the Dutch Barge Association no time at all to respond:

No, not for me. I could not recommend it. Insurance is unobtainable. You would have to seal the boat like a tank and you would have to face the possibility of losing it if the worst came to the worst. There is nowhere to have charts readily available to the steerer and if it went down anyone inside would be locked in a tomb.

Quite poetic, really, said Monica.

The second nice man took a fortnight:

I personally have not taken a narrowboat any further to sea than round the estuary to the Medway. SO I CANNOT AS-SIST ANY FURTHER THAN THAT.

I'm not sure he's for it, said Monica. I'd better ring Clive about these two, I said, he won't want to go now.

Clive rang back, said Monica that evening. It's all over then, I said. No, said Monica. Did you tell him about the tomb? I asked. Did you tell him about the insurance? Yes, said Monica, he sounded a bit like Kipling–

> *If you can make one heap of all your winnings,*
> *And risk it on one turn of pitch-and-toss,*
> *And lose, and start again at your beginnings,*
> *And never breathe a word about your loss . . .*

But it's their home, I said. They haven't got a house like us. I wonder what Beryl thinks?

DON'T TELL ANYONE, BUT ON A NARROWBOAT you live where you like. Sometimes people come and ask for money, but not often. You can always move on, but we paid our three pounds and there we were, swaying gently in the June sun, opposite the pitched roofs and balconies and boat-houses. No one in Henley had a better address.

I went for a jog with Jim. He was balky because it was hot and Monica had gone somewhere without him. We got lost in the town and wandered round underdressed like one of those dreams. Then we found the river again. The evening sun was at our backs; the line between water and air had melted and there were four carp hanging below us. They were velvet black, each more than a foot long, idling in the sunshine. I felt good, the way you do when something is explained that had not made sense before.

I decided to run round the meadow and let Jim off the lead. A whippet running as hard as he can is fast indeed—sometimes he goes through a door only he can see and comes out somewhere else. His ears go back, his eyes fix on his mark, his legs reach under him and there is such power in his footfall that you can feel him drum the ground. All the time he holds his balance so he can jink or turn and as he runs he seems to be smiling. There is something desperate about a whippet running—he does it as an artist, everything about him is compromised for it, and he is the best in the world.

It makes you happy to see something doing what it is meant to do, whether it is lazing under the water or running in a green meadow.

That evening I told a fisherman about the carp. Jim had tried to eat his maggots and his sandwiches and I felt I should offer a little conversation. They grow to forty pounds round here, he said. They were black, I said—are they really black? Yes, he said, they are black. But not underneath. Underneath they are gold.

WHAT ARE YOU TRYING TO DO, MISTER? ASKED the little boy in Abingdon. I am picking nettles, I said, wincing as they punctured my rubber gloves. What for? the little boy followed through. To make nettle soup, I replied. Nettle soup is good for you. It has vitamins. You must profit from the gifts of nature. My basket was full and I walked out of the nettle patch towards the children, smiling and pulling my fingers. They ran away, shouting for help.

Nettles are always with us and nettle soup is not hard to make. You take some fat bacon and fry it up in a saucepan, and add some chicken stock. Then slice in some mushrooms and one large potato and add some single cream. Then if you wish add the nettles. It doesn't make much difference if you don't.

On a canal boat food comes and gets you. The crabapple and the curious pear themselves into your hands do reach; nuts tap you on the shoulder; ruined orchards beckon you in. Monica makes blackberry crumble, stewed blackberries, blackberry jelly. At a lock she gathered two pounds of aromatic fungus—for all their enterprise the southerners do not play mushroom roulette. Near Abingdon I flung a rope over a branch and Monica spread a blanket on the ground. We pulled in rhythm and hundreds of black plums fell on Jim. Then there is Monica's home-baked bread. You could throw one of her sandwiches through a corrugated iron sheet.

If you would let me make beer in the engine-room we could live off the cut, I said. At least it might get you into the engine-room, said Monica. What we need is protein—what we need is rabbits. That whippet has got to be good for something. What about lamping, like the gypsies—you can borrow my torch. (My wind-up torch had recently attacked me, then exploded.)

So I set out into the dusk, gatherer turned hunter, by the light of my faithful hound Jim, the fastest dog in the world, and a kitchen torch with a half-mile throw. It seemed like a winning team to me.

The field was big, and there were dozens of rabbits grazing a yard from the hedges. I aimed the torch. They stopped chewing and sat transfixed, their eyes shining. Jim began to scream softly, like a fiend in hell watching a likely soul go over the wall. I cried havoc and let him slip. As he approached at forty miles an hour the rabbits stepped into the hedge, and when he had gone they stepped back out again.

After some time I put Jim on the lead and we considered our position. Then we saw some baby rabbits ten yards away, lolloping around. They were the size of chocolate Easter bunnies. My heart filled with lust. I realized the enormity of what I was going to do but still I did it. Jim rushed at the babies and knocked two of them over, then stood and looked at them as they hopped into the hedge.

Back at the boat Monica was waiting with a scissors. Jim went to his kennel, looking straight ahead. Where are my rabbits? asked Monica. Not much out there tonight, I said. You are a pair of losers, said Monica. I did not answer—I was too ashamed. I am ashamed still, and glad that Jim won't talk.

THE ANCIENT CITY OF OXFORD ALLOWED US A good address: a little out of town, under Folly Bridge, by the cricket ground, opposite Christchurch Meadows. It was raining but we kept to our plan for a walk, in full mating plumage. Jim was wearing a paisley bandanna, setting off his butch leather collar and lead. Monica sported her Drizabone Australian hat, looking like Ned Kelly's reckless sister. I was appearing, for the first time in public, in a Breton sailor's cap. I had not dared wear this on the *Phyllis May* in case someone asked me a question about boating. Our caravan poured up the towpath to Isis Lock, where Oxford bares its backside to the canal.

Fifty years too late the university had laboured and brought forth a business school and we passed under the vacant stare of the new building–death's mightiest powers have done their worst. But The Broad was still broad and The Turl was still not, and Jesus College was rather as it had been for the last four hundred years. The sun came out and the Japanese tourists fell like corn before the sickle of Jim's lead.

We processed back to Folly Bridge and behold–a pub selling Fuller's London Pride–

> *I often wonder what the Vinters buy*
> *One half so precious as the Goods they sell.*

As we settled by the river Jim began to snicker and we looked around. A chap nearby had put a basket on his table and was taking out a chicken. He stood the chicken on the table and he and his lady chatted with it as it stalked about and crowed and they all shared a packet of crisps. I'm so glad we had this walk, Monica said–the weather picked up, you liked the beer, and there was a chicken.

The next morning we went to the pensioners' matinee at the Odeon. The grey ones were creeping in from all over the city like lichen across a damp floor. There was a long queue. Don't worry, said Monica, some of them will have died before they reach the ticket office. I expected the ticket lady to say Sorry sir you can't possibly be that old, but she was a trusting soul and let us in. For two pounds each we got a free cup of coffee, and a chocolate-flavoured biscuit as a further gift from a grateful nation.

The film was about the writer Iris Murdoch growing old

and going mad and dying in Oxford. This happened very slowly. The audience took it well, considering. There was a choking and a commotion near the end, and I guess someone didn't make it, but most of us pulled through.

WE NEEDED NEW FLOWERS FOR THE ROOF OF the boat and the garden centre was in Summertown. This is a stifling suburb in North Oxford, full of academics who hate each other, and go mad and die and have long films made about it like Iris Murdoch. You don't get well from the Summertown blues.

Jim and I fought through the bawling Saturday tourists in the Cornmarket and headed north up the Banbury Road. Here the streets were empty, except for two Goths. They were big chaps: black-leathered, riveted and chained and tattooed, their hair like quills upon the fretful porpentine. They lurched towards us, staring, talking about us, laughing. Should I keep going, step aside, or just fall to my knees? They stopped. One of them, the one with pointed teeth, addressed me. Great dog, man, he said. Excellent dog, agreed the cross-eyed one. Peace, man, he added. Peace, I replied. Peace and love.

There were just enough geraniums in the garden centre to fill the planters, although some were bright mauve and if you looked at them too long you got fits. I needed a taxi and sometimes taxis won't take dogs. I climbed in with Jim. Folly Bridge, I said, and waited to be put out on the pavement with my dog and my geraniums. But first gear was engaged, the left foot slowly raised on the clutch, and we moved forward.

The driver spoke. Lurcher, is he? No, I said, straight whippet—a better pedigree than I've got. I had a black Labrador, said the driver. Oh yes, I said, what colour? Black, he confided. She reached sixteen, then she died. A good age, I said. Yes, he said, cancer. I couldn't take her to the vet, I couldn't do it so my son did it and when he carried her out she turned and gave me a look just a look and she knew. His voice broke. They know, I said. Yes, the driver said, they know. Two years before that she had meningitis, he sobbed, cost me three hundred pounds, then she died anyway. This is the best place to put me off, I said.

The geraniums looked good on the roof and as we turned with the current, back towards Reading and the Kennet and Avon navigation, Jim stood up there with them, sniffing, seeing ahead.

Back in Abingdon, alongside the meadow, a candles and linen dinner from Oxford market, with wine from the *Phyllis May* cool cupboard, whose depths no man hath sounded. On the hi-fi Chet Baker was singing of love.

Would you have recognized her, if you had met her in the street? asked Monica. Fifty years is a long time, I said, but she wasn't very tall and her eyes were blue–Monnie, I said, we'll go down the Kennet and Avon, that's fine, and then we'll come back up the Kennet and Avon, like we said. But I'm not going up the Bristol Channel to Sharpness, it's bloody mad, and that Channel business is madder. You forgot about the seasickness. I get seasick looking at postcards of yachts. And when I take travel sickness pills I get visions of universal love–I mean my judgement goes. I would try to get out and walk. That's because when we got off the ferry you drank the free samples in the French supermarket on top of the pills, said Monica, and got pissed at half past eight in the morning.

But you can't expect me to take you out to sea if I am an invalid, I said–it's not me I'm thinking of, it's you and the poor defenceless dog. Of course, sweetheart, said Monica, of course, you are the skipper. Try some of this jam with your ice cream—it's still warm. I made it from the plums we shook down on Jim.

THE KENNET AND AVON NAVIGATION RUNS from Reading across Wiltshire to Bristol, and if you care nought for your safety, through to Avonmouth and on to the bounding main. The first fifteen miles run in part along the river Kennet. The navigation is the biggest of the waterway restorations. It is a hundred miles long with a hundred and twenty locks and rises three hundred feet and falls four hundred, and is not to be taken with a merry laugh.

In Reading we moored near an island with trees in the centre. A stone hit the boat, then after a while another, then another. We climbed out; I took a photograph of the kids on the island, and rang nine nine nine. The police were charming. They asked where I was, as they were not familiar with the town themselves. They explained that if the people of Reading stopped murdering each other, and returned each other's cars, and the five-hundred shortfall in the Thames Valley Force was made good, they would be among us within minutes, truncheons flailing. How big were the stones? I don't know, I said, about the size of eggs. Just a minute sir—have you got the stones table, Audrey? What sort of eggs did you say sir? Hen's was it? Hen's, oh well.

Two small children approached the boat. Please missus it wasn't us threw the stones. Me and my sister are down from London and we are on your photo but it wasn't us, really it wasn't, please don't tell. Come and meet Jim, said Monica, and don't worry, darlings. They stepped down into the fore-deck and Jim rushed off and came back with his rabbit of plush to show them, and jumped them and licked their spectacles.

Then a dozen more people arrived and stood around very close, shouting. They were kids, all shapes and sizes and colours. One of them said It's because I'm black, isn't it, that you hate me, so fuck you. Another boy was six feet tall, fifteen stone, with breasts. You took a photograph of me without my permission, he said. That's against the law and I find it personally very offensive, and I am going home to fetch my big brother. Another said I will tell you who threw the stones, his name was Jason Salvadori. Another said No it was Colbert Aventura. A Spanish-looking boy said It's a disgrace you coming here and behaving like this, so fuck you. A little girl of eleven with bleached hair and jeans said Fuck you both, coming here and causing trouble. Fuck you, they all shouted, fuck you both, and your boat, and your dog.

Pursued by stones, we cast off in the dusk and moored downriver opposite some houses with lights. A figure came along the bank. I saw the metal on his coat. Good evening officer, I said. Nice boat, said the stranger. He laid seven cans of Special Brew on the grass and settled down.

When a midnight duck came to manicure us, rat tat tat along the waterline, we started up in dismay, but we made it to the morning. Perhaps the wino was a plainclothes man. Audrey, is Gary free?—he likes a drink by the canal.

THE NAVIGATION TO NEWBURY IS A BASTARD. The main obstacles are twenty locks, designed by twenty madmen. They have earth sides barbed with stakes and rotting weeds, or scalloped sides to bang you, and they leak and they creak and torrents come at you as you try to moor up, and torrents fill your boat if you get inside the lock, and the beams stand at head height and none of woman born shall move them on his own. The locks are big enough to take your boat and alongside it the *Ark Royal*, should that happen along, and they fill at the speed of the church clock.

Then there are the boater-operated bridges, most of which work, but all in a different way. You halt the traffic on an arterial road, turn a key and wait while nothing happens. Economic life in the region comes to a halt and it's *Hoot hoot* and Who do you boaters think you are eh?

We were hit with tropical heat, and flies that had escaped from a nearby biological warfare establishment. When the trees closed in the flies struck from the rear, biting my calves and thighs and my hand on the tiller. We met a lady with her swollen arm in a sling, and my wounds ached for a week. A mooring pin snapped and put us across the cut, and a bearded fool took loud offence because his dog wanted to bite Jim. Monica had sunstroke and I had stomach cramps.

Then came the rain, the Noah rain. It caught us off the boat and we were drenched and redrenched and it caught Jim off the boat and we found him lying sodden under a hedge, waiting for the end. We walked to the only pub within miles and it was flooded and I left our keys in a swing bridge.

We made it to Newbury and found the Nag's Head—

Superior Wines and Spirits, Traditional Ales, Welcoming Atmosphere, No Dogs, No Soiled Working Boots.

We woke to the sniggering of ducks, the mad laughter of geese, and the pigeons calling Fuck you two, your boat too, your dog too, boots too, boots too, boots too.

• • •

MY MOTHER CAME BACK AGAIN LAST NIGHT, Monnie, I said. I got up for a pee and there she was, standing in the shadow in the middle of the boat. When her own mother came back it was always a warning something awful was going to happen. Do you think this was a warning? Perhaps I should tell Clive we are not going to sail across to France or up the Bristol Channel or anything like that. Even if you make a promise, when someone from another world arrives and says Don't do it then perhaps you are let off—perhaps it's a special arrangement.

I shouldn't think so, said Monica, you promised in this world not the next. How was your mum? I couldn't see, I said, I was frightened and went back to bed. Frightened? said Monica, frightened of your own dear mother who loved you so much?

I know, I said, I loved her too. It's just the way she keeps coming back from the dead.

AFTER A WORLD OF TOILS AND SNARES WE were now on the Kennet and Avon Canal proper. There was no break in the navigation but a new spirit of place. The locks worked; they had moved apart and our ten coach windows were filled with blue.

Most canals are enchanting at all times of year—let me count the ways—shall we say of Wiltshire that like Ophelia with fantastic garlands did she come, of crow-flowers, nettles, daisies and long purples. For a further blessing we arrived at the Long Pound, fifteen miles without a lock, at the summit of the navigation before you begin to step down to Bath, Bristol, and the sea. Bored?—read the names on the map. Draycot Fitzpayne, shouted Mannington Bruce, you Cuckoo's

Knob, you Clench, you Littleworth on your White Horse, how Dare you speak so of my Honey Street?

A nerd gongoozler had said to me You'll have a busy day when you go down the Caen flight har har. We left Devizes early and picked up a little narrowboat with a couple who seemed to know what they were doing. The gentleman had a bike and whizzed up and down opening paddles. We got to know them a bit as we descended, as you do when jointly faced with a fearful ordeal. There are twenty-nine locks in the Caen flight.

Robert was a photographer who specialized in the Kennet and Avon. I cover the waterfront, I said. You like the old tunes? asked Robert. Yes, I said. We talked about jazz. We had both played a bit and Robert still went to jazz festivals. One of his friends had stood in a coffee queue next to Gerry Mulligan. Gone, said Robert, and not very old. And Chet Baker, I said, the marvellous boy; jumped out of a window—heroin. Mel Tormé sang 'I Cover the Waterfront', I said—he went into the velvet fog not long ago. Billie Holiday sang it better, said Robert—drugs, forty-five. We were speeding down the flight and at every lock another seat on the bandstand was vacant. Benny Goodman, Sid Phillips—It's the wood in the clarinet that does it, said Robert—in the end it gets them in the throat. What did you play? Clarinet, I said. As we came to the end of the Caen flight Ken Colyer breathed his last, in a caravan, in France. We were down in four hours but it seemed less, because of the music.

In Bath the boater gets the best seats, looking out over the town, and the footlights come up in the morning on houses and spires. Robert came by on his bicycle and hammered on the roof. Humphrey Lyttleton is OK, he said. Thank God, I said, something beside remains. We'll take you on a tour of Bath soon, he added. Fine, we said, and never saw him again. We guessed it was the hips–Robert played the sousaphone. He was not a big chap and in the end it gets them in the hips.

Monica took me to the abbey for communion–inexplicable splendour of air and light and stone. Beau Nash's tablet explains dryly that as the social leader in Bath he had the advantage of God, who is untutored in fashion or degree.

Monica has a genius for churches–Saxon churches in the woods, Victorian sunbeams. Memorials: a widow buried with her sons in the First War, a pilot lost over the North Sea. When I read the dead hero's tablet I could feel the cold.

And I was playing in the street again and saw the Junkers 88 bomber and the two Messerschmitt 109s coming in over Pembroke Castle (*In here Terry, now, now, now*) and on Llanreath hill the oil storage tanks explode, and all the fire and the bursting smoke.

AS WE WERE LEAVING BATH A TALL THIN OLD guy came along the quay. He had blue eyes with a sea mist, looking at something over the horizon. I've got a narrowboat, he said–I sailed it across the English Channel twelve years ago. My God, I said, you must be a hero. He smiled inside his beard. It's not everyone does it, he said. I have met someone who has sailed the Channel, said Monica, and shook his hand and asked if she could kiss him. I can't believe it, I said, that I've met you–was it in all the papers? Most of them, he said. Was it hard, said Monica, was it dangerous? Pretty hard, he said, and pretty dangerous–I planned it for years. But I had the time–the captain of a container ship doesn't always have much to do. So I studied the charts and the tides and did the modifications and everything was fine. Did you enjoy it, I said, or were you too scared? I was scared all right, he said, but I enjoyed it—so did my son, who came with me in his motor torpedo boat.

DOWN INTO THE RIVER AVON AND YO-HO-HO for Bristol. A tidefall marked the banks. We moored for lunch by Fox's Wood and way up under the trees a large group in dark blue was intent on a close ritual. Perhaps boater-murderers, end-of-the-worlders, whippet-racers practising without dogs. After a couple of hours we decided they were probably scouts. But where are their hats, I asked Monica, where are their neckerchiefs, their woggles? Where are their socks with their little tabs? It's illegal to scout without a proper hat. Everything's changing, said Monica, and they're not going to ask if it's all right with you.

Jim set off to destroy the local wildlife. He had caught nothing that had not already passed over Jordan but he always made a fuss and a scurry and often some jet fighter zoom and swerve. When he returned Monica said Oh look and his front foot was bleeding and he couldn't walk. We burned down the current towards Bristol and at Hanham lock a notice asked us to report to Steve. We stroked his cat in the lock office and Monica told him about Jim and Steve insisted he drive us to his vet.

The waiting room was full. Dogs, cats, fish in jars. A girl with a cardboard tube—her pet snake or a pair of ferrets. Jim looked around, dividing the patients into those he could chase, those he could impregnate, and those he could eat. He rolled back his lips and made for a hamster. Foiled, he settled on his haunches, licking his foot and looking pathetic.

On the surgery table he shivered and rolled his eyes. Goodness me, said the vet, it is a little vippet. And he has lost a nail, poor vippet. Ah the vippets, they are always injured.

A vippet, when he runs he goes mad. He bandaged Jim generously. Is he too thin? Monica asked—he's getting thinner and thinner and people are stopping me in the street. There are bits of him you can see through. The vet pinched Jim's bum and Jim turned and looked at him accusingly. He is a vippet, said the vet—they are born to be thin, they are born to run, but see the muscles. That is a strong vippet, das ist ein fit vippet, das ist ein gut vippet.

Steve drove us back to the boat. I will show you the memorial to my dog, he said. Oh Lord, I thought, he's a nutter, he's going to show us his dog's headstone at the bottom of his garden. There it is, he said.

By the road was a cream stone erection in antique style, some thirty feet high. Not bad, eh, said Steve. Not bad at all, I agreed.

She was half Labrador and half Alsatian, said Steve. I used to know what she was thinking. When she went I put on my yellow fluorescent jacket, and took a spade and went to the little plot behind the old gates to the town. No one sees you in a fluorescent jacket—you are an invisible man. So her memorial is the old town gates. One day I will go invisible again and put a bench there.

IT TAKES A WHILE TO SAIL INTO THE CENTRE of Bristol, and half a roll of film. Passing through Steve's lock we had entered the floating harbour. The harbour doesn't float, the boats do—I wish people would say what they mean. We moored on a pontoon in St. Augustine's Reach, among masts and bright buildings: crowds on the quays, the sun, the seabirds flying. That evening as Jim dragged and stumbled along the quay the very drunks raised themselves in the gutters to cry out and shed a tear.

Ring the pilot, said Monica, we'll go down the river Avon and up the Bristol Channel. And we'll ring Beryl and Clive and they will come with us. I'm not going back up the Kennet and Avon canal. Remember the vandals, remember the locks, remember the bridges, remember the flies. The flies, I thought, the flies.

But listen to this leaflet, I said, from the harbour office—

The Severn estuary has the largest tidal range in Europe, up to 14.8m at Avonmouth, with stream velocities up to 8 knots. Canal and river craft are strongly advised to avoid spring tides. If your engine fails you will be carried along by the tidal stream with little or no control of your boat. In severe cases craft can be literally rolled over and over on the sandbanks.

It's the September equinox now, I said—it's the spring tides.

SLEEP WELL, ROBIN? I ASKED CHEERFULLY. There was the dog, said Robin—it was dreaming, and the clock, it was chiming. I thought The poor dog hardly whimpers as he chases across the fields of heaven and the clock was chiming the watches and this old guy is supposed to be a sailor.

Next to the armchair where Robin had chosen to spend the long watches of the night where all is sin and shame Jim came out of his kennel, stretched, grinned, and farted. From the cabin came the early morning noises of Clive and Beryl, and Monica began to offer breakfast. It was four o'clock in the morning and very dark.

The water in the harbour was fast asleep with all the lights out. Robin had said we would get under the bridge before the Avon lock with our wind generator up but we couldn't and Clive was shouting Stop her there Terry for God's sake. We sucked to the side of the lock like a matchstick in a bath and sank to the level of the river. The keepers held the ropes–Nice boat, nice flowers–and went home to bed.

In the gorge there were lights in the air and lights in the water and we were sailing on ink. I steered with Robin at my elbow. He was tall and skinny, and he had put on a Breton sailor's hat.

Clifton Suspension Bridge was a luminous ribbon in the sky. Be careful no one jumps on you, Robin warned, and they piss on you too. I could think of one or two who would get up early to piss on me from Clifton Suspension Bridge, but their chance passed them by. Gently down the Avon on the ebb of the biggest tide of the year, eight miles of Parker Quink Permanent Black.

The M5 to the west goes over the river at Avonmouth. A dismal highway over yards and wharves, but now an arc of light from horizon to horizon, white and gold, on matchstick pillars. In the river shining vehicles sped *to the island valley of Avillion, where falls not hail, or rain, or any snow.* Behind us the sky had turned pink and lavender.

Under the bridge and across Avonmouth harbour, past South Pier Lighthouse, and into the Bristol Channel. We turned left, going away from Sharpness. Narrowboats are not made to put out to sea, certainly not on a spring tide, and the tide spat and slapped at us and the *Phyllis May* bucked and swayed. Jim began to whine–What the hell's going on? Beryl pulled him out from under the table and stroked him as he looked at her in despair. May there be no moaning of the Jim when I put out to sea.

I wondered if Jim had more sense than I did, and I hung on to the tiller as the waves and the current yanked at it and I felt scared and sick. We wallowed south-west along the coast and turned inside the Portishead breakwater, watching the tide rip by, sending fingers to snatch us and throw us spinning into the Atlantic. Through the sea lock, into the marina, and as day broke we fell into our beds and chairs and kennels and went to sleep.

Twice a day the Severn fills, the salt sea-water passes by. In eight hours we would be out on the new tide, which should carry us up to Sharpness lock, and on to the Gloucester and Sharpness Canal, where the sea can't get you any more.

At Portishead the estuary is five miles wide, narrowing to one mile at Sharpness. The first bridge is at six miles, and the second at ten miles, and Sharpness is twenty miles away.

IN THE MERCHANT MARINE THERE ARE TWO hundred words for slow. As we waited at the sea lock a tug entered the other side at the speed of continental drift. I stood at the tiller for an hour with Robin. It was not easy for either of us. The sun was hot, I was nervous, and I was not interested in talking about the immigrant problem. Also I wanted Robin to man the tiller only when there was danger and Robin had decided to sail the boat all the time. And he was falling all over me when I needed to manoeuvre and how can I say to a bloke of sixty-two who had commanded oil tankers You can't stand there on a narrowboat for Christ's sake?

When we got out of the lock we were late and Robin told me to go hard. The engine began to bellow and we headed for the first great bridge on the horizon. The sea was blue, and there was no swell.

If we arrived at Sharpness after the top of the tide we would not be able to get into the lock and we would have a night on the mud. The prospect of this, with Jim and Robin aboard, was dreadful indeed. I brought the engine up to eighteen hundred revs, about six knots plus the eight-knot tide. Warp nine—*She cannae take much more of this Captain Kirk—ye cannae change the laws of Physics.*

I have got Sharpness here, said Robin, his VHF radio to his ear—they think we'll be too late for the lock. I remembered what Joe had said—Run at normal speed, don't hammer the engine and it won't break. I put my weight on the throttle handle—two thousand, twice cruising speed. Warp ten—Sorry Joe. In the pandemonium of the engine-room Clive watched the dials and prepared himself spiritually for changing a belt in an estuary on a spring tide.

The lower Severn Bridge crosses the channel where it is three miles wide. It hangs from cobwebs between two white towers. As we rushed onwards it retreated further and further away. Robin had said it would take fifteen minutes to reach it but after half an hour it had almost vanished. Then out of airy nothing it began to take form, inhabiting the sky; the cobwebs turned to girders, the towers to sunny cliffs, and Monica drove the *Phyllis May* under the first of the great bridges.

In the front deck Jim lay in his bed in his life jacket looking like one of those orange-and-black liquorice allsorts. If you can imagine a terrified liquorice allsort then you have him spot on. I had argued a spell on the tiller for Beryl and we were drawing near the next bridge: smaller, simpler, white and beautiful. When I looked back Robin was on the tiller again. My greatest challenge still lay ahead. I had decided to drive the boat under this bridge myself.

I worked along the gunwale and stood by Robin, crowding him, ready to elbow him into the current. He held on to the tiller and put his radio to his ear, nodding and frowning. That's Sharpness again, he said, we mustn't slow down.

Righto, I said, but you are going to let me take her under this bridge. Robin looked at me, wishing he had been on Clifton Suspension Bridge earlier, but he moved to one side. As we passed the middle of the bridge I gave a wave and a shout.

Up Slime Road we rattled through a soup of sand and gravel, and into deeper water where surges whispered and bubbled—*Just one mistake, just one mistake, break a belt, break a belt.* Robin said It's going wrong, we are late. He took over again and showed Clive, whom he liked, where a big tanker had caught aground and rolled, lost with all hands on just such an evening. They catch, they catch again, and then they roll, and then they drown.

But the strife was o'er, the battle done. Sharpness would let us in after the blue freighter ahead. We sat in the front deck where the engine could scarce be heard and watched the evening come down. The smoke from a cottage rose straight into the air. The water settled to a rink of opal, overflowing every creek and spilling on the grass.

At Sharpness we waited in the stream while the freighter passed into the lock. Another demonstration from the merchant marine, that foster-child of silence and slow time. Then *Squawk*, and *Re-squawk. Come on Robbie boy, we'll squash your funny little boat in somehow squawk fizz.*

Our bedmate was registered in Estonia and was rather smaller than Jermyn Street. We crept under her side and her crew, fugitives from many a desolate Baltic wharf, looked down with disbelief on the thin boat, the orange dog, the bush hat, the flowers.

The gates opened into the canal and Robin came along the lock. Thank you Robin, I said as we shook hands—you have helped give us one of the best days of our lives.

• • •

THE GLOUCESTER AND SHARPNESS CANAL RUNS
alongside the Severn estuary. It's a ship canal—straight and
wide to Gloucester.

> *On one side lay the Ocean, and on one*
> *Lay a great water, and the moon was full.*

Robin told me he had only done one narrowboat before,
said Clive. Did they make it? I asked.

We drank and we boasted—We went past the Houses of
Parliament, and we went under the great bridges.

> *For lust of knowing what should not be known,*
> *We take the golden road to Samarkand.*

We'll take the narrow dog to Carcassonne—bunnies can and
will go to France!

Jim knew we were inland—I had not seen him wag his tail
before, but more than that, he was frolicking.

I've been thinking about the Channel, said Clive: about
roping the boats together. It's a question of the forces at play.
Oh yes, I said, the forces at play.

There's not going to be any forces at play, I thought. We
were lucky today—it could have gone either way. Sail on, you
mad bugger—for me, it's the lorry, and the crane into Calais.

Three
DEAD MAN'S WHARF

Stone to Southwark

Jim and I walked down to Aston lock to look over the edge of the world. The cut was frozen but in a few months the narrowboats would be moving again—*thanne longen folk to goon on pilgrimages.* We stopped at the Star for a pint and a bag of scratchings. The new landlord pulled Jim's ears—They say a whippet makes a good dog—what's he like as a boat dog? Terrible, I said.

I hear your friend Clive is taking you over the Channel, said the new landlord. Good heavens, I said, who told you that? Everyone knows, he said.

At home we had a second e-mail from the nice man with the beard and the capital letters. Perhaps he had remorse about the capital letters, for this time his letters were small. Ring the Royal Yachting Association, he suggested.

A weather window special, said the Principal of the Royal Yachting Association Dover Sea School, showing no surprise. It can be done—I took one across ten years ago. You must close up the front deck or it can fill and sink you. The ferries throw up waves three feet high, the Sea Catamarans six or eight feet. There is always a swell. It's the busiest shipping lane in the world. It's full of rubbish to get round your prop and the tides run fast. The Goodwin Sands is a very big place and very nasty. Your best plan is to go down the Thames and round to Ramsgate with a pilot and then across to Calais the next day with an escort boat. Sixteen hours to Ramsgate, six hours across the Channel. With two narrowboats it will cost you half as much, and it's safer. You can have any level of support from me you want, except the Rolls-Royce option. There is no Rolls-Royce option.

Do you think I'm crazy? I asked. If you want to go up the Matterhorn, said the Principal, you can go over it in a plane, you can go up it in a cable car, or you can climb it. It depends what sort of experience you want, how close in you want to get—I know which I would prefer.

They tell me I can't get insurance, I said. Write and explain, said the Principal—you never know. You'll find a shortrange radio operator certificate useful. You might look at a nautical almanac. I had not heard of nautical almanacs but supposed they gave you the lucky days for sailing.

I rang Clive—I think we're on! You see, he said, I told you so—it is a question of patience and finding a way. He explained about patience and finding a way, and why people from Dudley were particularly patient and always found a way. He rang early next morning to explain again, and make whooping noises. All night long he had been out at sea.

• • •

IN 1771 THE TRENT AND MERSEY CANAL REACHED Stone, and the Star Inn was soon built alongside. In 1777 the boatyard in Stone was opened. Like much of the town it is built of red brick, smaller than we build these days. It was made without art, and it is very beautiful. At half past three the setting sun washed the walls with flame.

We had known Peter and his wife Karen since they were children, a long time ago. In the office of Canal Cruising there was room for them both and Monica and me and a telephone and a jar of instant coffee. There was no room for Jim or for Jim's best friend, the boatyard lurcher, but they were there anyway, wrestling on the floor, growling horribly.

Beans? said Peter—you want us to fill your boat with beans? Any particular sort of beans? Baked beans? Broad beans? Perhaps runner beans? suggested Karen. No no, I said, let me explain. If a narrowboat is out at sea the weak spot is the front deck, because it is low down and enclosed at the sides. If the waves fill it we will sink, so we have to enlarge the drain holes. But if we enlarge the drain holes we could fill up from the drain holes. But I have the answer—we fill the front deck to the top with those little foam beans they use in parcels, and cover it over with a net. Then it will never fill with water—how could it?

The lurcher had won the wrestling match and had licked Jim all over and was starting to swallow him. Peter leaned down to pull them apart. That's a very good idea, Terry, he said, and I am surprised it is not standard practice. But we are only an inland yard and it may be a bit advanced for us. Tell you what, I'll put a removable wooden deck on the front to keep the water out and see what you think. Oh all right, I said, but if you run into trouble call on me and I'll help with the beans.

And look, asked Monica, would you like to come across the Channel with us? You have been so good and you might like the ride. And you can change a belt or mend the engine if things go wrong—Terry is so helpless.

Peter is a big chap and when he laughs, which is often, it is a seismic event. As we walked back up through the town cracks were appearing in the pavement.

At home the phone rang. It was Beryl. She and Clive were not coming. She had decided they couldn't take the risk of losing their boat.

It's their home, said Monica, and all their things—it's everything they've got.

We felt numb and lonely and afraid. But the adventure was all ours now, if we wanted it.

THE GENTLEMAN ACROSS THE TABLE WAS GO-ing down eight miles south of the Great Orme. But I had spotted him. *Pan pan seelonce,* I said slowly into the micro-phone. *Yacht sinkerman in fairisle jumper on deck waving. Sinkerman repeat Mayday. All ships all ships, seelonce feenee, go to 67, transmit for ten seconds and repeat. Pan pan medico—roger and out.*

The gentleman across the table looked as if the winter sea had just reached his Y-fronts. That really wasn't very good at all, said the instructor, a captain with a beard—he would have sunk while the coastguards were trying to decide what you were on about. It would have been kinder to ram him and keep going. Fortunately you were on the wrong channel and you forgot to press the transmit button.

We've got this dog, said Monica later. He's a very thin dog. Will he lose his core temperature and die? I don't understand, said the captain, we've all got to go some time. I mean, said Monica, the dog is on the boat. When we transmit *Mayday Mayday* and nature of danger, and number of crew, do we include the dog? When they send a helicopter do they need to know about the dog? We are very fond of our dog. He's only a small dog, perhaps they would winch him up as an extra. If it's the British coastguard, said the captain, tell them about the dog. If it's the French, find a moment to say goodbye.

In real life, said the captain, if I come up the estuary and call the coastguard it's *Joe you drunk get that tug out of my road was that your wife under a Dutch whelk fisherman on Tuesday?* If you say everything by the book they will know you are not real sailors, and finish their breakfast, and all is lost. Do you mean that what you are teaching us is no good? I asked. I'll explain that one over coffee, said the captain. We were given our examination papers. Does he want a pencil? the captain asked Monica.

The next day I rang the insurance company. They told me my details were lost but no doubt someone had thought it was a joke. If I wanted I could apply again har har. I sent a copy of my application, and a saintly letter forgiving the delay. This went to the holiest in the height of the firm. Most sure in all his ways, he decided the *Phyllis May* would be covered for the Channel crossing at a cost of £125.

WE'VE HAD ONE OF THOSE CATALOGUES, I said—I thought perhaps something for the voyage. But it's full of terrible things—penis-enlarging pumps, versatile trimmers to get rid of unsightly nose and ear hair, a bunion corrector that goes to work while you sleep, Soxon to help you put your socks on with ease, non-rustle incontinence pants. My

God—is this what happens next? If we go down in the Channel it might be for the best.

Yes, said Monica, we'll drown, then we'll be all right. But ring the Small Ships Registry and ask them where our certificate has got to. They will let us in at Calais if we have unsightly nose and ear hair and our incontinence pants are rustling, but they won't let us in without a registration certificate. Jim and I are going for a run.

EVERYTHING TO DO WITH A BOAT TAKES seven times as long and costs seven times as much. I allowed three days to polish and lacquer the brasses inside the boat, and finished three weeks later. My right arm had doubled in size, my shoulder will never work properly again and I think something happened to my lungs.

The night we finished Jim pulled me to the Star. He started a relationship with a lady of a certain age which became tender, bordering on passionate, but did not deliver any pork scratchings. Then the gentleman next to me took half a yard of raw black pudding out of his pocket, and with a schoolboy penknife from the forties, cut Jim a length. Jim had not tasted black pudding before, and this was the one they make in Adie's Alley off the High Street, the one with the sweet bits of fat. Jim sat back and looked up—this had turned into one of the best days of his life. The gentleman cut another length and gave it to him. Then he cut another and gave it to me. I barked and wolfed it down. I had another pint and my shoulder stopped hurting.

Sitting opposite was a chap with curly hair and muddy boots. Do you go lamping for rabbits? he asked. We did once, I said, but it was a bit quiet. Mine likes to chase squirrels, he said. Oh yes goodness me squirrels, I said—Jim goes mad. But they run away up the trees—I hear they are good to eat. Curly looked at me and spoke quietly, as if he had realized we were both Freemasons, or gay, or listened to the Carpenters—Look, my brother has got squirrels, all over his garden and in his roof. I'm going round on the weekend and we will get a couple of sacks-full. Not much mess—airgun. Lovely with a few carrots, bit of curry powder.

Monica, I said when we got home, if by any chance a chap comes round with a sack of dead squirrels you won't be nasty to him, will you? I mean show no surprise.

You shouldn't be allowed out on your own with Jim, said Monica. He can't look after you, he's only a dog.

I HEFTED MY NEW YELLOW ELECTRIC DRILL. They'll know us by the colour of our weapons, I said. Don't try to use it, said Monica, you'll lose a hand. Who will know us? They, I said: the poets, the gypsies, the circus performers, the philosophers. When we are in Paris they will all want to meet us. We don't know anyone in Paris, said Monica—who are you planning to meet? Gérard de Nerval, I said, with his pet lobster on a string; Arletty, the dark angel of the Hôtel du Nord; Jean Marais, the lover of Cocteau; Charles Trenet, writer of 'La Mer'; Louis Aragon, fearless poet of the Resistance.

All those people are dead, said Monica. Gérard de Nerval has been dead for a hundred and fifty years. And what are you going to talk about with people like that? Will you show them your electric drill?

IT SEEMS TO HAVE GONE FUNNY, SAID THE fifteen-year-old girl in the hairdresser's. Won't it do a ponytail? I asked. There's not enough of it, said the child, and it's all patchy. It's like those dandelion clocks you blow bits off, when it's late in the afternoon and it's nearly all gone. It's coming out of your ears. How long have you been growing it? Two years, I said, but it keeps falling out. What are you trying to grow a ponytail for? she asked. Well, I said, I used to be in business but now I'm retired, so now I can be myself; I can be free. I want to look like Willie Nelson, the country singer—he looks free. Oh, said the child, having a bit of a rebellion, are we?

It was time to visit Raymondo's parlour. Thank you for waiting, he said. I had spent an hour among a rout of twelve-year-old girls, bikers, babies, and people shouting in Estonian. We don't get many like you, said Raymondo. Nothing too fancy, I said, it's my first time. OK, said Raymondo, though it's not as if you will regret it when you are sixty-five. How about 'Mother' or perhaps a naked lady, very daring, or a big one, a shipwreck, across the chest, with drowning sailors. I think I would prefer one of those Maori ones with wavy lines, I said.

Here we are, said Raymondo, look at this. Black, lovely on the upper arm. What does it mean? I asked. What do you want it to mean? asked Raymondo. I want it to mean *Within my immediate social group, my sexual performance is above average*, I said. That's it, said Raymondo, that's what it means.

He broke out a fresh needle. This will hurt—more when I draw the outline, and not so much when I am filling in. He pricked the tattoo into my arm. He was very gentle. It hurt, but not as much as running up a hill. One more of us, said Raymondo, one less of them.

Monica kept taking my bandage off to look. A couple of days later she went across the road. When she came back she had along her arm a Chinese dragon. Monica is small, and it was a big dragon. She looked like the sign for a Chinese takeaway. Raymondo wanted it done in two goes, she said, but I had it done in one.

In the showers at Stone Master Marathoners she went down a storm with the other girls. At every chance she wore a singlet, particularly among her middle-class friends, who pretended not to notice.

They'll know us by the pictures on our skin, said Monica—and Raymondo said he'd do Jim. They'll know Jim anyway, I said, and he's already got the map of Indonesia across his belly and his privates.

I HOPE WE GET AWAY ON TIME, MONNIE, I SAID. I can't go down the High Street. People keep stopping me and wishing me luck. I don't know most of them. They shake my hand and look into my eyes, as if they are seeing me for the last time. I keep trying to explain that if it starts to look dangerous, it's the lorry, and the ferry, and the crane, but they don't listen. I don't like being a public figure before I have done anything.

Perhaps that's how it happens, said Monica. You know Roger Bannister, when he ran the first four-minute mile, I bet he never meant to. One day he turned up at Iffley Road running track and there was Chataway and Brasher and the rest of his mates, and they shook his hand and looked into his eyes and gave him his shoes. I bet he was scared stiff and would rather have gone to the pictures.

Can't we make up our minds? Monica asked. Everyone says different things, I said. Half of them say it can be done and half say we are crazy. And everyone knows someone who has been across and I spend days tracking them down and when I speak to them they haven't or they did it in another sort of boat. But it's too early to decide. Let's go to London—we've got four weeks to think about it on the way— we'll get across somehow and get to Paris too.

WE DIDN'T MAKE MUCH OF OUR PARTING, on April Fool's Day. We embraced Peter and his wife, who had brought the *Phyllis May* to the stage where they would almost have sailed in it themselves. The gentlemen who worked in the boatyard kissed Monica. One of them was crying—Monica had known his mother.

A couple of friends and our elder daughter came to wave us away. You'll be fine, Dad, said Lucy—just send an e-mail that you would like me to have the Nepal carpet with the lotus flowers. Me, not Georgia. Georgia can have the wooden lion from Nigeria. But you'll get across, don't worry. And Clifford can have your watch, if they find you. It's waterproof, isn't it? You don't know to what sort of depth, by any chance?

The Trent Valley was grey and green and brown, with willows, alder, poplars, and the blackthorn fired with white sparks. We moored at Weston and when we woke there was mist on the cut and the fields sifted with frost and the early sun in his glory.

Boating in the summertime is great, but it is not like the real thing. In the winter I pull branches out of the cut and fill the log-box that says *Phyllis May* on the front side and *Kiss Me Again* on the backside. Each log is handmade and I grieve for them when I open the stove, but you've got to let them go. They give heat you can hear, heat you can smell, heat you can see, heat that makes toast.

After breakfast I turn the key in the engine-room, rise like a centaur through the hatch, close the door behind my bum,

put on my Russian hat with the flaps, and arrange my properties on the roof—map, binoculars, radio, boathook, camera.
I push the throttle handle and the prop grips the water and I
swing the tiller and the stern moves out from the bank.
Straighten up, and Hurrah for the North-west Passage.

I like the heat from the engine warming my legs. I like the
Knock knock Here Terry and the coffee passed up and the
plates of ice vibraphoning quarter-tones along the hull and
the sun and the snow on the banks, and the fields that climb
out of the valley, outshining the bright clouds. I like the
trees, veins reflecting no light, and the barbed wire of the
bushes. One morning I saw a kingfisher scatter snow from a
bush and head straight up. The sky was blue, but not as blue
as the kingfisher.

At dinner we drink red wine and the sleet wobbles down
the window and the radio croons and the stove roars and the
wind generator moans and trees sigh and whistle.

We are in bed, warm in our steel Anderson shelter, when
the Jerry rain machine-guns the roof. The storm rocks Jim in
his cradle, and behind the stove Monica's horse-brasses clink
and glow—*the antique shapes of kings and kesars straunge and rare.*

IF YOU FALL UPON HARD TIMES, OR EVEN IF
you don't, you need not starve in Rugeley: a Lilliput town of
squares and flowers. Every other shop is a charity shop, selling CDs of Milt Jackson playing upon the vibraphone, or-
phan volumes of the *Oxford History of England*, T-shirts from
ruined car dealers and little glasses with Spanish dancers. In
the indoor market they do all-day breakfasts for a pound.
The tea, the tea—it's made from the bits that are left on the
factory floor, the bits with all the flavour. The eggs are sunny
side up and so is the service. The bread is real bread, the

white floppy bread we had in the war, and the margarine is made from boiled cows, none of your sunflower lite crap. The bacon is chewy and salty—excuse me, I must visit the fridge. Goodness, that's better. South to Fradley, in light snow.

THIS SPRING WE WOULD TAKE A DIFFERENT route—the Coventry Canal and the Oxford Canal and down the Thames to London. At Fazeley Junction near Tamworth Jim and I went to the newsagent and when we came back Monica had gone ahead. Jim could tell she had not gone towards Birmingham, and pulled me down the Coventry Canal and at a fast walk we caught her up.

Sometimes when I follow another boat on a still morning I can tell if they are having tea or coffee—I can tell if their bacon is smoked. For a dog it must be like that all the time. Jim knows what has happened in the past because it leaves traces. He can hear things we can't hear and he can see in the dark and he can see into the future. He knows what I am going to do before I know myself. He can tell where I am going to sit, and gets there first. He knows forty minutes before I take him to the pub. Dogs tell by changes in your brain waves, and by your quick, nervous movements.

At Polesworth we moored on the side of a hill and walked round to the main street, always seeing the canal a couple of hundred yards away across the valley. The big second-hand bookshop had gone—why it was ever there we could not guess, because Polesworth is a small village and poor. We walked on in the spring sun and saw Jim across the road. As he was on his lead at my feet and I was holding the lead this puzzled us. We looked again and he had gone so we followed the imposter up a lane towards the church.

There were two imposters, both fawn like Jim: the ears, the whip tail, the muscle, the delicate feet—two imposters just the same. And there was another whippet, a bitch. No potter could have caught her brindling in his glaze, no painter her sadness, no sculptor her grace. Jim greeted his fellows with enthusiasm. Their owner seemed unmoved. They are mine, he said—whippets.

Going back to the boat we saw whippets round corners, behind hedges, and just over the valley, nearly out of sight. By my troth, Monica, I said, this is a funny place. There are three dozen whippets in the world and most of them are here.

Back at the boat we let Jim off for a run. We don't often let him off on his own, but there was a long field and no road nearby. We went into the boat and had a cup of coffee, musing upon the whippets we had seen, and on the whippets we had seen before them.

It was only a chap with whippets, I said. People have whippets. We've got one ourselves. I know they are not common but they exist—I mean where did Jim come from—there must have been at least two in Grimsby or he could not have taken place. It was just a chap with whippets and the others were imaginary—nervous whippets. It's the Channel stretching our nerves. We didn't really see them, they were round corners and things. I saw one, said Monica, a black one. He looked at me. He had a pink tongue—oh just a minute.

Don't worry, said the lady on the phone, I've got him, he's going to be all right. My God, said Monica, he has run off, I bet he was on the road, he could have been killed. Where are you? she asked the lady. I'm on the towpath, by a long grey boat, she said, the *Phillip Moy*. There's a propeller on top and primroses. We looked through the window and there was a lady with a phone to her ear, and Jim held by the collar, wriggling.

When you have eliminated the impossible, whatever remains, however *improbable*, must be the truth, said Monica later. There is only one explanation, my dear Watson, that fits the known facts. The lady had been out for a walk and she met a chap who had lost a whippet. A fawn whippet. She promised to look out for him. Then she came across Jim by the boat. She grabbed him and read his collar and rang the phone number. It's a question of too many whippets, really.

We sailed away and looked back and there were whippets running over the hills and fields: fawn whippets, black whippets, whippets broken in white and brown, or brindled in colours no potter will catch.

THE WATERWAYS GUIDE SAID ATHERSTONE WAS a pleasant town, with a strong eighteenth-century feeling. A wide towpath with mooring rings, coal barges, warehouses with broken windows, gardens of rubbish. A bed of narcissi coming into bloom. The local youth walked by and shouted and scuffled and went away. Jim and I walked into town.

The off-licences were netted in steel and the gutters were drifts of cigarette butts. In the newsagent's the packets carried new warnings—

If you smoke you will die but first your sexual organs will wither and drop off—If you smoke one cigarette from this packet you are a fucking lunatic—If you smoke you will become incontinent and hair will grow out of your ears and you will be unable to put on your socks.

Does it make any difference? I asked the lady. No, she said.

Some youths charged by in a red car. They shouted abuse

at Jim and me and pressed on to the next village to kill somebody. A young woman stopped me—A dog like that: would he
be a good guard dog? He looks a nice dog but would he look
after me? Would he keep me safe, I mean round here? Is he
fierce? Does he bark? He can bark, I said, but he won't. In fact
he can talk, but he won't. But he's all boy, I mean he's a spir-
ited dog. Jim laid back his ears, looked up, and grinned ab-
jectly. He's not very frightening, is he? said the young lady.

We were inside the pedestrian area but a red car came
thumping at us over the kerbs. This is it, I thought—no
December years, no France, no Carcassonne—raped and
eaten by the youth of Atherstone. But it was a different car. A
pale gentleman with bad teeth leaned out. The dog, he
lisped, I like that dog—how much would you have to pay for
a nice little dog like that? There's a pretty little dog, he said
to Jim, and took out his wallet. Then a woman in the passen-
ger seat started to hit him on his arms and shoulders and he
let in the clutch and thumped back towards the road.

Jim and I strolled on, marvelling at the spherical women
with black leggings and their cloned daughters, waddling
like coots between the boarded shops. A brown lady offered
a happy smile and a leaflet for a kebab house. We stopped
for a pint. On the bar was the *Daily Stoat.* It didn't take me
long to read it and I wished I hadn't.

What was Atherstone like? asked Monica, as we waited for
our lamb shishka to come along the towpath. A pleasant
town, I replied, with a strong eighteenth-century feeling.

That night the local youth let the coal barges off their
moorings and drained the pound behind us. They ragged the
bed of narcissi and threw the broken flowers across the towpath. Monica gathered them and put them in water and as
we left Atherstone the sun shone through them and filled the
boat with perfume.

• • •

THERE ARE PLACES WHERE THE CANAL IS crowded—Great Haywood near Stone, Little Venice in London, Braunston Junction on the Oxford Canal. But normally it's the loneliness, doctor, the loneliness and the ducks. We sought a mooring at Braunston—the junk shop, the pub, the butcher, the church on the hill. Early communion on Easter Sunday—the new minister, her voice gentle, enough people there, not all old.

After deciding the width of the canals the eighteenth-century engineers chose to have as few locks as possible and to follow the contours. But contours do not go anywhere in particular and sometimes the navvies digging the cut found themselves back where they started or further away and the investors were writing letters.

The Oxford Canal around Fenny Compton is so tortured that I looked up from the tiller and saw the *Phyllis May* going round the bend in front of me. But perhaps I was distracted, because we had sailed past a moored boat called *Elizabeth Jane. Jane Howard was so beautiful that continuous problems arose*, wrote Robert Aickman, saviour of the waterways. *Little in the way of completely normal business was possible when she was in the room.* I set out backwards to have another look at the narrowboat *Elizabeth Jane.*

When I sail the *Phyllis May* in reverse there is snaking and roaring and smoke and sometimes I get a good crowd. I covered the hundred yards to the moored boat and stopped in a whirlpool of foam. The couple tying things on the roof looked at me. Elizabeth Jane, I shouted, oh ho, well done. There were giants in those days, eh? The Inland Waterways Association and all that—Tom Rolt the dreamer, and Aickman the activist. Hated each other of course. And Elizabeth Jane

Howard—campaigned for years with Aickman, snuggled up in his narrowboat. She was married to Peter Scott but he preferred blokes half the time so she took up with Aickman but he was mad half the time so she married Kingsley Amis but he was drunk half the time. Always got it wrong, Elizabeth Jane. Absolute cracker—good writer too—could have had anyone in London. In fact she had one or two. All those toffs and artists after the war knew each other of course. And fancy you calling your boat after her—marvellous idea—I agree we must show respect.

Elizabeth Jane is my wife's name, said the gentleman on the boat. We don't know any of your friends. He and his wife went inside their boat and drew the curtains. I dropped into forward gear. It had started to rain, and it was still raining when we got to Oxford a fortnight later.

ST. BARNABAS IN JERICHO TOLLED THE SMALL hours and I stared at the ceiling. I had been reading a life of the novelist Angus Wilson, who took a hundred pages to go mad and go incontinent and die. At breakfast Monica said I'm bored. Yes, I said, I think I am too.

The rain won't stop, said Monica, we've got colds and we can't breathe and we can't run, we're getting fat, it's freezing and the wind is blowing us into the bridges. The towpaths are muddy, the grass and trees are soaking, the spring flowers have drowned. I can't move the lock beams because I'm too little, the lift-up bridge lifted me up into the air, I dropped your new aluminium lock key and your best flowered jug over the side. The cut is deserted and lined with rotting boats, the pubs in Thrupp wouldn't have Jim, the fish restaurant in Jericho didn't have any mussels, the mussels I bought in Oxford market were off, we have run out of logs and I miss my kids and my grandchildren and my friends in Stone. There is no one to talk to and no one has rung us and no one has e-mailed us and I'm frightened about crossing the Channel. We could be months in London, like a dentist's waiting room. We've done this canal before, we've stayed in Oxford before. You wanted to live full-time on the boat—you must be mad. I've got cabin fever. When I go, which could be quite soon, I want to be cremated—I've had enough of wooden boxes.

I know, Monnie, I said, but Isis lock may be the last narrow lock ever—you can throw away the lock key—I mean the one you haven't already thrown away. We'll scarper down to London on the current—the Thames will look different going south. We'll see friends and the weather will change. In a few weeks we could be on new canals, in a new country, with a new language and a great new adventure.

If we don't bloody drown, said Monica. She started to cry, and Jim started to cry. Let's go to the pub, I said, and Jim stopped crying.

In the Old Bookbinders they brought a bowl of water for Jim and they sold scratchings and Greene King IPA and had peanuts in a barrel and good white wine, and a young man who lived on a boat asked about our journey and told Monica she was very brave. I bought him a pint and he explained that although he was not in a position to buy one back he could offer us good karma for the crossing.

AT ISIS LOCK IT WAS GOODBYE THE NARROW world. Three generations of a French family leaned over, chattering, as we dropped into the river. I told them in French we were going to Paris but it came out wrong and they replied in English that the weeks of rain were over.

Near Folly Bridge a rat swam by—not a water vole, a rat. He was desperate. I was so sorry and wondered if he was leaving the *Phyllis May*. But Monica was waving from the bow and Jim was on the roof and the sun was shining. A couple of American girls on a bridge—Where are you going? Paris, I said, and they shouted Oh my Gard oh my Gard, and Have a nice trip.

At Abingdon on our mooring a varnished dinghy coughed alongside. It had a wood-coated boiler, a coal fire, a chimney, and lots of tubes. There was room for a gentleman in overalls who was spinning little wheels and pushing levers. I thought I'll ask him if he will make me a cup of tea from his boiler and we will have a laugh together and then I thought I bet everyone asks him that and he will take offence and it will spoil the day and give us bad karma and we'll drown in the Channel.

Is it nineteenth-century? I asked. No, he said, I finished it on Thursday. It's lovely, I said. I made it all up, he said. See that flask on the side of the boiler? That's my kettle. That's where I make my tea. Not too much milk for me, I said.

We moored by an old orchard, a cruiser behind us. We are going to Goring, I said. Oh, we live there, said the man on the cruiser. There are three pubs—one is very good, one is not bad, and one is worse than the others.

Jim and I went to the worse one. It was like a normal pub, but worse. At the bar was a thin chap with a ponytail and dark glasses. My best friend had a dog, he said. The dog was sixteen, and he was blind, and he was deaf, and he couldn't walk very well. Coming down the stairs he used to fall most of the way so they put a duvet at the bottom. With a bit of luck, I said, one day Jim and I will share a duvet.

A powerful man in his forties, in a dark jacket and an earring, came in, and his dad, who looked the same but younger. Dad watched Jim finish his bag of scratchings and then he went down on his hands and knees and Jim put his paws on his shoulders and licked his face. They don't get any fatter, said Dad—I used to have one and people made remarks. I said Jim can't handle food—I gave him a second bag of scratchings last night and he was sick.

Have you been blind for long? asked Dad. I'm not blind, I said, I can see. Son bought a bag of scratchings which he gave to Jim. I'm a landscape gardener, said Dad—I was in an office and now I'm free, but it's hard in the winter. He bought a bag of scratchings and gave it to Jim.

They got up to go. You haven't drunk your beer, I said. Never mind, said Dad, I don't. Have you been blind for long? They both shook me by the hand and said how much they had enjoyed our conversation and Jim stood up tall and they kissed him.

AT CAVERSHAM BY READING AS WE LAY, THE back of the boat filled with greasy water. The engineer from the boatyard explained that I had forgotten to tighten the nuts that stopped water coming in where the drive shaft goes out to the prop. We had been taking in water all the way down and the bilge pump had worn out. He knew the famous adventurer who had gone across in a narrowboat. He had his air intake up here on the roof, said the engineer, and his exhaust up here too, so the waves couldn't get in.

But my exhaust is only inches above the water, I said, and I don't know where my air intake is. To be honest I don't know *what* my air intake is. He showed me. It was a pipe on the side of the engine, low down. I'm worried about the exhaust, I said. It's OK, said the engineer, there's a U-bend.

If the adventurer had his exhaust up here there must have

been a reason, I said to Monica a couple of days later. I don't think I have gone into it enough. I can't get it out of my mind. It's keeping me awake. A big wave will swamp the engine through the exhaust and we'll go sideways and she'll roll and the windows will come in and we'll drown. But the boatyard said there is a U-bend, said Monica. The Principal of the Sea School said there is a U-bend. But why did the adventurer have it on the roof? I said—there must be a reason.

It's the fear, said Monica. Remember what you were like before you went on a big research job overseas. It's really about the big thing but the fear gets you on a small thing and you rush around looking for a lefthanded camera or an exhaust on the roof. We used to call it displacement activity. This is worse, I said—this is like falling apart from the inside.

WE WERE GETTING NEAR NOW, AT MAIDEN-head. We rang the Teddington lock-keeper about our passage down the tidal Thames to South Dock. The Thames Barrier has been up a lot this spring, he said. There has been rain and the tides have been bad. You are not going to have an easy trip—the piers and pontoons have been swept away. Perhaps you can slip in at Limehouse, hang on the wall and then go down to South Dock on the next tide.

Around the horizon there were headlands of cloud, and cliffs of rain. We sailed from downpour to downpour, and the electric silences between were lit by rainbows. Storms of swifts, devil birds, buzzed us like Messerschmitts. A ragged cormorant blundered into the air. Monica was still not well— the locks and bridges had pulled her muscles and she ached with fever.

When we reached Teddington I called at the lock-keeper's cottage. The answers to your questions, he said, are free mooring tonight, the Tide End round the corner, and six o'clock tomorrow morning.

The barmaid in the Tide End was the one on the left in Atomic Kitten, the one with the eyelashes, the one that makes you go all wobbly in the knees. Jim and I sat down next to an old man. My brother had whippets, he said. They were big whippets, bigger than your whippet. But whippets are small, I said. There's no such thing as a big whippet–they must have been greyhounds. No, he said, they were whippets, the big ones, bigger than him. I was a sailor. I was stuck on the Goodwin Sands. It took three tugs to pull us off–it's a graveyard.

A creature walked out between the stools and legs at the bar. It was an English bull terrier, not much taller than Jim, but built like Staines Town Hall. She's called Samantha, said her master, she's all right. I thought–Just as well, she could throw him over her shoulder. You can call her Sam, he said. Sam was white, with a black spot on her nose and black ears. Her head was shovel-shaped, and the muscles of her jaws reached halfway down her back. She was slitty-eyed, and her eyes were on the top of her head like an alligator. She reminded me of a girl I knew who used to play hockey for Yorkshire.

Sam licked Jim's nose and nibbled him behind the ears and rubbed her shoulders against him. Jim backed under the table. Would they like a drink? asked Atomic Kitten. Jim drank, but Sam would not, so her owner poured a pint of lager into the bowl. Sam emptied the bowl in one draught and looked around the room for Jim, and set out towards him, moaning. Jim hid behind the ironwork, his eyes wide. She's all right, said her master, throwing his weight on the lead. Like a graveyard, said the sailor as we left.

I did miss you tonight, Monnie, I said, you would have loved Samantha.

AT SIX O'CLOCK TOMORROW MORNING THE tide was against us, with half an hour to run. Here we were in a new-washed dawn, going towards the sea.

Twickenham and Richmond offered woods to sail through, doubled in the river. The tide had flooded the parks and I could hear the bells of drowned churches. The current went slack and then it began to run out and we went faster and faster into the sunrise. There were no other craft except racing shells like long-legged flies—singles, pairs, fours and eights. They came out of the blazing river and went any way they wanted, but we missed them as far as we could see.

In your own boat the seventeen-mile journey to Limehouse, under the bridges of London, is a thousand-dollar ride. The day brightened and a wind nudged us as we sailed downstream. Through the parks of Kew and Chiswick and a long sweep down the boat-race course to Hammersmith, where the river is wide and the bridge carries the road on cables slung from its shoulders.

On the right the Star and Garter at Putney, where I would come off the river and rub my swollen wrists and drink beer and joke with the lads from our eight and put sixpence into a machine with a glass bowl on top. It filled my hand with warm peanuts and I could taste the salt, fifty years later.

Hammersmith Bridge is a rugby forward, but the Albert Bridge is satin and lace—slim Gothic towers, the fairest of them all. The tide was running mad, climbing the pillars of the bridges and streaming for a hundred yards behind. It was windy now: waves splashing. A vessel came behind us, a water taxi, at forty miles an hour. We were going under Chelsea Bridge so I couldn't turn into the wake and it yanked at the tiller, nearly sending me into the tide. The *Phyllis May* flung from side to side, hit by the reflection from the river walls, and then by the second bounce.

Battersea Bridge, illuminated by monks in green and curling gold; Vauxhall orange and red, twisted from steel, a painted toy. Behind it the MI6 building. MI6 is a secret organization and it is now known that the arrogant heap in Vauxhall is paint and plaster, set by the river to deceive our enemies. The real headquarters is in a bunker underneath Rugeley–the entrance is through the curtain at the back of the Oxfam shop.

Clouds were coming down as we passed the Houses of Parliament, but the early sun still fired the gold on Big Ben and the dewdrops on the London Eye, the spider's web over the river. On the Jubilee Footbridge a line of people walked across the sky.

I slowed down because we didn't want it to end, but here we were at Blackfriars, then Tower Bridge, then at the Tower of London, then we were swept past Limehouse lock. I turned and crossed the stream, which wanted very much to carry us out to sea, and pushed back against the current. Soon we were stationary along the wall before the lock, the engine balancing the tide, the water hurrying under us. Then I put my money on the engineers of Bordeaux, gunned the engine and went hard right. The prop shuddered and bit the water, and with a great noise I took the boat straight into the corner pocket.

The new lock-keeper said to Monica That wasn't bad–narrowboats get caught across the entrance–but I wouldn't go down to South Dock this afternoon. The tide is coming in against the wind.

• • •

I TOOK JIM FOR HIS WALK IN THE LITTLE PARK near the Prospect of Whitby, and there were four barge trains and three trip boats, all throwing up Bondi waves, which crashed into the walls below us. The tide was coming in and the wind was kicking up the water and I thought Oh my God.

Because Greenland Pier is in the way I would have to go past South Dock marina and then turn to come in with the current behind me—in other words out of control. I could not moor and rope the boat in because the pontoon had been washed away. But I had told South Dock we were coming and we could use the experience of waves. Should I ring up and ask how best to get in? I lacked the courage to do that.

So at three o'clock that afternoon there we were again in the Limehouse lock. The gates opened and the fury of the waters was revealed. My heart went into spasm and I couldn't breathe. We're clear, shouted Monica, and we set off for the impossible landfall.

But the boat was steady because we were going straight at the waves and twenty minutes later we passed Greenland Pier and turned and crabbed into the lock without hitting the walls and rose up into the basin.

We could be here for months, said Monica. I'm nearly better now. Shame really—Southwark looks a good place to be ill.

THE POOL OF SOUTH DOCK IS GUARDED BY iron gates. They will open for boaters with the secret code, except sometimes. There are notices outside—*please do not feed the boaters*. Around the pool are apartments for people who can afford to live by the river. A few of these buildings have a crazed grandeur, but not many. Behind them are Southwark and Lewisham, where the pavements are broken and tower blocks gnaw the sky.

We walked for a mile along the river but saw no one. The boaters had forgotten the secret code and the rest of the population were frightened of each other. Imagine the terror for a teenager stopped in the street by a lady banker and asked about the Hang Seng Index.

It was a long way to the shops and a long way to any grass and we were bored and frightened. Jim got into a fight with a Staffordshire bull terrier and stood his ground like a fool and lost some velvet from his ribs. The wind changed and it became sunny and hot. A week passed in inches.

MY MOTHER CAME BACK LAST NIGHT, I SAID. What did she say? asked Monica. I'm not sure, I said, it wasn't a very clear appearance, but it was something about the air intake. She was unhappy and it made me frightened. It may not have been your mother, said Monica. We are right next to Dead Man's Wharf, where the bodies come in. It could have been somebody else's old ghost. What else did she say? She said I must go to the lavatory before we set out, I said. It was your mother right enough, said Monica.

> *Bifel that, in that seson on a day,*
> *In Southwerk at the Tabard as I lay*
> *Redy to wenden on my pilgrymage . . .*

An e-mail arrived from the Principal of the Dover Sea School—*Thursday morning, 10.30 to 11.* Tomorrow we'll put on the storm deck, said Monica. And ring Cousin Ken, perhaps he'll come and take some pictures.

On Wednesday I swallowed sea-sickness pills and we went to bed. I was hanging on to a buoy, the green tide ripping at me, Jim in my arms. We were losing our core temperature and my fingers could not hold. Two bitter breaths and we would faint and it would be over.

Thank God they got Monnie off, I said to Jim, and he licked my face for the last time.

Four

THE SEA CAT

England to France

The Thames was low, running up. It was a bright day and there were no waves. This will do for the money shot, said Cousin Ken–Canary Wharf in the background and you for the open sea. Then I'll run down to Dead Man's Wharf and catch you again with that rotting pier in front. Ho ho, he said, it'll be a killer.

We walked on with Jim and I thought about fear. The slow fear in the corner of your brain, the fear that punches you in the stomach, fear of the *horla*–the empty human shape that passes across you in the mirror and then you go mad, the fear that dries your mouth and trembles your voice: the shadow in the dark room, the nightmares of death. A killer, said Cousin Ken–two centuries of photography, all leading up to this.

In Pepys Park we let Jim off the lead but it was hot and he was lazy and began to wander about. We walked on in silence. Ken shouted–He's on the road! I ran hard and stopped Jim with a shout and caught his collar. Sweat ran into my eyes and soaked my shirt. My lungs burned, my heart stuttered, and the sunlight went off-key like a film badly developed. I thought–It was only a hundred yards and I'm supposed to be fit. I couldn't speak and Cousin Ken held me up. You're dehydrated, he said. Hot day, too much beer, too much coffee, too much walking the dog. No, I said, it's the sea-sickness pills, or the fear, or a heart attack.

We walked slowly back towards South Dock and the day lightened. I was more frightened than at any time before. Not about the heart attack, nor the roll of waves, nor the panic of drowning, but whether the Principal of the Dover Sea School would turn up and take us to Ramsgate. I had met him only once; I knew he had a pending job for Norway, and he was not answering his phone. I had so much experience of arrogant boatyards and I remembered my last pilot. If the Principal did not come I would be helpless and defeated and the fear of that humiliation drove me into myself and shortened my breath.

When we got to South Dock he had not arrived, and it was eleven o'clock. Father Christmas, in jeans, came along the quay–They say you are going to Ramsgate. Yes, I said. But you haven't got a keel, he said. They roll over. No they don't, I said. Have a good trip, he said.

At ten past eleven two men stood smiling on the quay, and Monica rushed to punch in the secret code. The Principal was huge and black-haired and black-bearded and the pilot was huge and bald all over. I had just shaved off my hair after the fiasco of the ponytail and we were a murderous bunch. The Principal tied down everything on the roof. You want to keep the flowers up there?—why not, you are an inland boat, you show 'em. He jumped up and down on the storm deck. Monica gave Jim two sedative pills and shut him in his kennel. We put on our life jackets and harnesses and Monica put on her bush hat.

THERE WASN'T MUCH SPACE IN THE MARINA and I was off form and it took us half an hour to reach the lock gate. As we went out on to the Thames the sun went dark again and my heart revved up. This time it's the fear all right, I thought, but I wedged myself upright at the tiller and dragged in enough air to talk to the Principal at my side. Death itself would not stop us now.

We began to punch the tide behind a couple of yachts motoring to the sea. We waved to Cousin Ken as he made photographic history on Dead Man's Wharf and we worked out the only way three people could stand on the back counter of a narrowboat without having sex.

Long ago, in the first London Marathon, Monica and I had run past the sailing ship *Cutty Sark* and seeing it gave us courage. The voyage round the coast to Ramsgate would take all day and most of the night, sometimes out of sight of land, and could be the most dangerous part of the crossing. But when the starting gun has fired you are not afraid any more.

Our long meander round the Isle of Dogs brought Canary Wharf alongside again and we remembered how the towers looked at dusk from South Dock, green and transparent. Goodbye, Dead Man's Wharf. With luck we would be in Ramsgate before morning and, should the weather hold, tomorrow we would pull out the big one.

• • •

THE NINE HELMET-SHAPED TOWERS OF THE Thames Barrier are fifty yards apart. They swelled up and they swelled up. They shone silver in the sun: clothed in white metal, mystic, wonderful. The engines inside roll titanic gates from the bottom of the river, turning them on axles, so when the North Sea is hounded up the Thames by an east wind London is not engulfed. Look, the yacht is going through the wrong way—he's against a red light, no he isn't, it's changed, oh hell, just go through. We passed the axles of the gates on the waterline, and looked up and up, for each helmet is as high as a five-storey house.

What does she cruise at? asked the Principal, into my ear in our rough manly embrace. About eighteen hundred revs, I said. That's fine, he said—keep a bit in reserve. I swung down into the engine-room through the back hatch and Monica took over.

In the saloon the pilot was asleep in my chair. Jim was whining in his kennel. I opened the door and he fell out, crying and fighting against the drug. I'm sorry Jim, I said, but I'm doped up too. I carried him on to the sofa and he tried to lick me and looked around dazed—he wanted to be on the scene. The water was rushing just below the windows and the engine and the wind said you are on an express train, but this one doesn't sway.

I made a cup of tea. The pilot woke up. I've been across in worse than this, he said. See this lump hammer, I said—if we run into trouble chuck it through the window and go out after it. There's no other way out except the back—it's a tomb. Very handy, said the pilot—two sugars please. I took some tea up to the Principal and Monica, then I had a cup of tea, then

I had a carton of tomato juice, then a bottle of milk, then a low alcohol beer, then a pint of tonic water.

Through the window an orange inflatable. The Royal National Lifeboat Institution, thinking we had been swept down from Richmond while making whoopee in the cabin, had arrived to suggest we return to quieter waters. The three young men in black wetsuits could have represented their country in any event needing beauty and strength and a full set of teeth. They recognized the Principal, who had taught most of them, and tagged alongside joking with him and wheeled away with a roar and a flourish of spray. The blue freighter that had shared a lock with us at Sharpness over-took us, or was this one a bit more rusty? We felt the wake, but hardly.

BELOW THE BARRIER THE THAMES ESTUARY IS industrialized, in which there is no shame, and the banks are flat and far away so you can't see what is going on. It's mag-nificent, but it's not the Trent and Mersey Canal. No flowers, no green fields, no trees, no pubs, no families of fowl, no towpaths, no lockside chat. And no Moby-Dick heaves his body from the deep, no flying fish leap aboard, no dolphins frolic, no forests of weed under the glassy cool translucent wave. Just blue-grey water, with a fine smoky finish, but just water, miles and bloody miles of it. And you don't get any-where—nothing on shore gets nearer or further. It's like wait-ing for a kettle.

The pilot suggested another cup of tea and said he had spo-ken with the Principal and the *Phyllis May* was steadier than they expected—too long to pitch and ballasted like one of those toys. I looked out of the window and a yacht lurched by.

Yachts have keels but they are fat and plastic with rounded bottoms—they roll. And they have masts to tip them over. The *Phyllis May* is thin and heavy and hunkers down and each side is straight like a sixty-foot keel and she hardly rolls at all. Up yours, Santa Claus. The pilot went back to sleep.

Ah, here's something. After three and a half hours the Queen Elizabeth Bridge across the sky. It was loaded with cars going very slowly. We could turn on the traffic report and have a laugh. A year ago such a bridge would have been one of our best moments. Now it's a bridge. That's right, Jim: sleep, my pretty one, sleep, my little one. Time for a drop of tonic water.

AFTER SIX HOURS WE WERE OPPOSITE CANVEY Island and out at sea. You couldn't see Canvey Island, but the Principal said it was there and I am sure it is an excellent place. But we could see the chimney at the entrance to the Medway, and it took only a day and a half to pass it.

I held the tiller and struggled with the cramps in my hand. If I relaxed the muscles they hurt and if I squeezed them they hurt and I tried to think about something else. I had left my harness below—there was no need to walk the gunwale, because the front of the boat was closed and there was nowhere to go. And despite what they said in the books I had taken the crotch strap off my life jacket. *He is going to be all right, Mrs. Darlington, his crotch strap saved his life, but he is not the man he was. Oh, you want us to throw him back?*

We passed the wreck of the American munitions ship *Richard Montgomery*, which went down in 1944. It held its arms out of the sea imploringly, but no one will blow it up. It is left as an ornament along the way, perhaps to save some sailor's sanity. *Here Taff, look at the nice masts sticking up—can't be far from land now, nice masts, not boring like the old sea—oh God, take him back down.*

There were waves now—force three or even four, said the Principal. The boat climbed the swells and smashed down, but there was in the hull such strength, even grace, and from the engine such power driving us on, that I felt in control and exhilarated and looked for bigger waves to climb.

We had forgotten to take the wind generator down and the three-foot propeller screamed and fizzed. Steer by the shadow of the generator pole, said the Principal, like a sundial. This was a new skill and an hour passed as I learned it. The Principal kept tapping into a sort of mobile phone that told him where we were. We could have had a compass on the top here, he said, and I thought, That's a good idea, a compass.

The sun was going down and the wind dropped and I began to steer from some clouds, which were high up so I hoped they were not moving too much. Then there was a ship but that was no good as a mark because it came and went across our horizon. Other ships were further out, cities of containers, slowly moving away. We were opposite Whitstable but out of sight of land.

Ah, there it is, said the Principal, the buoy. On the horizon was a speck the size of a flea's earhole. Go for that, he said. I looked and it had gone. There was a cloud though way up in the blue, and I headed for the cloud, hoping it was not going anywhere in particular. I braced my legs against the sway of the boat, and enjoyed the waves, the pearly water, the setting sunlight, as we drove into the dusk.

SIT DOWN AND HAVE A PORK PIE, SAID MONICA. It was night, and the boat was bumping and moving sharply.

We braced against the furniture. Jim slid off the sofa in a heap of legs and Monica picked him up and comforted him. The pilot slept in my chair, his forearms like marrows, his tattoos faded to pastels. The water under the windows was black, and there was foam. You could see nothing else.

At every wave the propeller was breaking the surface, grinding air and water, and the boat shuddered and the engine roared with pain. I sat in Monica's chair and went to sleep. Monica curled up on the sofa with Jim and went to sleep. The boat rose and smashed and roared, and the booze in the cold cupboard tried to break its way out.

MIDNIGHT AND WE HAD BEEN GOING FOR twelve hours. I woke to the sudden death of a bottle of beer, put on my life jacket, stumbled back to the engine-room and heaved myself out of the hatch. The Principal handed over the tiller and we settled into a position that you would find in any reliable marriage manual. I put my weight on one leg then the other, leaning on the side of the hatch, riding the boat as it roared on. There was nothing but the night, and I can't see at night.

Watch out for that buoy, said the Principal. What buoy? I said. We're not there yet, said the Principal, but it's a red one—it doesn't show up because it hasn't got a light. I strained into the darkness, looking for a buoy you couldn't see, and wondered what it was like to run into a buoy at night. I worked out the chances of hitting it and felt they were low but found little comfort. It's over there, said the Principal, pointing into the encircling gloom—we missed it by five miles—better steer a bit to port now. I swerved to the right then to the left. We turned on our navigation lights but our front light on a stalk blinded me, and I was shaken when a fishing boat came across us heading for the shore. I could just see the yellow oilskins and nets. We blacked out and charged on incognito.

From the bow of the boat for twenty yards on each side flew ribbons of light, rushing away in the dark. Scarf on scarf, streamer on streamer. Like every schoolboy I knew this was caused by millions and millions of micro-orgasms in the sea. I drove for hours through the radiance, crashing from black wave to black wave, surfing the night, trailing scarves of king-fisher blue. I was Hawkins, I was Hornblower, I was Bader, I was Cats Eyes Cunningham, I was Bannister, I was Moorcroft, I was the masked rider of the plains, I was Jumpin' Jack Flash, I was the new and undisputed King of Rock and Roll.

That's Margate coming up, shouted the Principal, and on my right a thin row of street lights had ignited.

GOING ROUND THE COAST YOU STEER FROM buoy to buoy. The Principal, stout Cortez with his eagle eyes, guided me until the buoys revealed themselves as dull full stops of light, an hour away, fading out and in. The North Foreland was not sheltered as we had been told nor treacherous as we had been told—it was like the rest of it, with a bit of a right turn. We peered ahead and beat on into the night.

The final buoys were at the entrance to Ramsgate harbour, and there is a sandbank to go round. From the Principal's radio squawked the voice of the harbourmaster—

We are full, sod off. And we don't do dogs. There's no room, I say, no room. It's Friday tomorrow and it's a bank holiday weekend. People are so thoughtless. Look, I've had a terrible day.

The Principal, who probably taught the harbourmaster to walk, jumped off and found some balloon fenders and a place to moor and we all went to sleep as dawn rose.

AT BREAKFAST I WAS BEING LICKED BEHIND the knees. Jim rubbed his muzzle against me, and sauntered down the boat, stealing a piece of toast off the table. He was making a crowing noise. He jumped on the pilot in my chair and tried to interest him in a little romance, nearly waking him up. Then he found landfall on the pilot's huge thighs. He's drunk, explained Monica—I only gave him one pill this time and it has removed his inhibitions. He hasn't got any inhibitions, I said.

It was a hundred-year day. Sun off the sea, a breeze tapping the rigging on the yachts, a few gulls. No other narrowboats—we were in another country. People off the yachts took pictures and talked of us among themselves and some told us they liked the boat and said we kept it well. We had painted the roof white for the Mediterranean heat and this had given it a holiday look.

After enough paperwork to tie Britain into the Single European Currency the fuel barge filled our tanks. The pilot came up from the engine-room rubbing his eyes. Where is Jim? I asked. He's hiding in a drawer, said the pilot—he has eaten the marmalade and one of your socks. Monica and I and the pilot arranged ourselves on the back counter.

I'll take her out, said Monica, and revved backwards into the quay. The engine hasn't used a drop of oil or water since Stone, I said, give her a burn. Nineteen hundred revs, and we thundered past the harbour wall and into the bay. Monica and I kissed—Here we go, here we go, here we go, we can't believe it. I'll take a break, said the pilot.

In the wide waters outside the harbour there is a yellow buoy. Nothing else for miles–just a yellow buoy. The buoy looked very big as we grazed it. It sort of fascinated me, said Monica, and it's the current. Yes, I said, it's the sea. It can move faster than we can.

To our right, between us and the coast, the thirty-seven-foot steel escort boat–businesslike, blue, with rails. The Principal was at the helm and his crew was a young man with an earring, who looked like Douglas Fairbanks Junior as a pirate with a heart of gold. The *Pedro* had two engines, each strong enough to pull us to safety. But it was not breakdown that was in our minds, nor tempest on this lovely day. It was the waves, the waves, the seven-foot waves from the terrible Sea Cats, and the ferries, with their bow doors open and a drunk at the helm. If they drown their own passengers what will they care for us?

You go down the coast a long way, nearly to Dover, past the Goodwin Sands, before you turn left to cross the shipping lanes at right angles. On our tide it took two hours and seemed longer. I thought there were always gulls and gannets out at sea but it was desolate, except for some sad brown birds floating in front of the boat–the souls of drowned narrowboaters.

At last the escort began to inch left and we followed her. The Principal shouted–Look at those breakers! A mile or two away on our left the white teeth of the Goodwin Sands–it's a graveyard. Come over towards me hard, shouted the Principal–those gulls are not floating, they are standing up!

A gongoozler was making for us at twenty knots–half a million quid of motorboat with smoked windows. As I turned he turned too and I had read that if their profile does not alter as they come near they will run you down. At last he turned away, without a wave or a signal. Mind your own bloody business, I thought.

A hand came up from the engine-room with a piece of paper with drawings of ferries. So you can recognize them, said the pilot. And there they were, hunched along the horizon, the tools of corporate manslaughter, the runners aground, the sad cafés, dirty hotels foundering under the weight of thousands who would never know if they had crossed the Channel or not. The threats, the enemy, the beasts that could run us down. But they sank under the horizon, and we headed for the South Goodwin light vessel, a flea on the rim of the world.

It took us an hour and a half to reach the South Goodwin light vessel and an hour and a half to get away from it. Every glance over my shoulder and it was still there. I was fed up with the South Goodwin light vessel. It was getting me down. It will be there all my life, even on land, like an old enemy trying to outlive me, like something I did a long time ago and can't forget.

WE WERE ON OUR OWN, OUT OF SIGHT OF England at last, but we could not see France. Was it still there? Had it gone away while we were planning and delaying? Had we missed our chance? Oh come on, come on, we have come so far and we are nearly there but something will go wrong—dear God how long. Will we ever get there? On the *Pedro* Douglas Fairbanks flashed his Hollywood teeth and the engine rumbled Of course, of course, of course.

The sea was oily blue and moving lightly in small mounds and dips. The sun shone. This is as good as it gets, called Douglas Fairbanks—and we are over the first shipping lane.

A ship came up from the right. It was white and monumental and moving very fast. We were toads under the harrow, we could do nothing. The pilot had come up through the hatch like a genie. Keep going, he said. But we are done for, I said. No, said the pilot, that is a big ship. It is two miles away. It will pass a mile in front of us. We kept going. Now T-bone it, said the pilot—point at the middle and keep going. We pointed and kept going. Nothing happened—the ship did not get nearer or further away and we were heading straight for it and we would squash against it like a fly on a windowpane. Oh the noise, the confusion, and what about Jim, and I didn't e-mail about the Nepal carpet.

Suddenly the ship had gone, offstage right at a trot like Falstaff, and we were alone. It works nearly every time, said the pilot. For us it worked every time, as the factories and apartment blocks came thrashing by.

Where is France? said Monica—we're lost, I can't stand it. It's there in the mist, I said. We sang 'La Mer', and we sang 'Blue Skies', and Monica sang 'Plaisir d'Amour' in French like she did when we were young. We sang 'La Mer' again. You're in the wrong key, I said. I'm going downstairs, said Monica. She was still there half an hour later when the French coast came in sight. Where were you? I asked. Making tea for the pilot, said Monica, and Jim is drunk and I was seasick. And you were nasty to me about 'La Mer'. And we are nearly there and I can't stand it. I know, I said, I can't stand it either.

Ferries were coming up from the right along the horizon. I didn't know there were so many ferries in the world. Far away a Sea Cat, smaller, faster, its huge wake almost dying before it reached the *Phyllis May*. We drove on, getting no nearer to anything. The tide is wrong, shouted the Principal from the *Pedro*–take her inshore out of the stream and we'll go up with the ferries. Head for that white dot, said the pilot at our elbow, that's Calais.

Still we got no nearer and the sun was setting. I thought– Six knots against a seven-knot tide isn't going to get us far, and I remembered the Channel swimmers who had given up a hundred yards from the shore. On the cut it is only five minutes from one place to the next and you can tell you are moving because you can see the scenery going by. But this is lost in the desert, adrift on ice floes, flailing through outer space. France was a long way away and it was staying there. The wind brought back fumes from the toilet tank and we were tired.

AT LAST WE COULD SEE A BEACH AND SOME buildings. The ferries began to appear huge behind us and on our left. We felt the wakes but they were slowing down. The Friday sky was full of orange vapour trails. I pushed the engine harder. Our bow wave rose and we moved slowly along the shore, and arrived three weeks later at the Calais harbour wall.

What does it feel like to have made it? asked the pilot. We haven't made it, I said. Hang on here, said the pilot. Four ferries came across the setting sun behind us and into the harbour and three ferries came foaming out.

On the *Pedro* the Principal put his radio down and shouted–*Go for it, Terry*! This is it, said the pilot, *now, now, now*! I felt nothing and saw nothing except where I wanted to go. I rammed down the throttle–flat out for the first time. The engine nearly threw itself out of the boat, plates fell off the walls, Jim howled drunkenly, Monica put an arm around me, and the *Phyllis May* headed for Calais harbour.

The bank holiday crowds on the quays cheered and waved and pointed. As we came near the entrance a Sea Cat came out at thirty knots and its wake came for us six feet high like a running grave.

I had seen that wave when I had first spoken to the Principal, and I had seen it come at me up the cut a hundred times. I had driven into it as I sat in the Star with Jim. I had slept with it and woken with it. I was not afraid of it–it was my big dipper ride, my impossible dream, my Everest, my last enemy, my best friend. I turned and drove straight at it and the bow of the *Phyllis May* broke into its green side and was swallowed, and then threw itself up and out, and then crashed down with a scream from the engine and a wall of water coming along the sides and over the roof. The tiller wrenched at me but I had it cramped into a grip that was not going to break. The wave dropped under the stern and the next wave came but it was all over, we could handle that. I turned into the harbour, and drove along the pier, collecting fishing tackle, worms, and curses.

Monica kissed the Principal and the pilot and Douglas Fairbanks and called them lovely men and I clapped them on the back and Jim came to wriggle against them and have his ears pulled–and they were gone.

We were safe on our mooring. We were there. We had made it. In seven and a half hours we had made it. We turned to each other and were silent. We embraced. Monnie, I said, I would just like to say–A great hammering on the roof, a shouting–Come out, English, we know it was you. We have returned and it is clear. We know what you have done to our boat. You are guilty like hell. Shame on you, English. You are found out, English, you are discovered and we are here. Come out, English, come out and face us!

Excuse me a minute, I said to Monica, I'll be right back.

Five

MINDFUL OF HONOUR

Calais to Armentières

$\mathcal{A}$ man who has just sailed the Channel in an inland boat against informed advice does not need to assert his dignity. I felt Olympian. The pontoon was working against the harbour wall and a fat man in a white T-shirt was jumping up and down, and a thin man with a Zapata moustache was treading his feet like a heron. Both were over six feet tall. The fat one raged–You know what you have done, English, you cannot hide. *Monsieur*, I said, please explain. The heron came up close and shouted pungently–You lie, English, you lie, you are perfidious–our dinghy was here and now you are here and you have stolen our dinghy. He drew his arms back like a disco dancer, moving from one foot to the other, preparing to knock me down.

What nationality are you, *messieurs*? I asked. Belgian, they said. Have you been drinking? I asked. We had dinner with our friends on shore and you have stolen our dinghy and we cannot get back to our boat, they shouted. Now listen, *messieurs*, I said. I am English. In fact I am an English gentleman. English gentlemen don't tell lies. I looked straight at the fat one—I am telling you that I know nothing of your dinghy, and wish only to help you in your misfortune. He looked back—My God, you are telling the truth. Now let's go on board and have a whisky, I said.

We got on board and Monica got out the whisky and I went through to the engine-room with the fat one and started the engine and cast off and switched on the big brass tunnel light. The dinghy was drifting along the wall on the other side of the basin. We sailed across and soon the huge Belgians fell into their boat and paddled away into the darkness.

Did you have a chat with the heron? I asked Monica. Yes, she said—he told me it was very good whisky and it was a privilege to meet us. He said he had disgraced his country and his family and himself and he loved our Queen and fancied the Duchess of York, and then he started to cry. He didn't finish the whisky but said he would return. We left the half-glass on the kennel for a couple of days and then I drank it.

NEXT MORNING JIM STEPPED OUT ON TO THE pontoon and threw himself flat—You fools, we're going over! He has an athlete's balance but he is a land athlete. Each time we left the boat we had to carry him along the boards and then up the long ladder to the quay. He liked it when we did that. If the tide was out it was a steep climb but he felt warm and would relax, but not too much.

Aren't yachts supposed to be in the water, I said to Monica, and aeroplanes in the air? Around the basin a hundred craft were on stilts, and in the sky above us someone was frying bacon. The basin was in a waste of concrete, and the *capitainerie* was a kilometre away. Over it a bar which was clean and bright and enough to put you off drinking for life. Under it the pontoon with the fuel.

Your boat, *monsieur*, what luxury, said the young man filling our tank—we have not had one in the yacht basin before. How English, your boat of the canals, with the flowers, and the thin dog. You came on a lorry? No, I said, we sailed.

You sailed across the Channel in your little boat of the canals like a cigarette? You sailed standing on the back in the waves? It is not possible. My God—*sans doute c'était un défi personnel.* Yes, I said, without doubt it was a personal defiance.

I CAN'T GET THE E-MAIL TO WORK, SAID Monica. We can't tell anyone we made it—they'll all think we've drowned. If we had drowned, I said, it would be on the news. But no one knows, said Monica, and I can't tell them, because you said in South Dock forget about the laptop and the mobile phone and the e-mail because nothing matters except getting across alive and now I have let you down and it's all your fault. It's so complicated, I can't cope, it's all gone to hell, and you should be ashamed how you mess me around.

We're tired, I said, it's a reaction after the crossing. We'll ring the kids and Peter at the boatyard. We'll send everyone else postcards—postcards are fine.

You made it then, said Peter. They made it, Karen! he shouted. Don't sound so surprised, I said. The engine didn't miss a beat all the way to Ramsgate, and all the way over the Channel. And your storm deck went right through a wave and out the other side and we never shipped a teaspoon of water. We didn't need the beans after all, though they would have helped. And no problem with the exhaust—we blew bubbles all the way.

I'm glad you made it, said Peter—we thought you were mad. And you can be a funny bugger and take offence and I was worried that if the modifications hadn't worked you would never have spoken to me again. If the modifications hadn't worked, Peter, I said, I would never have spoken to anyone again.

We sent the postcards and people phoned us and the e-mail started carrying congratulations. We were safe, we could move on, but the fear of the crossing had been the centre of our universe and now the galaxies of our brains were rushing apart, sending hopeless messages into the void.

We had not thought about our route, or the wide waterways or the huge locks and barges and the currents on the rivers or which way we were going and if we could moor in Paris and would we have enough strength for the terrible Rhône and we thought the engine needed work but we didn't know how to check. We decided to leave at once, we decided to stay for weeks; we couldn't think, we couldn't make sense of anything. The tide lifted us up into the sunshine and let us down again and cuckoos called and called and it didn't seem right there were so many cuckoos.

MUCH OF CALAIS HAD BEEN REBUILT IN THE dark days of low-rise concrete. Jim was not allowed on the beach and we wandered among the bad restaurants and the bad smells. Next to the yacht basin was the Citadel, with bushes and walks and flowers and among tall trees a raised sunlit lawn. The Sangatte asylum centre had been closed down and the asylum-seekers lay on the lawn or stood in the bushes: dark, accusing, waiting to cross the Channel; their journey so much more brave, more desperate than ours.

But every day yachts were arriving in the basin and we began to spend evenings with couples who told of drug-runners and broken masts and making love in storms. A boater could not but be gay in such a jocund company. Their steepling poles and folded ropes amazed us, and their bows that feared no distant sea.

In the early mornings we returned to our steel tube, our flowers, our hangovers, pleased that such people wanted our company. We would stay for a while until we were ready, and the *Phyllis May* was ready.

IT WAS TEATIME AND JIM HAD JUST BARKED. Jim can bark, but he won't, so we looked out of the window. On the pontoon were three men with guns. They walked down the boat, talking quietly. They stopped at the back and read the fairground lettering–**T and M Darlington, Stone**–and stood without expression, waiting for a sign. One of them made a phone call. Then they went away. After forty minutes they came back and did the same things again. Should we surrender? asked Monica–we're outnumbered and they're armed. But one of them hitched up his gun-belt and rapped on the boat–Customs, he said. We asked them on board and Jim sniffed their blue trouser legs.

There were two Young Guns and Top Gun, who was in his late twenties. Top Gun looked terrified. We had been here for ten days and we all knew there could be no point in a visit except curiosity. In such a rare and British craft perhaps we were related to the Queen, or were friends of the Duchess of York, and could ruin his career. He kept touching his gun, and I wondered if he was going to put a bullet through Jim to steady his nerves.

He filled in a long and boring form with Monica, both of them standing at the table. He stuck to English and did not smile, keeping his dignity in front of the Young Guns, who stood around and patted Jim and looked at the pictures on the walls. Then Top Gun stepped back and addressed us. He spoke as if he had been rehearsing for some time in a mirror. Welcome to the canals of France, he said.

We felt thoroughly welcomed, officially welcomed, as if by The France herself, by Marianne, interpreted by Catherine Deneuve in a flowing nightie. As the boarding party left one of the Young Guns whispered Pretty boat, *monsieur*–the woods, the brasses–first I've seen–my God. He shook my hand before Top Gun noticed and patted Jim on the head.

THERE IS A STORY ABOUT A SAILING SHIP THAT arrived in an unknown bay. Nearby some natives fished from a canoe. They looked at the ship–white sails, oak walls, ropes and spars–and they comprehended it not. So they did not see it, for them it did not exist, and with their catch they paddled back to the shore. I am like that with the engineering on the *Phyllis May*. Sometimes I pass through the engine-room, and sometimes I lift the boards and look at what is beneath, and I comprehend it not. So I see nothing, and I paddle back to the shore.

You need to do things in the engine-room, said Monica, we have done two hundred hours since Stone. It is not as if we were dropped off a lorry, all sorted out. There is a book, I said, somewhere.

The book was written in many tongues, filled with grainy photographs of steel intestines and warnings—

If you touch this it will bring a slow and painful death. If you do that it can seriously affect your health and that of those around you. This you must do at once—there is not a moment to lose. And that you should have done twice a day since you came on board and God help you if you haven't.

I spent an evening laying out my props like a conjuror, talking to myself and rehearsing my movements, and the next day I changed the oil. I had not changed the oil before and I didn't make it look easy. The next day I filled the batteries with a gallon of distilled water. The batteries did not want to be filled and it took me all day. You'd think they'd make them easier to fill, I said to Monica—it's bad design, not thinking about the customer.

In the book it said we should change the oil in the gearbox, and adjust the valve clearances, and the engine-room stank of diesel, and the lights in the saloon were dim, but I had paddled to the shore.

JIM SAT STARING UP THE STEPS OF THE RESTAU-rant by the sea, pathetic and outraged. The waitress went in to consult the *patron*. She returned—Unhappily we take only small dogs—a *lévrier* is too big. But he is not a *lévrier*, said Monica, he is a whippet, a *lévrier nain*, a dwarf greyhound. Desolated, said the waitress. We dined next door. As we were leaving, a gentleman of a certain age threw himself to the floor in front of Jim, who snuffled him and licked him. The gentleman stood up and took out his wallet. A foxed Polaroid showed a young man on a sofa with his arm round a girl and a dark shape over his shoulder that could have been a cushion, a fault in development, or the *horla* himself. My whippet, he said–his name was Black–he could fly. Yes, said Monica, they can fly. He was racing down a lane, said the gentleman, when a Belgian in a four-wheel drive came very fast at him and would have crushed him. But Black flew, right over the four-wheel, right over the Belgian, and he was safe, because he could fly.

The gentleman shook my hand and his three friends shook my hand and they all shook Monica's hand and they shook each other's hands and they shook Jim's hand and they shook the waitress's hand and they shook the hand of an old chap who was trying to get through to the gents. They said *Bonsoir Sheem* and the gentleman bent over Monica's hand and kissed it.

WHY AREN'T YOU IN THE ENGINE-ROOM? ASKED Monica. Why do I have to keep reminding you? You know there are things to do. I'm not right yet after the crossing, I said, I keep seeing the South Goodwin light vessel. But anyway I am a civilian, I don't know anything about it. Things don't work for me–they won't come apart and they won't go together. Can't we leave and take a chance? We always leave and take a chance, said Monica, and we always break down. You must take an interest. We are not on the Trent and Mersey here–there are no boatyards and no engineers and you might need spares. The people in the sky have been waiting eight weeks for a gearbox. Why are you no good at anything? You're useless. We should never have bought a boat. Other people know how to look after their boats. We'll never get to Carcassonne—we'll never get away from Calais. We're trapped, with the bloody cuckoos.

I went to the two-masted yacht moored next to us. Can you advise me, I asked the skipper, a Dutchman, where one might hope to find the drain-hole for a gearbox? He laughed and gripped my arm and his eyes bulged—he looked like Mad Mozza's father. At the lowest point, he said—you are not an engineer? No, I said, I am more at ease at the conceptual level. Talking of myself personally, said the Dutchman, I am a lecturer in the marine diesels. I will look at your engine-room. Oh no, I said—it's OK—I have the book.

Your gearbox is fresh like the daisy, said the Dutchman. You changed the engine oil through a wrong hole. Your batteries are maintenance-free and cannot be refilled and they are at the door of death. Your water separator is pissing diesel into the drip tray. Your big alternator is fallen off. Your windmill generator isn't generating. Your valves are for adjusting. Your tunnel light is broke. You have no connection of the electricity with the shore. You have not a battery charger. You have an engine like the lion but you have been running for two hundred hours and everything else is gone to hell. But have no fear, I will make it all like new.

No, I said, you mustn't, really you mustn't. I like to do it, said the Dutchman, I insist I do it, I must do it, I will make no charge. Why are we here, if it is not to be kind to one another, and help the poor, and the lonely, and the inadequate, and the weak? That's nice of him, said Monica. There is no such thing as a free lunch, I said.

In the mornings I held spanners and passed rags. In the afternoons I wobbled after the Dutchman on his wife's bicycle, seeking spare parts where there were none, falling on to the pavement, crazy with heat and fatigue. I minded the bikes in the sun as the Dutchman, who had no French, spent two hours in a confectionery wholesaler trying to buy an oil filter. When Monica and I tried to catch a nap he banged on the boat, when we sat down to eat he called us over to see his screw cutter. In the dead of night I mopped out the drip tray, trapped under the engine block as in a car accident. When we ate together the Dutchman trained Jim to put his head in his lap and made me jealous. If I told a joke he was there first with the punchline. One morning I woke and he was lying between me and Monica, his eyes bulging, a spanner between his teeth.

I said to him Ryk I feel so obliged, so helpless—you won't take anything and I want to do something to repay you but I am no good at anything—all I can do is write reports and poems and things and what bloody use is that? No use, said the Dutchman, no use at all.

More and more problems were being found, more spanners to be held, more fruitless errands, and the days were passing. We realized the Dutchman would never let us go and we had to leave Calais while we had our reason. We said that we must leave next day and organized a dinner to thank him and his wife helped pull him from our engine-room by the ankles.

In the restaurant I opened an envelope. It wasn't much of a poem, but Ryk didn't interrupt as I read it.

> *I sing this song when the days are long with no*
> *clouds in the sky*
> *And we are afloat on our narrow boat with a*
> *pub to steer her by*
> *We lay by the quay, Mon, Jimmy and me, with*
> *not a single care*
> *But a sudden call from the harbour wall said*
> *English boat—beware!*

For it was Ryk—he was strong and quick and
his eyes were shining blue
Oh my dears, I am full of fears of what will
happen to you
Your lights are low, your fuel won't flow, you
have no batteries
Your tunnel light is a dreadful sight and your
little dog has fleas

Your valves they bang, your pipes they hang,
your plugs and wires are wrong
Your diesel drips, your voltage slips, your flexes
are too long
Alas the day, if you sail away, you will surely
meet your maker
Your block will smash and will fall with a
crash on your water separator

But here I am, the Holland Man, and I will
sort you out
I am strong, I am quick, and my name is Ryk
and I leap on board with a shout
Pass me my spanner, pass me my hammer, and
pass my coffee too
And you will see the Zuider Zee need never
frighten you

So here's to Ryk, who's strong and quick, and
both his eyes are blue
He'll sort you out with a cheerful shout and
make things work like new
But when you try to say goodbye and thank him
for what he has done

> *He says no fear, perhaps a beer—then a wave of*
> *his hand and he's gone!*

Ryk laughed and read the poem out loud himself and laughed and read it out loud again and laughed and folded it carefully and put it in his wallet and took it out again during dinner and looked at it under the table and folded it carefully and put it back in his wallet. To my surprise I had found a currency he could accept.

RYK WAS ON HIS DECK BEHIND A PIANO-accordion, fingering a merry tune about clogs, and his wife was waving. The gates at the end of the yacht basin were open and the *Phyllis May* headed for the Calais Canal, where the slow heartbeat of the tides would move us no longer. We would berth at Audruicq in four hours' time.

We knew little about the French canals, but we had heard the water was sweet and there were ducks and grass and draught beer of a sort, sometimes less than a kilometre away. The maps said that if we could sail seven hundred miles we would get to Carcassonne. It was the end of the beginning.

Across the sunny basin, waving to the other boats, through the gate and under the bridge, out past the pontoon of the stamping Belgians. To our left the harbour entrance and the sea. We turned right past two bloated ferries and the wind hustled us into the grand old lock that led to the last sea basin—the lock that is left open so you just sail through. But today it was not left open. It was closed at the far end, and there was a red light.

In the front deck Monica was on the phone to Voies Navigables de France. It's shut all day because they are diving, she shouted—we have to go back. I can't go back, I answered, there's the shame, there's the accordion. Two men on the quay yelled–Twenty minutes and you'll go through. Ask them do they work here, I shouted over the wind. Yes they do, Monica answered, they say we can pass–I don't know what is happening. Behind me a freighter was coming in from the sea. It came towards the lock and entered it, and as I slowed for the end of the lock I lost steerage and the wind drove me across its path.

The end of the lock began to open, and I waited for the red light to change. It didn't and the ship was coming on me like an avalanche. I had a choice–I could jump the light and sail through into the last basin, meeting God knew what on the other side, or I could risk being overwhelmed by the freighter. I slammed down the throttle. As I did so the bridge over the lock broke apart and its supporting girders came at me, ready to rip us open like a can.

I don't think I panicked but I came close. We bolted for the centre of the bridge, and escaped just in front of the freighter, the wind screaming and pulling us across its path, the girders passing by my shoulder. The next basin was empty and we went hard right and let the freighter pass. There was a lot of it and it took a long time. We fought the wind to reach a quay and tied up and had a cup of tea and a shudder as the boat heaved and thudded against the wall.

Monica shed a tear and said Those buggers at the VNF. It was our fault, I said, we should have checked at the last moment, and perhaps we were never really in danger, there was more room than there seemed. We had another shudder and another cup of tea, like in the war.

We were joined by a yacht and a motor cruiser. Five o'clock, said the lady on the yacht, and they'll let us out the other end into the canal. She had just crossed the Channel. You came across in that? she asked–in that thing?

We sailed down in convoy and waited at the lock as the wind tore along grey and yellow hills on the quay and strafed us with sand and gravel and dust. At half past five two men in rubber suits appeared on top of the lock. It opened, let the other craft in, and shut in our face. The wind blew us across the basin by a welding yard, and cinders and dirt howled over us. I thought–Across the Channel in a narrowboat to be smashed up by a freighter or choked in a sandstorm before we reach the canals. But the gates opened and soon we sailed out of our first lock in France, on to fresh water. I raised my camera to record the basin and Calais Town Hall. I had run out of film.

Ten minutes later we were in a café. A Ricard for Monica, a beer for me, a bag of crisps for Jim to chase around the floor. In the corner a friendly wolf–blue-eyed, a malamute. In seven hours we have come five hundred metres, I said to Monica. At this speed we won't live to get to Paris, and Carcassonne is in another star system. But here's looking at you, kid.

The landlord dropped to the floor and lay there for a while with Jim, as is the custom in these parts. When Jim had licked his face he got up and said–I will tell you a story about my sledge dog Lady. One morning my wife woke me up and said My darling, Lady has been killed–a car accident, it's all over. *Merde alors*, I said, and jumped from my bed. So young, I said–there is no hope? No hope, said my wife–so young, so beautiful, so much loved, the blue eyes, the beauty, all is gone. I held my wife and together we wept. We wept and wept–my heart was breaking, *monsieur, 'dame*. Poor Lady Di, said my wife. Lady Di, I shouted, Lady Di! *Monsieur, 'dame*, it was the poor princess Lady Diana who had been killed, not my Lady with the thick fur and the blue eyes. The Lady Di was not much connected with me, and I was very happy. Most fortunate, I said.

• • •

NEXT DAY THEY LIFTED FOUR BRIDGES AND
we fled down the Calais Canal into Flanders. Why did Hitler
let the British get away at Dunkirk? my son Clifford had
asked me at Christmas. He was forty and beginning to ask
awkward questions. Hitler wanted the British Empire as an
ally, I said, and the RAF had Spitfires and Hitler didn't have
the guts and he was mad. He stopped the tanks at Watten,
thirty kilometres south of Dunkirk. The panzer leader
General Guderian was speechless. Did any narrowboats go
over? asked Clifford. No, I said, their engines were too small
and the canals go only to London.

As the *Phyllis May* sailed through Flanders I thought of my
children and my grandchildren and the people who had died
to save their inheritance. Along the dykes and drains millions of poppies bloomed, under a huge sky.

Little diagrams in the *Navicarte* waterways guide said that
nothing lacked in the town of Audruicq. There was a supermarket, a restaurant, a hospital, tennis, swimming, a camp
site, canoeing, walking, cycling, and horse-riding. There
were floating pontoons, and the lady mayoress would give
you a kiss. Across the turning to Audruicq there was a
chain. We gave up and moored on the bank. Three *péniches*
came by—black transport barges, over three hundred tons, a
car on top, wheelhouse high above us. At speed they could
suck us into their cooling systems and spit us out like a stick-
leback. But they slowed down and just tore out our mooring
pins.

The next morning our first canal lock, shared with a
péniche. We cowered in front and when he came out we let
him go ahead. He waved and led us south down the Calais
Canal, in the sunlight.

There was such depth that the *Phyllis May* would have gone faster along the green straights and round the long bends between poplars, but we hung back, and rows of white clouds got to Watten before us.

THE DUNKIRK–ESCAUT LINK IS PART OF THE *grand gabarit*, the French wide-gauge canal system. It runs through Watten, where Hitler lost the war. It's as broad as the Thames at Windsor. Thousand-ton barges, three times the size of the *péniches*, sweep the water up the canals and drains which run away into the marshlands. Sometimes the barges are alone, sometimes in twos, sometimes in threes. The French waterways are wider than the British, and older, and nearly three thousand miles longer. We turned under a bridge into a backwater, and tied up behind a restaurant.

I ordered a large beer and the waitress brought a glass four inches high, filled just above the mark with an icy liquid. You can't quaff French beer. You take a little into your mouth and the bubbles force it into your bloodstream between your teeth.

I still can't get my mind straight, I said to Monica. There is a kennel on the lawn with a sheep in it. That bouncy castle wasn't there when I sat down. What is that machine splashing around by the *Phyllis May*? It looks like a cross between a paddle steamer and a lawnmower. I swear I saw a submarine in the cut and a camel looking at me through the bushes. It's the strain. I'll be better when we move on. We've been three weeks in France and we've got nowhere. Tomorrow we'll start to motor.

Tomorrow our water tank emptied two hundred gallons on to the bedroom floor *Squish squosh* and it would take a fortnight to repair. A bottle of fish soup exploded in the cupboard. I was bitten on the sole of the foot by something with two fangs, which made me itch into my armpits. I couldn't walk or bend down because I had pulled something structural in my backside when under the engine for the Dutchman. Jim lost another nail and was standing on three legs and every time he tried to scratch himself he fell over. The boat stank of fish soup and dirty water and I was sitting around like a cripple and we could do nothing but wait for the water-tank repair and it rained day after day and Monica had an attack of the summertime blues and cabin fever.

You must go home, I said—it's been three months. You always planned to have a break. Go tomorrow—you'll be in Stone for lunch.

In five weeks in France we've come twenty miles, I thought, and lost half our crew. Bloody good start.

WIDOWED, UNCONSOLED, JIM AND I SAT ON the pontoon and watched the machine with a paddle wheel. It had come about the duckweed. It flailed around for a couple of days, but did not bother the fish. Nothing bothered the fish—they teemed and chased and flopped and I wondered if they might come into the boat one night and get us. There are catfish in the French canals that will swallow a dog, and lampreys that can empty you and spit your husk into the water lilies. I have seen them in an aquarium, grinding their teeth against the glass. When we had watched the machine for a while I would go and mop up dirty water and fish soup until I started to feel sick, then we would watch the machine again.

Jim had decided that until Monica returned he would stay on three legs and eat nothing but chips. The only thing more pathetic than a whippet is a three-legged whippet, and he got a lot of attention as he hopped through Watten.

The town has one main street, varied, unkempt, Flemish.

Shops, brick and off-white houses, narrow pavements. The street is called Rue Charles de Gaulle and halfway along there is a square. Here a plaque records the general's speech from London of 18 June 1940, declaring his contempt for Marshal Pétain, who the day before had announced an armistice with Germany.

Rulers thrown up by chance have found themselves able to sur-render, overcome by fear, mindless of honour, delivering the land into slavery.

Close by the plaque there was a restaurant. At the bar a big man with white hair, and his younger friend, who was small and smiled and smoked. Jim lay on the floor grieving, waiting for chips.

Your town was not destroyed, I said—I mean not like Calais or Abbeville—most of your buildings are old. There was no fighting in Watten, *monsieur*, said the old man. The troops passed through and then they passed through again. But night after night there was bombing. A couple of kilometres away in Eperlecques we have the blockhouse, built by slaves, for the V2 rockets. After the bombing there was nothing left of Eperlecques. Here fifty people were killed—people I knew. Louis Gokelaert was killed and his wife and five of his six children. Two were twin girls, one year old. Planes were shot down—one was a Spitfire, another was the American one with two engines, the Mitchell B-25. One man went down with the plane. Three jumped but one of the chutes did not open. Many of your airmen are buried here.

We had Germans billeted on us—the last one was Austrian—his cap had a feather. He got us coal and wood. He knew we had a radio. You could be deported if you had a radio.

Up here you were not under Pétain's Vichy government, I

said. No, said the younger man, we were not part of the Free France. In Britain we did not think Vichy France was free, I said. No, no, of course it was not free, said the old man—but you must realize, *monsieur*, the Marshal Pétain was the hero of the first war, of the siege of Verdun, the turning point.

In the war you were part of Belgium, I said. Both men rose from their seats—Belgium, never, *monsieur*. Belgium? We are The France. No, I said, in the Second World War the Department of the North was administered by the Germans from Brussels. Ah yes, it is possible, they said, and sat down.

Did any of your family fight over here? the younger one asked. Yes, I said, two of my uncles. One was a stretcher-bearer in Normandy. He was twenty-four. The other was a paratrooper at Arnhem. He was twenty-seven. They were both killed. But look at your infantry who died while we were getting away from Dunkirk. And in the Resistance there were many mindful of honour.

Yes, said the old man. Six from round here were betrayed for a few hundred pounds and condemned to death for help-ing a Canadian airman.

Before her judges, Madame Illidge took a proud and noble stance, saying—I regret nothing. If it were to do again I would be more careful and work alone.

When the judges left the courtroom, they gave her a military salute.

I wonder if Louis Aragon knew about Madame Illidge, I said. His ballad—the one that spread across France during the occupation—we know it in England too.

One word and you can live
One word and you can save

Your body Only give
One word and live—a slave

If it were to do again
I'd do it—count on me
Her words rise from the chains
Speak of the days to be

There were many, said the younger man, and not just on the last day. He shook my hand and lit another cigarette and bought me a beer and folded his newspaper and patted Jim and went out, all in one movement.

WHEN MONICA CAME BACK JIM THREW HIM-self against her again and again, and then he threw himself against me—You fool, you fool, you let her escape, but here she is—I got her back and I forgive you, you fool, you fool. He started eating and walking again. Even when he was standing around he did it joyfully.

He seems to have expressions, I said. Of course he has expressions, said Monica. But he can't really have expressions, I said. The human face has dozens of muscles, and he hasn't got room for that many and they'll all be different to ours anyway and he's only a dog. Look at him, said Monica. Jim was lying on his back, his paws bent over, his body doubled, making the growling noise he makes when he would like you to pat his stomach. He was smiling broadly.

You know, said Monica, I feel fine now I've had a break and realized what is going on. I never really thought about what it would be like if we got across the Channel. I thought it would be a holiday. If we had spent half our life on boats and we were thirty, perhaps it would be. But for us it's new, and it's hard work, and it could go either way. I feel different now—I expect nothing but hardship and pain.

I'm sorry the boat was in a mess when you got back, Mon, I said. It's just that I met these chaps in the town and we talked about the war and they came to see the *Phyllis May*. And then the old one wanted his girlfriend to see it and the younger one wanted to show it to his mother. Then there was the vet and his wife who came along for coffee and Malcolm from the yacht next door told me about his alcoholism and his operation and how he sailed over the Channel and when he got over he was so tired he fell on the pontoon and broke his arm in two places. And a French family on a cruiser took me into Dunkirk in their car. And I left my glasses in the restaurant and the *patron* brought them back and we had a beer.

You're anybody's, said Monica, you're just an old tart. I like talking to people, I said, but they all start talking to Jim anyway. You've seen how they kiss him and he licks their faces. You've got to speak to them.

I'll tell you something about the French, I said. You get an English couple on the *Phyllis May* and they will sit where you put them, and they will talk in normal voices and in their turn, unless they are drunk or dicks. The French love the boat but when you show them a seat they take no notice. They come right up to you and shout at the tops of their voices. If you move back they corner you up one end of the boat and you have to listen to them and answer them properly. If you do not they pull at your clothing.

Jim was still on his back. Smiley Broadling, the horizontal hound.

• • •

ON OUR LAST DAY IN WATTEN JIM AND I WALKED down the canal. The café was called the Relay of the Fisherman and it was one of those waterway cafés that sells fishing tackle and bait. Outside was a notice:

Worms of mud	*2 euros*
Worms of flour	*2 euros*
Worms of earth	*2 euros*
Worms of wood	*2 euros*
Worms of compost	*2 euros*
Worms and chips	*3 euros*

On the way back my younger friend from the restaurant stopped me. He was carrying a box with an antenna, and a book. Thierry, please keep this book about the war in the region. War is not funny but there is a story—the Germans built hundreds of planes out of wood and put them in the fields to one side of St. Omer airport. The RAF came and dropped bombs on them—wooden bombs.

Thierry, it has been exceptional. *Bon voyage*—we will think of you both and Sheem. I will return now to my little submarines.

We walked back to the boat past the notices for a circus. It had left town, taking its camels.

THE FRENCH FAMILY THAT HAD DRIVEN ME into Dunkirk had given us a map marked for a voyage to Armentières and into Belgium. You have to visit the Ardennes, they said, they are very nice, and I had said, Of course, wondering who they were. We were to go across south-west Belgium and approach Paris from the rear.

Jim knew we were leaving before we did. As we cast off he

stood in the middle of the boat, shivering, ears folded, eyes brimming—Look you know I really really hate this boating business—I am an athlete, an artist, I need space. I need a stable home environment, friends, room to grow.

South to Arques, down the Dunkirk—Escaut link, on the *grand gabarit*, down the great water. So much sun, so much sky, so much green towpath: rich fields, people waving, or astonished and waving back—*Beau bateau, beau bateau.*

This is it, we are boating in France. This is freedom alley, this is Route 66, this is the golden road to Carcassonne. Burn it, burn that diesel baby. A full fathom under us—now we haul ass.

Look behind you, said Monica, squeaking like the pantomime clown, look behind you—if a big barge comes up it could be goodbye. I kept looking but after a while I stopped. We forced on alone, and when a barge came towards us we almost welcomed its giant company. It moved to one side and I turned into the wash and enjoyed the counter kicking beneath my feet.

Wearied by betrayal, Jim had gone to sleep in his bed out on the sharp end. A whispering, a whispering over my shoulder—My God, within feet, a barge! But its thousand tons came by slowly, light of foot, and there was no wash. The lady on board held up her little girl to see us.

After three hours we reached two locks. These were not Earth locks—these were the locks of the biggest planet in the universe. One was thirteen metres deep—a black hole from which no light emerged.

I don't want to go in, said Monica, I can't see anything, I'm scared—but the signal was green and she did. An arch spanned the lock, and there in a window was the tiny head of the *horla*. Behind us a guillotine ground down like the portcullis of hell. We tied to a floating bollard in the darkness under the girdered gate and I thought When they open the gate paddles that will be it—overwhelmed and sunk in seconds. But water came from beneath and quietly we rose. In twenty minutes we were back on Terra, safe on our blue bauble hung in space, with its trees and its sun and its gongoozlers. We turned left off the *grand gabarit* into the river Lys, moving at summer's pace.

In the river Lys the long plants lay all the same way and the sun played across them and oxygen bubbled from their leaves. Fish flicked and rolled. This could have been an English canal, but it was better. The water was clearer, the navigation was wider, the sun was brighter, the poplars more towering, the flowers bolder, the views larger; there were water lilies, there were no other boats. Maybe it was not really better—how can you compare?—but for sure it was the Hollywood version, in widescreen and colour with stereophonic ducks. Central Casting had supplied some ecstatic gongoozlers safely distant on the banks, and fourteen herons in a fifty-yard stretch. *How many herons did they say, Nat? They didn't? Oh hell, better send the lot, and if you get a chance spread 'em out a bit this time willya?*

Aire-sur-la-Lys has a shallow pool where only a dinghy or a narrowboat can moor, and we did, with our gangplank. The town was once rich but now it is dirty and broken, the shops scattered among empty houses. We walked around, jumping away from the cars. In England cars go quickly on main roads, and in side streets and car parks they don't. In France there is no alley so humble that a little car will not rush down it, no turning so tight that it will slow a Frenchman down. They hurtle across car parks as if on a motorway. They come up behind you on shrieking motorbikes. They come at you out of drains.

• • •

WE TURNED INTO THE MARINA AT ARMEN-
tières. *Hinky dinky parley voo*, said Monica. It was the four-
teenth of July. We were the only boat with bunting and flags,
and the French boaters approved, though alarmed by the
flag with the red dragon, perhaps because the dragon was six
feet long. Where's the party? we asked. Tonight there is
dancing, *monsieur*, said the *capitaine*, and fireworks, in the
town. Jim is good with fireworks, because they take place on
land, and we all went to town.

In the main square a young man dressed as a junkie was
bellowing into a microphone. He seemed to be telling jokes.
The French male normally converses at a full shout–give
him a microphone and he goes nuts. The noise was reaching
across Belgium. A dozen people were standing around looking the other way. There was a hot-dog stand and flags, but
there were more flags on the *Phyllis May* than there were in
Armentières. Now and again the young chap would sing a
rap song, accompanied on keyboards by a man in a
butcher's apron and on bass guitar by a lady in a flowered
dress and a forties hairstyle, who was quite good.

We walked past the war memorial. Marshal Pétain accept-
ing a bunch of stone flowers from a little girl.

Rulers thrown up by chance, mindless of honour.

Back at the boat we heard artillery, and the crackle of machine guns. On the pontoon it was night and there was
smoke and red and yellow fire over the town.

Then the maroons went up and the sky bloomed with
chrysanthemums, and ran with silver rain.

Six

THE DARK TOWER

Courtrai to Waulsort

The dick and Jim looked at each other without enthusiasm. I used to have a dog, said the dick, and he died. I don't blame him, I thought, but Oh hard luck, I said. We had tied up to our first pontoon in Belgium, at Wervik just over the border, and the dick and his wife banged on the roof and I went out on the deck and thought I know these guys and have forgotten who they are God how embarrassing.

Come in, I said—we're just making some coffee—how have you been? The dick settled down and I realized I thought I knew him because he looked like Ronnie Kray, the famous murderer. His wife was slim and dark and looked like a girl who used to race in the Midland Veterans Cross-country

League—the one called Barbara who had little black shorts. The dick was gathering speed.

We have been here six years, he said, and in the winter we go to Portugal. We have a Dutch barge, much bigger than yours. We know all about everything round here and you have just arrived and you will find boating in Belgium very difficult. Jim walked into the cabin and went to sleep.

Have you ever been conjoined? asked the dick. No, I said, I've been straight all my life. The dick did not laugh. The thousand-ton barges, he said—you can get conjoined. What happens is when they go through the water they leave a hundred-and-fifty-ton hole behind them and if you are an inch too close you get sucked down into the hole and you stick to the side of the barge and you cannot get off and you stay like that until the bargee notices you or until you are knocked off by a lock or a passing boat. It happened to me. I was conjoined and the bargee—he's my friend now, old Gaston—saw me and left me there for ten kilometres and then just as we were going into a lock *whoosh* he reversed and blew me off. Goodness we laugh when we talk of it now. Very amusing, I said. Then there is the poison gas, said the dick.

It happens at Charleroi, he said, a week away, on the Sambre. Right in the middle of the industrial area there is a steelworks and the fumes are so bad you close all the windows or you die. We steer standing on the back in the open, I said. Ah, said the dick, so you do. There are very few mooring places round here, and they are full of Dutchmen. You have a long boat, though not as long as mine, and the Dutch will not move an inch to let you in. They become violent.

Can't I moor on a wall? I asked. The dick laughed, and his wife laughed. Moor on a wall, with thousand-ton barges coming by? When you leave Courtrai your only hope is to go to Antoing which is ten hours away and when you get there it's a small basin and the Dutch will not let you in.

I've got a washing machine and a dishwasher on my boat, said the dick's wife.

NEXT STOP COURTRAI–*KORTRIJK* IN FLEMISH– designer shops for watches, designer shops for shoes, for underwear, for chocolates. Designer shops for corkscrews; designer shops for hamster cages. A bright square with a loony brick tower in the middle. Mercedes and BMWs, and designer cars you could slip in your pocket. The people were a foot taller than in Armentières. They wouldn't speak French but some had English and they had their own quacking tongue.

We had a bad meal in the square. We can't possibly do ten hours tomorrow with eight locks, said Monica, we'll be exhausted–it's not safe. We have never done ten hours in our lives–we do an hour a day if we are lucky. Remember our motto–*Start slow and then give up.* We've got no choice, I said. There are no marinas until Antoing. And if we do get there the Dutch will become violent and beat us up. I suppose we could go home.

When we got back to the *Phyllis May,* next door there was a fine old barge, a Hull keel, with a fine old British couple who asked us on board for a *digestif.* We've had a look at Belgium, they said, and we are going back to France.

IT WAS A LOVELY MORNING FOR EXHAUSTION and violence. The couple next door were holding a Welsh flag and waving. It was like leaving for the Falklands–I wonder if any of our lads will come back?

The river Lys had become the river Leie and soon we were on the Bossuit-Kortrijk Canal.

Like the British canals, the Belgian canals are the old work of giants, but these giants had machines. The canal was fifty yards wide and a fathom and a half deep—green verges, metalled towpaths, poplars in rows, all their green tongues talking. Grebes, ducks, cormorants, moorhens smaller than our own plump race. Herons, Canada geese, Greylag geese and little brown and white chaps I must look up one day. No coots. Plenty of water for everyone. Locks a hundred yards long; the *Phyllis May* sometimes alone, sometimes alongside a cruiser, sometimes crouched under a barge.

We had bought our boating licence in Flemish Belgium, but now we had crossed into French Belgium—Wallonia—where it was not recognized. So at every lock Monica had to put on her life jacket, climb up a slimy ladder in the lock wall, climb up the lock tower and have a form stamped. The Flemish and the Walloons might hate each other, but that is no excuse for taking the piss with the poor boaters.

I had never done a four-hour shift on the tiller before and I felt grand. Lunch on a lock mooring. Moor right at the end, said Monica, you never know what will come along. What came along was a container barge ninety-five metres long—it would have taken one of our nation's noblest athletes, his blood frothing with performance-enhancing drugs, ten seconds to run past it. Its length was painted on the side, and a message pointing out that it carried the freight of sixty-eight heavy lorries and although it might not look much was a damn good thing in every way. It came by and it came by and I thought There is not enough room on the mooring, there is not enough room in Belgium, he will swing his back in and there goes the *Phyllis May*. But when he swung his back in, there was room.

A crewman threw a rope from the boat towards a bollard, a rope as thick as a lamprey, and missed, just like anyone else. He threw the rope to me on the bank and I caught it and put it over the bollard and the skipper of the barge levered the boat in against the rope, springing it in just like anyone else. He waved at me and smiled. I have done four hours on the tiller, I thought. I have been waved at by the skipper of a hundred-yard barge. Right, bring on the Dutchmen. I'll knock the buggers into the cut.

Monica took over and I went to sleep and when I woke the poplars seemed a hundred feet high, marching for miles round sweeping bends. Some poplars were pillars and some were pompoms. They looked a richer green than they were, as things do when you are waking up.

We passed under Tournai's thin stone arches and arrived at the little basin of Antoing. We had taken seven hours. On the quay five Dutchmen took our ropes and pulled their boats along to fit us in and asked if they could take pictures of the *Phyllis May*.

But in Tournai the canal had choked beneath us. No birds, no fishermen, no glassy cool translucent wave. Just stink, just dullness, just death.

NIMY IS A SMALL PLACE NEXT TO MONS AND the Nimy–Blaton–Péronne Canal runs between Nimy, Blaton and Péronne as it should, but the other way round, right to left as you read the map, if you follow me. Anyway what the hell it sort of goes across south-west Belgium. Péruwelz is a town to one side of the canal.

The *capitainerie* in the yacht basin looked like a chicken shed after the fox got in, and they had swept up a bit and put in a few tables and chairs and some leaflets in a rack and some Jupiler *en pression*. There was the *capitaine*, who was a jolly young chap, a couple of men of a certain age, a spherical woman in black leggings and a drunk. The little guys who live in the forks of the creeks. The weather was heavy, the canal smelt and there were flies.

Jim looked at me—At least make an effort, can't you? There had been no scratchings since South Dock. *Monsieur*, I said to the *capitaine*, you have not a savoury snack for my dog? Some biscuits of cheese? Even some crisps perhaps? Sheep? asked the *capitaine*, for the dog? The French for crisps is sheep. He went away for twenty minutes and came back with a green and purple packet containing air and some white pads stained with rust. He may have driven into town. I offered the packet to Jim. He lay down and closed his eyes.

The woman took the drunk for a walk but he fell over and she sat with him on the grass. She lit a cigarette. Is it a greyhound? asked one of the older men. No, I said, it is a whippet, a racing dog, the dog of the English working man.

I went to England once, said the other—I walked along the pavement and then I came home. Go over again, I said, walk on some grass, build it up gradually. Then the next time, said his friend, *sortez le grand jeu*—buy some chewing gum.

My word Belgium is a hot country, I said. Ninety degrees—I don't know how you get through the summer. No, *monsieur*, in Belgium it rains three days in five. This is a hundred-year heatwave—the dog days, the *canicule*. One of them bought me a beer. Where did you learn to speak French, *monsieur*? Hanging around in Lille with my penfriend and his mates, I said, when I was a boy. And my wife was a French teacher.

Can you explain to me about the Flemish? I asked. Why don't you Walloons like them? Is it because they have the rich towns in the north and the money? We don't mind them, they said, it's the different language that's all. But it's crazy that such a small country is in two parts like this, I said. How did it happen? It was a long time ago, and it was your fault, they said—you were in charge after Waterloo, you made our nation.

I was in Armentières a couple of days ago, I said, and it was the national day there—not much celebration in Armentières. When is your national day? Today is our national day, *monsieur*, said the *capitaine*.

The drunk struggled back to the bar. As he passed he snarled at us. Jim does a bit of light growling, but I have not heard him snarl, and Jim is a dog. Is that gentleman often drunk, I asked, or is he celebrating? Alas, *monsieur*, they said, for him every day is a celebration. The spherical woman put her hand on the drunk's shoulder and lit his cigarette. Jim snapped at the flies and I finished the bag of sheep.

THE CANALS OF BELGIUM WERE PLANTED WITH poplars and served by huge ports and wharves and boatlifts made of clockwork that would balance a *péniche* in each hand. Now the wharves are desolate and the springs of the boatlifts are broken. Soon enough the green poplars will fall, and only the loony towers of Belgium will be left. In little Antoing, in tattered Mons—medieval turrets, baroque belfries, a Fabergé egg in a spire; a princess looking out, combing her bright hair. And the new work of giants—silos and fractionation columns and twisted chimneys, smoking and defecating along the water. Towers with no princesses. We pushed on, urgent to escape, until Childe Roland to the Dark Tower came.

The boatlift at Strépy-Thieu is an intergalactic cockroach in the sky, a *War of the Worlds* spaceship on stilts. We passed between the concrete legs and tied up in a tank a hundred yards long in an avenue of cables a hundred yards high. Each hank of cables was gripped at wharf level by a robot soldier, his electric guts clicking behind a glass panel. We shared the tank with a cruiser and a thousand-ton barge—there was plenty of room.

A humanoid in blue across the water made a sign for the damfool paperwork. It took Monica a long time to walk round and a long time to walk back. A line of gongoozlers giggled as I took a picture of their heads against the sky.

We held our ropes and waited and nothing happened but after a while the fields and hills below had been pushed away. Give me a place to stand and I will move the world. It was a blank experience, like the Channel Tunnel, like having a tooth out under gas, like Shakin' Stevens. Far away the gate opened and we sailed out two hundred feet higher, on to the top of a hill, the body of the cockroach tower behind us. Beneath the boat the water still lay dead.

From behind their smoked windows in the tower the aliens watched us leave. They are the size of sheep, but shaped like maggots, and so strange are their minds that they deal directly with the European Commission in Brussels—We will replace your missing billions and help restore order in your society and then we will clean up your canals—trust us—you have nothing to lose.

Ha ha ha, ha ha ha—the fools, we will swallow them up.

THE *PHYLLIS MAY* LAY UNDER THE WHARF LIKE a toy. Monica climbed the ladder in the wall. I caught Jim, snapped him into his life jacket, and hoisted him on to the roof. I climbed after him, using the brass step in the side of the boat. On the roof I had put the log-box, the one with *Phyllis May* on the front side and *Kiss Me Again* on the backside. I rested one end of the gangplank on the log-box and the other end up on the wharf. Then I chased Jim along the roof and picked him up like a handbag by the strap on the back of his life jacket. He dangled—not too tense, not too loose—he is a good dangler. I stood him on the gangplank and pushed him. Monica took hold of the handle of the life jacket and pulled him up along the plank on to the wharf. She unsnapped the life jacket.

Jim took a few steps along the wharf and pissed over his right front leg. Then we all went back by the same route.

What am I supposed to do, I said to Monica as we turned out the light, with an animal that pisses on itself?

AT CHARLEROI ON THE RIVER SAMBRE WE sailed through a steelworks, as the dick had foretold—twisted towers, hills of scrap, and all the fire and the bursting smoke. It was a bright day and the wind blew away most of the poison gas. The works groaned and clanged and grabs swung over the water, greedy to pick us up and drop our tasty steel hull into a furnace. When we went round a corner I could see they had got the boat in front, but I swerved and accelerated each time the grabs came near and we made it through.

That night we moored by a deserted coal-wharf and Jim ran away up the slag heap because he had not had a run for days. I brought him back covered in coal-dust and Monica stood him in the bath and washed him and rubbed him with a towel. He growled and grinned and wriggled against my chair and ran about the narrow floor. But in the morning he shivered and looked betrayed. I'm a whippet, I need green grass, I need pubs, people to love, something to chase, something to steal. Monica and I were tired and bored too.

We pushed away from the coal-wharf and under the

hammer of the sun we followed the stinking Sambre through a waste of towers and turned south on to the river Meuse at Namur.

WE HAD STOPPED DRINKING FOR A TIME BEcause we were getting fat. We took this decision in the middle of a heatwave in a country famous for its beer. Having made our resolution we no longer had a choice—like nonalcoholics everywhere we were helpless in the net of our folly. We started running again, and left the *Phyllis May* under the seven-arched Pont des Jambes, attended by a grebe, which surfaced now and again to check she was still there.

In Namur the splendour falls on castle walls, the shops open, the Dutch in the motor launches along the quays fold back their canopies and start frying bacon, and machines arrive to dig up the roads.

We jogged past the lock, along the embankment by holiday apartments and old houses with mansard roofs and towers. I was going well, but I was having trouble with my shadow. It had lost some of its shape and was throwing the left hand and not getting much lift. I slowed down and it regained its form, though it seemed hardly to be moving. Monica and Jim had pulled ahead, and Jim came back to see what had happened, and then raced back to Monica. Soon after he reached her his shadow caught him up.

Hello hello—my boat is over there, come and have a beer. We went across the river and took a glass of fizzy water with an Irish couple who used to own a marina in Hull. I like your boat, said the gentleman—low in the saddle, long bow, open layout. You too have a very fine boat, I said, and four times bigger than the *Phyllis May*. Eighty years old, a Dutch Tjalk, said the gentleman. I found her rotting on a mudbank.

Worked on her for five years. She's lovely, said Monica—all curves, like one of those seaplanes, the Catalinas.

We sailed her across the Channel, he said—I still have bad dreams. My wife went by train—she said she wanted someone left for the grandchildren. You came across on a lorry? No, said Monica, we sailed.

Goodness, said the marina owner—you are very brave. Oh I don't know, I said. But yes, he said—I am an engineer and I understand these things. It's a question of the forces at play. A sixty-foot narrowboat is fine until you get two waves exactly sixty feet apart. Then the bow is on one wave and the stern is on another, and it snaps in the middle like a rotten carrot. The famous adventurer, whom I know personally, had a base plate made of twelve-millimetre steel, so it would not snap.

I said, I have not heard of this before, are you sure? Heavens yes, said the marina owner. Eleven narrowboats have gone down in the last few years. It's in print in *Boating for Fun* magazine.

They were ever so nice, said Monica, back on the *Phyllis May*—but why didn't you tell me about the breaking in the middle? We could have lost the boat, we could have lost Jim, we could have been drowned. You're irresponsible—you're a lunatic—I knew I should never have married you.

Some people said we were stupid, I said, and some said we were risking our lives, but no one said a narrowboat had ever been lost. Our base plate is ten-millimetre steel—the sides are six millimetres and the roof four. That's normal. How can a tube like that break under its own weight? I drove her round the North Foreland in a force four and she was like a rock. Yes, there are eleven narrowboats snapped like carrots lying on the bed of the Channel, and there is a panther on Dartmoor, and a double-decker bus on the moon.

• • •

I TOOK A TANKARD DOWN FROM ITS HOOK IN the galley and it felt hot. I patted Jim and he felt cool.

> *Me seemes the world is runne quite out of*
>   *square,*
> *From the first point of his appointed sourse,*
> *And being once amisse growes daily wourse and*
>   *wourse.*

The air is thirty-eight degrees, I said, so everything we touch is hotter than our blood. It means the rules have changed— we have to lose heat all the time, and so does Jim, or we die. Thank you doctor, said Monica.

We listened to a news bulletin—the French Ministry of Health had been asked about the heatwave and said there was no problem. Then someone noticed that there were a third more corpses around than was usual at this time of year, and there were apartment blocks full of people who would not answer the door. It was the *canicule*, the dog days, the worst heatwave ever recorded. Jim lay near the engine-room, where the boat was deepest in the water, his bald belly hard against the deck.

For our last night in Namur we went out to dinner and had a pizza. The restaurant staff were charming and there were people at the next table eating pizzas like ours, full of water and tinned artichoke hearts and cardboard mushrooms. We were thankful for the four rows of teeth under the table, but we paid, smiled, and left a tip. I had decided before we left Stone that on the waterways I would be relaxed and cool, never standing on my dignity. I was doing well—apart from a rather good riposte to a vigilante dick on a lock in

Leicestershire. The policy was working OK but I am not sure I recommend it—before I go to sleep I sometimes think of the bastards I should have pushed into the cut.

We walked down the main street. We could have gone straight to Paris, I said—we have lost a lot of time. The Belgians confuse me. The Walloons, the French ones, have that stupid paperwork at the locks and the Flemish speak English you can't understand, addressing you like an escaped lunatic. Sometimes they won't even say hello. The Flemish boaters in Mons smile faintly and look away, like some toff giving you the freeze. Was it my T-shirt? Perhaps *Stone Master Marathoners* is Flemish for *You Are a Belgian and Your Face Is Like a Bollock.* But think of the *capitaine* in Namur who wanted to drive us to the supermarket. Yes yes, said Monica, all very true—oh my word.

A thousand people came down the middle of the road behind us, sweeping along on Rollerblades. Some of the blades flashed and spun with electric lights in the dusk. The skaters made little noise, concentrating on speed. A couple fell down to show it was not as easy as it looked. There were pretty girls and hairy young men in black Lycra. Then a thousand cyclists, silent and intent, following the rest of the rout to the Pont des Jambes. Then the skateboarders. There were children following up in the rear, and a speaker van playing an American disco tune that had been huge twenty-five years ago. When we got to the bridge they had all vanished.

WE SLIPPED A COUPLE OF EUROS TO THE GREBE and headed south into the Ardennes. High hills covered with oak and beech and ash and birch and poplar and chestnut and rowan. It was hot and the Meuse smelt bad.

Please advise me of one thing, *monsieur.* Certainly, I said—

my dear chap. While Monica was up in the lock towers there was time to chat to gongoozlers, who were rarer than in England. This one had spectacles with steel rims. Please tell me why you British will not commit yourselves wholeheartedly to the Single European Currency and the European Community, asked the gongoozler. You are not being reasonable and I wish you to explain.

Well, I thought, it's a change from Is this your boat? The decision whether to enter the European Currency is not mine alone, I offered, but when my firm did research for the European Commission it was not an orderly house.

I have a herd of Charolais beef, said the gongoozler, the best in this region. Three times a week I take my daughters to piano lessons and come down and watch the boats. I cover the waterfront, I suggested. Yes, indeed, said the gongoozler, but tell me *monsieur*, why do you insist on siding with America all the time? They are imperialists. They will take everything and we will have nothing left. You are a European, why will you not stick with us? In ten years Germany will rise again and he will be your big brother and France and Belgium will be your friends, and together we will stuff the USA. Do you not want to stuff the USA, *monsieur*?

When I was a little boy, I replied, the Germans dropped bombs on me. They tuned the carburettors of the bombers so they roared in and out and frightened me and they put whistles in their bombs to frighten me some more. They drove us from our homes so we slept in the fields and they machine-gunned the cattle so they swelled up and lay with their legs sticking out.

When the American soldiers came they gave me chewing gum. It was the little red squares, with the cinnamon flavour—not so easy to get these days. I am a simple man—I go with the chewing gum.

Too simple, said the gongoozler—there are new generations, they will decide.

WE WOULD SPEND A FEW DAYS IN DINANT—
the jewel in the belly button of the Belgian Riviera. Churches
under the cliffs, houses climbing between trees, and by the
pontoons a street of restaurants. On the quay a notice—

Go away, tomorrow we are entertaining the
jet-ski world championships.

A jet-ski is a motorbike that has been modified so it sinks
more slowly. It is used for sexual display and to generate
waves. We untied and sailed downstream a quarter of a mile
to the Casino and drew the curtains and switched on the fan
to sweat out the afternoon. We had bought the fan in a
French supermarket—it has Bluesky written on it, which we
pronounce Blueski, in the Russian way, and then we laugh. It
is not easy to find things to laugh about when it is thirty-eight
degrees.

The Casino was made out of red bricks and didn't look
much like a casino, or anything else really. A lady knocked
and asked us for money for mooring and pointed to a notice
on the back of a post—

Go away, tomorrow we are entertaining the
jet-ski championships.

There is a mussel-house by the main quay, I said—they
cannot mess up mussels and chips. We walked back down
the riverside through tree-trunk men with ponytails and
wet suits, and brownskin women with great breasts, and

four-wheeled motorbikes, and vans painted with flowing devices, and roaring generators and cables, and we ate messed-up mussels and chips, and ice cream from a stall.

When you buy an ice cream Jim stares at you. He stared at me so hard I gave him my cone when it still had my scoop of pistachio inside and he wouldn't give it back.

The next morning we sailed down to take some pictures of the town in the mist. The twenty thousand jet-skiers were not around. They were asleep in each other's arms, in their vans and under their terrible machines.

HIGH, WOODED HILLS, WITH ROCKY BLUFFS and fields by the river. I'll let that thousand-tonner go ahead into the lock, I thought, and follow him. Now I'll put my bow alongside and tie up to him—oh the lock paddles are opening and the water is pouring in fast and his back is swinging into us—reverse, reverse quick! More rope, more rope, more rope! Are we clear Mon? Are we clear? Oh thank God. A thousand tons at one mile an hour is a lot of foot-pounds. One chap with a big steel launch was hit by a barge and lost the middle of his boat. When you hear these tales it makes you feel sort of hollow.

What are those guys like in the towers on the locks with their silly paperwork? I asked Monica. Are they polite? Some have epaulettes, she said, but some are really nice, like that chap who wished us *bon voyage* on the Tannoy as we went out. He visited England when he was a young man and he walked down Kensington High Street and Carnaby Street and he said he would never forget the girls' flared trousers, the *pantalon*. None of us will ever forget the *pantalon*, I said.

· · ·

BY ELEVEN O'CLOCK IN THE MORNING IT WAS too hot to travel. It was too hot to stay alive. I looked out for some shade and pulled under two trees, hacking and sawing. We roped up and had lunch, drew the curtains, switched on Blueski, and lay down until the evening. It was cooler then but the air was heavier too. After dark we closed the windows against the mosquitoes, and sprayed the boat with flyspray, and went to bed.

Under the net I dreamed I was suffocating so I slept in the saloon with Blueski, naked, with sweat running down my sides and my eyes prickling. In the night my mosquito bites swelled up and I had to take tablets.

In the morning there were new bites, in rows, and I had sprained my wrist sawing our way into the shade and I had to clean my teeth with my left hand. Life contracted to the four hours before eleven in the morning.

WAULSORT IS A LITTLE RESORT ON THE Belgian Riviera, south of the belly button. We moored and plugged in and walked the long pontoon with Jim and met the *capitaine*, a thin man with no front teeth. He had a magpie on his shoulder. I didn't know quite what to say. Perhaps Goodness you have a magpie on your shoulder, but he would have known that already. I could not say What a fine magpie, because it was a runt, hardly a magpie at all. Jim was pulling towards another magpie on the path. I wouldn't let him do that, said the *capitaine*, that one can be a bit violent.

The *capitainerie* rivalled Péruwelz for simplicity. It was a shed with water that poured down the roof to keep it cool, and down your neck as you came in. There was a cat with five kittens in a box. In pens outside there were goats and two dogs bred to hunt mammoths. They barked in a dark bass and Jim tried to copy them, and did rather well. Pumpkins glowed in a little garden and ripening tomatoes begged you to steal them–went down on their hands and knees. *Nine bean rows will I have there*, said Monica, *a hive for the honey-bee*–it's like the Lake Isle of Innisfree.

I work the chain ferry, said the *capitaine*–just stand at the quay and I will take you across to the village where there is a shop. Each morning I will fetch you bread. There is a fine bar and restaurant just here on this bank. Concerning the magpies, he said, there are usually too many in the nest and the strong one throws the weak ones out. I fed these two and they stayed with me. The one on the floor flew at Jim, who jinked just in time.

We asked the bald Englishman on the barge next door about the water–there were fish in the shallows and people bathing. The waterskiers say it is not too bad, said the Englishman, but there are pockets of salmonella underneath and the divers don't like that.

Are you in this marina for long? we asked. Yes, he said, I have bought a big house nearby. The Belgians are poor but they will do anything for you. The people back home in Bolton are so pretentious. In what way? I asked. I asked him twice, but he did not tell us.

THE GRAND HÔTEL RÉGNIER LIES WRECKED on the shore. A hundred years have flowed through its Art Nouveau grace. Once it was six steamer trunks from Brussels and stay a month, but grass grows along the railway lines and the nettle has invaded the courts.

Forty years ago my husband bought the hotel, *monsieur*, but in the seventies trade began to die. In the nineties the Meuse came through the windows–the insurance paid ten per cent. If one of those curved windows is broken, one of the radiators fails, what do we do? They are works of art—one radiator is a thousand euros. But in ten days there is our big event—the dayflies will come down the river, *les éphémères.* They will come in their millions upon millions. They will be five centimetres deep on the terrace. They come every year, and they die.

At dawn we ran through the trees along the river. I blinked and Jim seemed to vanish. He was smiling and panting when Monica jogged back with him, and his eyes shone. We ran on together. Let's get out of here, I said. France is only ten kilometres up the river. I don't like Belgium. The rivers and canals stink. The moorings are derelict. The finest work of their engineers looks like a cockroach. Half of them don't speak to the other half, you can't get a pizza and you can't even count on the mussels and chips. The whole country has clearly come under the control of aliens. One day a giant maggot in the *ascenseur* at Strépy-Thieu will press a button and release the salmonella from the bottom of the rivers and choke the whole of Europe.

Ha ha ha, ha ha ha, we will swallow them up—they do not know we have no sense of smell. And Orgon, old darling, turn up the wick—forty degrees if you please.

Seven

THE DRUNKEN BOAT

Charleville-Mézières to Paris

Arthur Rimbaud glanced away–abstracted, beautiful, his hair uncombed. His museum in Charleville-Mézières has many rooms displaying the same photograph: in black, in sepia, in pen, in charcoal, in oils. There is not much else left of the young master, except his poetry. His most famous work is 'The Drunken Boat'–

> *I came on Floridas you won't believe.*
> *Among the flowers were the yellow eyes*
> *Of panthers with human skin! Under the waves*
> *Green herds that swim through rainbows from*
> *   the skies.*

Rimbaud's boat is drunker than ours, but he was probably on the hashish and you can't compete with that. I bought a poster and went for a haircut.

Thirteen thousand people have died in the heat, *monsieur*, said Sophia Loren, twisting her magnificent body so that each hair on my head could be considered—alas there is no air conditioning in the hospitals and in the old folks' homes. What style is your hair, *monsieur?*—we do not have such a style in France.

I had a ponytail, I said, and it went wrong, so I shaved it all off a few months ago. Since then it has sort of grown. Perhaps we will try it in a brush, mused Sophia, pursing her swollen lips. There is always hope. I will need much time, then we will attend to your *lévrier*. He is not a *lévrier*, I said, he is a whippet, the dog of the English working man. He does not need a haircut because he has no hair, just a sort of plush. Perhaps a shave, said Sophia, for the whiskers.

In the market I looked for a Johnny Hallyday T-shirt. The French take Johnny Hallyday seriously, as if he mattered, as if his real name wasn't Jean-Philippe Smet, as if he could sing rock and roll. The posters outside the newsagents' have carried his picture for forty years, and now his son's picture too, and France awaits his grandson. There was a navy blue T-shirt with Monsieur Smet's face in yellow. I could not wear it even as an ironic T-shirt. I put it back on the hanger and the black gentleman who ran the stall reached for his knife so I bought a couple of bandannas for Jim. I tied one round his neck—a chic camouflage design, but too big and only Monica can get the knot right and he looked as if he had fallen into the curtains.

The Café du Port opens right off the street opposite the Arthur Rimbaud Museum. At the bar facing the door was a lady of the late afternoon, with a spider tattooed on her ankle and a short skirt and a cigarette. I sat in the corner and Jim stood by me waiting for the scratchings that deep within he knew would never come. Over the speakers a young lady was making short screaming noises, accompanied by guitars. Opposite us on the bar corner was a man of about fifty, slim, with a serious face, and one arm. He turned right round to face me and I thought perhaps he was giving me the eye, but as he was cross-eyed, and I am too, we will never know the truth about that one.

The *patron* brought a beer across and I marvelled at the navy blue walls and the black ceiling and floor, and the silver air-extractor pipe big enough to escape through. No one moved—it was that moment in the afternoon when the day turns round: the pause in the pendulum swing. It was an Edward Hopper painting—*Dayhawks.*

Françoise Hardy came in, as she was long ago, tall and slim and lovely, and started filling in her lottery form at the next table. Behind the cross-eyed man there was a machine with a glass bowl on top. I fancied some nuts but the cross-eyed man had an arm on that side, so I didn't chance it. As we left Jean Gabin came in, with Edith Piaf on his arm. *Bonjour, milord,* she said. So much class, that Edith Piaf.

THE AMERICAN COUPLE ON THE BIG DUTCH Tjalk next door asked us over for a rum and Coke. It was a long time since I had a rum and Coke and as I drank it I remembered why. They told us about San Diego, their home town, which they said is always cool, despite a good deal of physical evidence to the contrary. They had spent thirty years afloat, sometimes at sea for months. You don't get bored, they said, there is a lot going on in your head, and on the boat, and with the weather. And they had sailed for thousands of miles inside the USA, on the rivers and canals. You can sail on the Intracoastal Waterway all the way down the East Coast, they said, though it is hot, and there are hurricanes, and alligators, and flies. There is a fly, a green one–if you knock it off it attacks you again. But you can sail from Norfolk, Virginia, down the Carolinas and Georgia towards the tropics. We came on Floridas you won't believe, they said, like Lake Okeechobee, and Mosquito Lagoon, and Indian River.

I had that turning feeling in my stomach you get when you think you might do something very exciting and very stupid, like squeeze the breasts of the prettiest girl in class, or take the narrow dog to Indian River.

THE PLACE DUCALE AT CHARLEVILLE-MÉZIÈRES was full of parked cars. I wished I could fill it with old refrigerators, so people could see what a seventeenth-century square looked like when it was filled with junk.

Up past the square is a photography shop. The owner of the shop was large and red with a moustache–a French dominant male, a type not known in Britain. You can tell him because he shouts all the time. A small audience follows him round, laughing respectfully and throwing him cues. In a restaurant he is the guy who joshes with the waiter. Often he is called Max. In Britain someone would say Oh don't be such a prick, but in France he is a part of the culture–the national substitute for a sense of humour.

I asked the young lady if they had a slide viewer, and she said they might–the last one in France, because no one looks into slide viewers any more. She went into a hole in the ground and I asked Max if Monica and Jim could come inside the shop. English? he asked. Yes, I said. English! he bellowed, and with a wave drew the other customers into the drama. He addressed me for some time in a language unknown to science, and I smiled and nodded and his audience looked on adoringly. Then he looked through the window at Monica and Jim and dragged from his memory a phrase he had picked up while in police detention for rowdiness in Hastings in the sixties. No sheet, he cried, purple with strain and excitement—no sheet. His audience laughed and applauded and fell silent and looked at me.

It is an English dog, *monsieur*, I said, so he is very polite. I assure you, no sheet. But it is better if you tell him yourself. You must do that in English, because he does not understand French. The audience muttered approvingly.

I beckoned Monica and Jim and they came in and stood in front of the counter. Max dredged his memory and came up with another word. Dog, he said. Jim looked at him expectantly. Such encounters could produce treats. Dog, said Max, you dog. There was a pause—his timing was impeccable. No sheet, said Max, and laughed and all the customers laughed. Jim lay down and gave up. The lady arose with a slide viewer made in Cardiff that cost seventy euros. We got it working and she showed us some slides of toadstools and we paid.

I pointed at Jim. There you are, I said, *monsieur*, no sheet. No sheet English dog, yelled Max. No sheet, all the customers cried.

As we walked back to the Place Ducale they were still shouting and laughing, *les Anglais et leur petit lévrier*, no sheet. We could hear Max shouting Dog, you dog, no sheet. They only charged us sixty euros, said Monica, and gave us the batteries free. The French do that sort of thing sometimes.

• • •

WE TURNED OFF THE MEUSE ON TO THE CANAL des Ardennes. Rivers take the low road, but on a canal you can see for miles from an embankment, or a hillside, or down the mirror of a mile-long straight. Rivers have untidy and hostile margins, but a canal has banks, and the Canal des Ardennes had banks where you could moor, and trees and sunny meadows, and hills standing back just like home, so far away. We moored in the wild and Jim took up his station in the long grass where he could guard the boat, and did not want to come on board again.

A scrap of black rag with a red spot squirmed under the water and ran away up the bank. It was a moorhen chick, in its first day of life. How can it know what to do? A water vole scratched itself and ate its dinner. It didn't have a broad tail like a beaver but an ordinary tail like a rat. It didn't have webbed feet either so it must be a good wriggler.

Plop and a line of bubbles and it submarined away. You don't know what is under that water, but it never stops moving. There is more going on down there than there is going on up here.

AT NINE O'CLOCK TWO GUYS FROM VOIES Navigables de France opened the top lock of the Montgon flight at Le Chesne, offered a few manly boating words to Monica and got on their buzz-bikes and buzzed off. We worked the rest of the twenty-six locks ourselves, pushing buttons and bars and dropping into the countryside. We finished six hours later without seeing another boat and found a mooring in a wooded cutting at Rilly-sur-Aisne and we were tired and had a hard time getting the ropes right and a *péniche* passed at the worst moment and nearly dragged us down, and a man with dark glasses stood on the bank, looking at us.

Jim and I went for a walk into Rilly-sur-Aisne and Monica settled down with *Le Charretier de la Providence*, a book about murder and barges and Inspector Maigret and his loyal assistant Lucas. In my mind was a beer, and in Jim's mind were scratchings and sex and fighting and stealing things and running away very fast. A child limped towards us on the dusty track to the village. He looked at us and said something I did not understand.

There was no bar in Rilly-sur-Aisne; there was no one at all in Rilly-sur-Aisne, but there were sounds coming from a cellar like furniture being moved and someone groaning. I saw the child again on the road back, and heard an urgent voice call him home. A cracked bell with a double chime told us it was seven o'clock.

After dinner the radio said that Mars was nearer than it had been for sixty thousand years. I went out on deck to look, but the trees hemmed in the sky. There were noises coming from the cut. There was flipping and splashing and white bellies came to the surface and sometimes a fish sprang out. When we went to bed the splashing got worse and kept us awake.

This place is creepy, I said. The village is deserted. That child was trying to warn us about something. Who was the guy on the bank? And don't awful things happen when the stars are out of their appointed course? I mean crazy things in the deep country. I know it sounds mad, but those fish scare me. It's like that story *The Birds*, but it's *The Fish*.

Sit down, Lucas—the minister woke me up. He's under a lot of pressure over these fish deaths—he's taken me off the killings in the St. Martin tunnel. Still not smoking? I couldn't do this one without the pipe.

This your report? Oh how horrible. Two of them this time, and a dog, but the dog had gone—catfish, I suppose. We keep people off the streets and do our best and then these foreign buggers come in with their boat and their dog.

So you checked them when they came, and they spotted you, but you went back after dark. Apart from the splashing it was almost normal. Then you went under the bridge for a pee, and you thought you heard something and when you looked in the boat it was too late. There was a forty-pound carp in the bedroom with its dorsal fin torn out, and nine bream had been flung against the wall and burst. God, they must have fought like tigers.

Not much soft tissue left, I suppose. Their faces—contorted with horror, as usual? At the end, when they are getting weak, they send the lampreys in.

Don't cry, Lucas—there was nothing you could have done. When this gets out God help us all. Kissed to death. Sucked dry in little French village. Welcome to France.

THE APPROACH TO REIMS WAS DOWN A LONG straight, with a search for fuel in an empty port, where the old work of giants lay desolate. We pressed on in the sun. At the port the *capitaine* was on the quay. He was charming, but he charged us twenty-five euros a night.

Our boat was under a motorway, with a main road alongside and another over the water. There was grass, shivering in the roar, and there were showers. Outside our galley window was a bench for the winos, who were replaced every forty minutes by Central Casting.

Say Nat, that last lot, they looked like accountants, for God's sake. Can't you get some really scuddy ones, ones that talk to themselves? And look, tell them to use a bit of initiative, have a good scratch, fight, throw up.

We had visited Reims before and liked it, but we were beginning to wonder.

Last time we had not visited the cathedral, because I was in a phase of no history or ruins, and I bought a coat instead. It was supposed to be *imperméable*, but the man in the shop lied. Monica has not let me forget about the *imperméable*.

We walked through a filthy underpass, and came out by the Lesbigay bar, which looked cheerful, but was shut. Big Funereal Surfaces was open. Entry was free and all were welcome and it offered permanent promotions on selected headstones, and ring this number if you die out of hours.

The cathedral stood at the end of the street, and in the manner of things at sea the more we walked towards it the further away it went. We passed by some failed shops and came into a drab square.

A doll's house gives you the illusion of size because it is big made small. Here the illusion works the other way. The cathedral does not look big, until you realize that the human figures carved on its façade are fifteen feet high. There is a sense of intimacy, and power, as if Jesus Christ had come to tea.

The interior could have contained the rest of Reims and over the west door the September sun shone blood and cornflowers through thirty-foot windows. Up under the roof was a round window and on a pillar a notice.

> *The rose window on the north side of the transept is the most beautiful of the cathedral's ancient windows. It has two themes, creation and original sin. Right at the top the suckling virgin symbolizes the salvation of a sinful world by a second Eve.*

The rose window was not triumphant like the windows over the west door; the reds and blues and greens were softer. Round the outer edge there were scenes of the creation and the fall of man, and the shapes seemed to move. I came on beauty that you won't believe.

When people die and come back they say they floated above the world. If they hadn't changed their minds they would have gone through the rose window.

Those guys a thousand years ago were saying the world could be saved from man's first disobedience and the fruit of that forbidden tree, and one day the battle against evil will be won, and the powers of hell cast down, and while you were looking at the rose window you had to believe them.

On the way back Jim and I waited outside the supermarket. On the noticeboard the picture of a little girl.

Estelle Mouzin—9 years old. Disappeared 9 January. Height 1.35. Green eyes. Long chestnut hair. Navy blue anorak, violet beret, red dungarees, black satchel.
Why, this is hell, nor am I out of it.

THE PHONE RANG. IT WAS GEORGIA, OUR younger daughter. Lucy said if you had drowned she would have the Nepal carpet and me the wooden lion from Nigeria, said Georgia. That's not fair. I don't like the wooden lion—I don't like its smile. I want the Nepal carpet. Lucy's got a new dog. It's a rescue dog, a French bulldog or something. It's got a mouth like a frog and teeth down its throat. Horrible fat thing—shits all over the place, dribbles, farts, and rubs my baby with its horrible snotty nose and licks her with its horrible pink tongue. It's out of control—it's worse than Jim, and it's ugly like hell. It's got bulging eyes. I had it for a fortnight when Lucy was on holiday. I took it for a walk down by the cut and it was the hot weather and it lay down and started to die. I dunked it in the canal and carried it home.

I bet it was heavy, I said—I remembered carrying Jim

home in a thunderstorm—so Lucy's dog is a disaster? No, said Georgia—she feeds it on the tit. What about the girls? I asked. They all love it, said Georgia. They all lie on the sofa in a heap, laughing and farting. When are you coming home? In a couple of months, I said—we will be home for Guy Fawkes Night.

HOW LONG IS OUR JOURNEY FROM STONE TO Carcassonne? I asked Monica. Sixteen hundred miles, she said—and five hundred and thirty locks. If I had known that, I said, I wouldn't have come. A thousand miles this year, to get to our mooring in Sens, south of Paris, said Monica, and six hundred next year to get to the Mediterranean and Carcassonne. Next year will be easy, I said.

Perhaps, said Monica, but we've been lucky. Remember the lady they told us about at Charleville, who got a rope round her and they nearly had to cut her leg off? And next year there's the Rhône. The Rhône is terrible. Sergeant-major Owen had a friend who lost an arm on the Rhône. The week we went up the Bristol Channel the Rhône drowned fifteen people, and they were in their homes at the time. On the Rhône even the fish get drowned. It's different over here—Mme Surribas was out walking holding her husband's hand in Lunel and she was knocked over by a flood and sucked into a drain. They found her three hours later, half a mile away, clinging to a pipe.

When we arrived, I said, and Jim and I went for a walk, we happened to spot a pub in the square.

A YOUNG MAN STOOD AT THE BAR—RAPT. HE had long black hair and three earrings in the same ear and looked like a gypsy who had stolen a pair of yellow Bermuda shorts. He was twirling in his hand a withered spray.

The flowers in the square are sensational, said Monica. Yes *madame* it is a competition, said the gypsy. Condé always enters and all the towns and villages take part. The open pillared place, full of lilies, said Monica—your market hall, I suppose.

The historical records are incomplete and I am personally of the firm opinion that no one is quite sure of its origin, said the gypsy. The building has been moved many times. There is a particularity about it which I will explain to you. It is made of chestnut, and there is a particularity about the chestnut that is known to few. Do you know this particularity, *madame*? Goodness, no, said Monica. The wood of the chestnut tree, I am able to inform you, said the Scholar Gypsy, will not abide the spider. So there are no webs in the rafters and no dead flies drop upon the merchandise, which is very satisfactory.

Poor spiders, said Monica at dinner—nowhere to go. Don't you worry about the spiders, I said—French spiders do very well. Arthur Rimbaud said he was consuming himself, but the spider in the hedge eats nothing but violets.

THERE WAS A SIGN ON THE CANAL BANK—*Dragage dans le bief.* I knew *bief* meant a canal pound, but I didn't know what *dragage* meant. Shall I get out my little black dress? I asked. No, said Monica, it's dredging—remember the brave Sir Peppermints? Yes, indeed, the day we lost steerage on the Macclesfield Canal and Monica was stranded on the wrong bank. A British Waterways green giant floated his toy dredger up and took her across and said I'm not much of a knight in shining armour but here—and gave her a chewy peppermint in a twist of paper, and one for me.

In France round the corner a floating excavator roared and smoked and threw its bucket into the cut with a whack like a whale's tail. It carried on roaring and brandishing until we were a few feet away and then backed off, snarling.

Round the next bend the cut broadened and there were four machines heaving up blue mud and dropping it into barges. The engines screamed, the mud fell in landslides, the buckets slammed and the cut threw up waves. On the bank and in the barges workmen leaped and shouted.

Then the French Air Force came in three o'clock high, at Mach 1. The French fast-jet pilot, denied a hero's death in the Falklands or Iraq, turns his rage on his own kind, harrowing the land with explosions, cracking open the sky and throwing down thunder, traumatizing babies in their prams and shocking to death the very voles in the fields and streams. Squadron followed squadron, the firmament full of sonic boom boys, yelling Take that, you babies, you voles, har har. If it happened in England the mayor would have a word with the group captain at the golf club. And the *dragage* would have been more leisurely too. Georgia told us that in the heatwave the labourers on the railway near Stafford took their sunloungers to work.

WE MOORED ALONG A GREEN BANK AT AY AND the boat filled with spice and vinegar, bittersweet and rotten. Monica had just unwrapped some sausages and we sniffed them and read the packet–

Since man first walked the shores of the Mediterranean, people have sought the savour and preserving power of the herb. And since the Gallo-Roman age, the peasants of the Franche-Compté have given a specific taste to their charcuterie.

Like most descriptions in France, it took the topic a fair way back. But the smell wasn't the sausage, it wasn't Jim, it was something else pouring down the cut on the south wind. I remembered Arthur Rimbaud and 'The Drunken Boat'—

> *I've seen vast rotting marshes—in their snare*
> *Ferments the body of a whole leviathan*

We looked in the reeds for a whole leviathan, or even a half leviathan, but couldn't see one.

Ay is in the Champagne region and we visited a *maison* that grew its own grapes. Since ancient man first tasted the sweetness of rotting fruit, said the gentleman, wine has been cherished, and since vines began to clothe the chalk mountains of Reims, my family has made wine here. We have records back to the fifteenth century, before champagne was invented. In the depression in the thirties no one could afford to buy our grapes so my grandfather risked all to bottle his own brand. Now we do sixty thousand bottles a year and we are the second wine on the list at the Savoy in London.

There was little to see: a press, the fermentation vessels, the cellar. The rotten-sweet smell was from the floors and run-offs in the fermentation rooms across Ay as the harvest worked in the vats.

A couple of cases have improved the trim of the boat and at Christmas I will drink with my family to grandfather Gosset, who pulled out the big one.

THE DENTIST LOOKED DOWN MY THROAT. NOT much left here you started with, he said. No *monsieur*, I said, most of my organs have been replaced more than once. Do not despair, he said, it is a minor infection—see. He pressed a button and a coloured screen lit up with a mountain range of defensive dentistry. The screen also gave my name, my height, my address, my credit card number, the maiden name of my wife, the length of my boat, and the name and colour of my little dog tied to the railing outside. The consultation took not five minutes. The dentist wrote a prescription and shook my hand warmly and the lady at reception asked Monica for a small amount of money and wished us every happiness. In the pharmacy I asked if I could drink alcohol with the pills. Yes, said the pharmacist, provided it is champagne.

The Bar du Midi in the square, like most French bars, presents a gripping contrast to our own public houses, *un contraste saisissant.* Every bar is a stage where we strut and fret but the production in a French pub is by a lighter hand, played for delicacy, not for tears and thundering laughs. The French find the dull and deep potations of the northern races rather vulgar. They are happy to be lightly intoxicated, perhaps at breakfast, or elevenses, or at lunch, but will not trudge to the pub in the mid-evening to get ratted. At times they drink coffee, which tastes so good that I often wonder what the blenders buy one half so precious as the beans they sell.

In England to look smart is evidence of dick-hood, but the French dress for the pub, especially on the weekend, appearing in high style as film stars from a long time ago. The women favour black, or leather and gold and high heels. They are often thin and sharp-featured. From their teenage years they have a ravaged charm, and smoke-broken voices that would coax an apostle off a stained-glass window. The older men choose an apache look, denim and moustaches, and the young men black shirts with trainers. Monica asked if she could have one of each to take to Carcassonne.

If it is not too late there are lots of children, and always dogs, which prowl around affably, and if they are small dogs Jim will come forth and play with them, and everyone will say Is it a greyhound, and Is he calm for my little boy to stroke him and Are you from Alsace?

Years ago I saw a television programme about lemurs. Lemurs are a sort of tall monkey, with long hooped tails, and they don't do much except bounce around, passing through their group hundreds of times a day: touching fingers, grinning, embracing, as if binding the troop together with ectoplasm. If a lemur is for anything it is for saying Hello. In an English pub greetings are offered reluctantly, but the French are rather like the jolly lemur. They enter—*Ah messieurs, 'dames*—they shake hands in all directions, or greet with multiple kissing and punching and embraces, each encounter precisely reflecting degrees of friendship or kin, acknowledging bonds and experiences beyond the war, beyond birth, keeping whole the ectoplasm that binds them.

THE VINES COVERED THE HILLS IN ROWS, LIKE scenery for a model railway. A dredger surfed backwards across our path, then forwards, then swerved, then stopped in a roar. Perhaps he had seen Monica in her bush hat. Frenchmen fancy English ladies of a certain age, like Jane Birkin, or Charlotte Rampling, and when they think they have spotted one they chuck their dredgers around like anything.

Monica for her part was so moved she beached the *Phyllis May* on the side of the cut and the dredger had to come and pull us off, so all concerned had a lovely time. No peppermints, but a smile and a wave.

French locks are automatic—you don't have to wind up the

paddles yourself. The large locks are operated by men in towers and the smaller ones by pushing buttons and lifting bars. Sometimes in the small locks Monica had to climb a greasy ladder with a rope between her teeth and hold the boat steady as the lock filled. Often you are faced with two red lights because the lock is broken and then you ring the Voies Navigables de France, and someone comes out on a buzz-bike and fiddles about, or someone throws a switch in Bordeaux and all is well.

At one lock Monica was on the phone for a while, laughing and joking. What is going on? I asked. The gentleman said my French was impeccable, said Monica. He said my accent was distant and calm and grave, like dear voices that once he knew and now were still. He told me he had just been left a nice house in Epernay and he was free on Thursday. What about the lock? I asked. I knew there was something, said Monica.

Down on to the Marne, which ambles towards Paris. Fish rushed about, arrows in the green, bringing the word. We moored at Cumières and plugged in and went to explore. The town had a restaurant but it was shut, because it was Tuesday. We had not realized that on Mondays, and sometimes Tuesdays or Wednesdays, or at weekends or at lunchtime, or in the late summer, or in the winter, everything is shut in France.

Dozens of champagne businesses behind brass plates and pretty white gates. We ducked under the wire as the general store closed, and bought a local paper. Coming back we met a man with a greyhound—the first we had seen since crossing the Channel. The greyhound was tall and he stood awkwardly. He's nice, said the owner, no problem. Jim sat back and swayed and wanted to play and dashed under the greyhound, and the greyhound didn't mind but he wouldn't play.

I had another dog, said the owner, a saluki, and he died. Now Oslo won't eat and he is ill all the time.

Two *péniches* were moored under the trees a hundred yards away—*Paris Un* and *Paris Deux*. Their cable slid into the power point on our municipal mooring. One of the bargees was walking his three spaniels, which fell on Jim and they rushed about. You crossed the Channel? asked the bargee. He was a little old chap, very oily, in overalls, with a deep voice, as if calling from the middle of the cut on a rainy night. We are waiting for a load, me and my brother and my father. My father bought this boat in Paris in 1932, and then the other one. They both carry three hundred tons. They call them *péniches* in the schools, but to us and everyone else they are just the boats. We do mainly cereals, but the harvest is bad because of the heat. We walked on and he went back to his boat. We all would have liked to talk longer, but there didn't seem to be anything else to say.

I opened the paper and there was a picture of M. Thierry Charpentier, kneeling the better to support a catfish, which was the biggest ever caught in the Lac du Der, up the Marne. The catfish weighed thirty-four kilos and was nearly two metres long. M. Charpentier had caught fifty large catfish in the last year, for reasons which were not reported, and this was the biggest. By his expression the struggle could have gone either way, so next time we could see a picture of the catfish supporting M. Charpentier.

The findings of the expert inquiry into the thirteen hundred heatwave deaths in France were also revealed. It seemed the doctors were away on holiday and the hospital wards were closed, because it was late summer. The head of the health service did not testify, because he was on holiday.

Nothing else happened in Cumières, in fact nothing at all

happened in Cumières, except the year turned and started to roll down into winter.

AT NOGENT L'ARTAUD WE HAD DINNER IN A *grill-crêperie* where there were many pictures of catfish like that caught by M. Charpentier, and carp too—Just take the bloody picture, Isabelle, my knees have gone. On the wall were heads of pike, sticking out, teeth ajar, as if to give us a song.

After dinner we had visitors from the big house by the pontoon. Laurence, said the gentleman, offering a bowl of biscuits, and Madeleine. He was a short balding man in his sixties and his wife was younger. After a scuffle we got them to sit where we wanted.

We meet a lot of lovely people, I said, but I get nervous and forget their names. So I have developed a technique of remembering by association, which I will share with you. Laurence, I will think of you always with a turban, like Lawrence of Arabia, and I will think of your charming wife Madeleine with a moustache like Marcel Proust, who made the *madeleine* famous. In that way I will have remembrance of things past. *Monsieur*, said the gentleman, my name is Georges, and this is my wife Laurence, and the *madeleines* are the cakes.

They asked us back to their house for whisky. Laurence had her own communications firm, and Georges helped her though he was retired. The firm was based in Paris, an hour away on the train. Times were hard, they said—five firms bidding for every contract. The recession isn't over yet—there are still ten per cent unemployed. And the law is set against the entrepreneur; you can't make a move, you can't win.

Georges wrote poetry, including translations of Portuguese fados–

> *Come and bring your guitar*
> *Then we will go together*
> *Singing our sweet fado*
> *In the streets of Bairro Alto*

He asked if we had visited the Arthur Rimbaud Museum, and recited part of 'The Drunken Boat'. He was seventeen when he wrote that, said Laurence, it's enough to make you think What's the use.

Do you write poetry, Thierry? asked Georges. I did, I said, then I went into market research. It is hard being a poet, said Georges, and recited the whole of Baudelaire's poem 'The Albatross'. I had forgotten how sad it was: the dying albatross, mocked by the sailors. As Georges reached the final lines I joined in–

> *The poet is the rider on the storm*
> *Mocking the arrow, prince of all the winds.*
> *An exile here on earth, tormented, scorned,*
> *Trying to walk, dragging his giant's wings.*

We shouted the lines together, two fat old men, and waved our arms, and for a moment it all made sense–the playground mockery, the teachers who hated us, the teams that dropped us, the girls who said no, the invitations that didn't arrive, the interviews failed, the contracts lost–it all made sense. We were The Albatross–what did we expect?

· · ·

HATTED AND GLOVED IN THE EARLY SUN, WE sailed down to La Ferté-sous-Jouarre, and arrived before lunch and walked up the high street.

The French have developed noise more than all other aspects of their culture, except perhaps eating and drinking, which itself requires communal shouting. It is not just their jet pilots who make the welkin rattle. If the French find a quiet river bank they bring out African drums. As their emergency vehicles pass, the birds drop from the trees. We went for a coffee and the walls heaved as Jean-Philippe Smet urinated on the grave of Elvis. Outside three people with little motorbikes and big helmets were brewing up a Canaveral roar. They racketed up the street and back again, and away along the Marne, their din Dopplering down as they neared Paris.

I wonder how those machines are sold?

Monsieur, that one is a nice colour, but it doesn't have the decibels. Now this one has the Fartblaster, which can be heard fifteen miles away. It deafened my uncle permanently and I can thoroughly recommend it. The bike in the corner brought great success to your friend Guillaume. On their very first date his new girlfriend said OK you can have me right here and now on the pavement, if you will just turn that fucking thing off.

There was something odd about the high street in La Ferté-sous-Jouarre. As usual there was loud music, but not the usual competing strains—the tune was reinforced by a speaker every twenty yards. This was official noise: municipal noise. The broken-beat lead guitar was the mayor, with the town clerk on bass. The song that followed was the lady mayoress, to whom love had given short measure. At lunchtime the shops shut and the music was turned off and I hope the mayor laid down his guitar and went home and showed a bit of interest.

As the afternoon sun moved along the saloon Jim moved with it like a sundial–Gnomon the Wonder Dog. Jim sleeps for twenty-three hours, and seeks to divide what remains of the day between running at forty miles an hour and going down the pub. We took him on to the lawns along the Marne. There was a baby in a pushchair starting to eat an egg sandwich.

A Newfoundland puppy tumbled by, with a black Labrador bitch and their owner, a lady of a certain age. Jim licked the crumbs of egg off his muzzle and leaped upon the bitch.

Ah *madame*, excuse me, stop it Jim, oh dear, said Monica. It does not matter, *madame*, said the lady of a certain age–he is young, it is the enthusiasm, it is the nature, who can complain–but she is old, she will say no. But the bitch did not say no.

Oh I do apologize, said Monica, pulling Jim back on to terra firma, I'm awfully sorry, oh dear, Jim that's not nice–*madame* I am desolated. No problem, *madame*, said the lady–he is a fine young man. She is honoured.

MONICA TURNED HARD LEFT, SWINGING THE tiller. Her jaw was set, her gaze ahead. The windmill generator fizzed and the *Phyllis May* swung from the hip and smashed into a wave, breaking it in two. That's the left turn across the shipping lanes, I said to the gentleman at the counter. That was the turning towards France, after the Goodwin Sands. That was the point where we were committed. Your colleague made a lovely job of this–look at the colours–I can feel the spray. It was me, *monsieur*, said the gentleman, I made this print. The sky was not straight, so I straightened the sky.

Outside in the square five brown lads surrounded Monica. Look at the dog—oh my God his muscles. I bet he's fast—how much did he cost *madame*, how much does he eat?

I bought a paper at the kiosk in the square. This was the third English paper I had bought in Meaux and the lady in the kiosk and I were getting close. I apologized for leaving the next day. The French say *Bonjour* and *Bon voyage* without thinking, and *Bonne journée* when they mean it. The lady in the kiosk struggled, the occasion deserving something further. *Bonne navigation,* she said at last, and we both smiled with relief.

I tied Jim outside the fruit shop. *Ah monsieur,* you are the big Englishman from the thin boat with the narrow dog and the little wife. I have seen you when I walked with Crusoe. Where is your narrow dog, *monsieur*? Why have you tied him up outside? You should bring him in so he can say hello to Crusoe. Crusoe stretched his polar body across the aisle, so no one could leave until he said so.

In the fish shop the lady weighed her two crabs, one in each hand, and frowned. One moment, she said, and went inside, and returned with both crabs cut in half. That one, *monsieur,* that one is the best.

Meaux has not decided which side of the river it is on. This is because it lies in the crook of the Marne, asleep in its turquoise embrace. The town was a mess, spread about, dug up, the cathedral wrapped in brown paper, but there was plenty of space in Meaux and plenty of time. Under the bridges chub rolled in the misty river. Teenage girls dawdled in pairs and threes, and now and then a man in a business shirt passed, walking almost quickly. Mooring and electricity and water were free in Meaux and each morning a roach came to manicure the boat.

On the banks among the flowers a madman chatted to

himself all day—When I say something, then that's it, it's finished, decision time; when I say something then that's it, it's
finished, decision time. Fish shot around in shoals, and when
they paused they changed colour and disappeared. If they
stopped somewhere patched, then they went patched as well.
Rivers are paved with invisible fish, looking at you.

The heat had returned, and I sat on the pontoon, and tid-
dlers tapped on my toes. There are towns that are off-centre,
towns that have run quite out of square, but in Meaux they
have straightened the sky.

GEORGES'S E-MAIL ABOUT THINGS TO DO IN
Paris has come through, said Monica.

> *To the left towards the west are Rouen, Le Havre, the open sea,
> the Channel, and Normandy with the shade of William the
> Conqueror, Queen Matilda and her tapestry at Bayeux, the in-
> vasion beaches, apples, cider, butter and cheese, the Atlantic,
> and a little to the right London Bridge.*

Oh Lord, I said, a French description. But we've got a
month, we'll find our way. A long day's boating and a night
at Lagny, among the holiday caravans.

The Saint-Maur underground passage goes in one direction, claims the *Guide Navicarte*. How can a passage go in one
direction? I asked. The people can go in one direction, but
not the passage. Perhaps this is a new mouth of hell, said
Monica, I guess that would go in one direction. It says watch
out for floating bodies because they are always plentiful at
Saint-Maur.

An early start for Paris, where Monica had booked us a
mooring in the Port of the Bastille. The suburbs of Neuilly

and Nogent were pleasant, with trees and high embankments, and the Saint-Maur underground passage carried traffic in both directions, with no bodies.

To drop us towards the Seine there were three locks a hundred yards long. We waited for an hour outside the first two and when we entered the keepers pulled the plug while we were still on the lock-side with the ropes and we had to jump back on board. In the third lock the water rushed in one end and out the other for forty minutes and the lock-keepers rushed up one end and down the other for forty minutes and then they regained control and let us pass.

It was seven hours before we turned right on to the Seine at the Porte de Bercy, and sailed into Paris under the *route périphérique*, five kilometres from the marina at the Bastille.

WHERE WERE THE BROAD AVENUES, THE famous bridges, the little streets, the quays lined with bookstalls? Where was Notre-Dame? Where was the bloody Eiffel Tower? On this burning afternoon, seen from the great water of the Seine, Paris was dunes of sand and clay, miles of wharves and gantries, chimneys, sad warehouses. It was Tin Can Island, Lagos, Nigeria—the heat, the desolation, the pirates.

Rafts of barges powered by and chopped up the water, and now there were hotels naked on the bank between the silos, now some moored boats, and there, my God, moored up on our left, was the South Goodwin light vessel, waiting its chance.

I'll get to the bridge before that barge and go through the middle, why creep along the side—there's plenty of water, it's wider than the Thames. Down with the throttle—let's rock and roll.

Now that's better–the many windows of the Pont de Bercy, the Charles de Gaulle Bridge flung over the water, the knitted iron of the Austerlitz viaduct. Watch that *bateau-mouche* turning across us: a greenhouse full of gongoozlers, like a row of stoats.

A red light on the right and a shadowy entrance–the Bastille lock. Monica jumped off and held our rope as the pontoon pitched and then the light went green and she jumped back on and we eased inside the lock. It was dark and we couldn't see the mooring points and Monica gave me the wrong call from the bow and I shouted at her. It had taken us longer to get from Lagny to Paris than from Ramsgate to Calais, and we were tired.

The *capitaine* was three men called Bruno and Guillaume and Bernard, who declared themselves ravished by Monica's boat, her French, her dog, her smile, her hat. The basin was overlooked by battlements and flowered lawns, behind them ornamented old buildings, concrete outrages from the sixties, and the sturdy glass keep of the new Opéra de la Bastille. Two hundred craft–Tupperware cruisers, steel barges, yachts. We rafted up to a barge with a child on board who shouted and shouted until as night fell his parents murdered him.

We lifted Jim over the rails and headed for the gold angel on the column in the Place de la Bastille. He was perched on one leg, ready to swoop over the basin, scattering stars. It's not an angel, explained Monica, it's Liberty, but he could swoop if he wanted, like Jim can fly.

At the restaurant on the bank opposite the boat Monica had a glass of champagne and I secured the largest beer legally sold in France, nearly four fifths of a pint. To get a beer of this size in France you need strong vernacular

French, the patience of Christ, a piece of paper and a pencil, and a pint glass in a paper bag.

You are so polite, *monsieur*, I said to the waiter, as our negotiations drew to a close. Why are you not rude?–all Paris waiters are supposed to be rude. Ah, *monsieur*, said the waiter, I am the exception that proves the rule.

It's been a hard day, I said to Monica. I love the drinking and I love the boasting and I love the herons and I love the grebes and I love the hats. I love the Breton cap and the bush hat and the Russian hat with flaps when it is cold but to be honest the boating is getting me down. Jim feels the same. He used to ride up on the bow but now he stays in his kennel waiting for it all to end. Enough is enough. Even Arthur Rimbaud got a bit fed up after reeling round the world for twenty-five stanzas–

> *For me, in Europe, I want just one pool–*
> *In perfumed twilight see the sad child play*
> *See him let slip to waters black and cool*
> *His boat frail as a butterfly in May*

Let's be like Arthur, let's give up and stick to the pools in the park. We'll leave the *Phyllis May* here and walk around Paris with Jim.

No we won't, said Monica. We'll walk but we'll go by boat too–under the bridges of Paris and under the streets as well.

Eight
A SILVER BOWL

Paris and the Seine

I am not a handbag—Jim hunched in his fluorescent orange life jacket, giving the betrayed eyes. I am a creature of beauty and dignity, the sportsdog of the English racing man. Do you realize I am the fastest animal in the world?

Oh come on Jim, I said, and picked him up by the handle and slung him on to the bow of the big barge alongside and clambered after him and on to the pontoon. I dropped his life jacket back on to the *Phyllis May* and we climbed out of the basin into the street, and walked across the Austerlitz Bridge and along the Left Bank.

Down on the quay there was The Albatross, in a black tracksuit, running hard, waving his arms, going for a take-off. He went behind some trees and I don't know if he made it into the air. If he did he would have headed for the Atlantic hurricanes, passing over Notre-Dame, a black cross against the blue.

Jim started to tremble. He had spotted a black and brown dachshund, polished like a conker. The two hounds rushed around, athlete and dwarf, getting on fine. Happily we have room on the quays, said the old lady with the dachshund. What is a dachshund like as a breed? I asked. He is very sensitive, *monsieur*, said the lady. He is frightened of cars, of people, of noise. If I go out of the room he cries inconsolably. In fact he is a great nuisance, my little Prévert. She looked at Prévert adoringly and Prévert looked right back–

> *I am what I am;*
> *That's what I'm for.*
> *You think it's a shame,*
> *You want something more?*

The last time I saw Paris was nearly twenty years ago. One of my executives had gone mad in the Hôtel de l'Arc de Triomphe. I had to coax him out of the bathroom and send him home strapped to a door and then finish his research job, so there wasn't a lot of time to look round. But I had been much taken with the outdoor sculpture museum overlooking the Seine. And *Here it is*, said the notices, *here it is again, right here, the outdoor sculpture museum, remember this, this is great.* The bushes had grown tall and Jim and I walked between them and there were empty plinths covered with graffiti and on one of them, outside his house of cardboard boxes, a man was laying a white T-shirt to dry in the sun.

Notre-Dame strained on its stone ropes, longing to throw itself into the Seine and sail away. The sun beat on its sides and tourists washed around like surf. I looked up into the wind but

The Albatross would be over Le Havre by now. It was time for refreshment, time to face the fury of the Paris waiters.

I sat at a pavement café and hooked Jim to the table leg while he tried to strangle himself, bring the table down, look for scraps, and check out the chances of sex. The waiter lurched out–a man with mop hair who had been put together from bits left over from a wrestling tournament. *Monsieur?* he croaked. I asked for a coffee and with a sneer he left me. He came back with my coffee and a bowl of water for Jim. I have a boxer, he said. Jim climbed up his crooked body and the monster put his arms round him.

Soon we were staring up at the Panthéon, which a tour guide was explaining to a group of Germans. I don't speak German so I still don't know what the Panthéon does but it is very big, on a hill, with a dome. It is the sort of place you are supposed to visit but Monica and I prefer the sort of place you are not supposed to visit.

In Venice on a package tour we were supposed to visit a lot of paintings by dead farts in churches but we bunked off and wandered around and were stopped in the street by a man in a black suit. I thought he was hustling for a restaurant but he was a bridegroom about to be married by the mayor in the town hall and his witnesses had not turned up–would we be his witnesses? Monica cried all the time and the bride's mother arrived when it was over and everyone cried a lot more. Only the mayor didn't cry–he was wearing a very expensive green and red and white silk sash and I suppose he didn't want to cry over it in case he spoiled it for the next mayor.

Down to the Latin Quarter, the sort of place you are supposed to visit. Rows of restaurants and cheap clothes shops, and hundreds of students. I know that student life is tempestuous, the skies lowering with girls and beer and essays, but to everyone else students are just young and boring as hell.

THE MONTPARNASSE TOWER IS ONE OF THE boldest works of the Glasturdi school of architects, who in the white heat of their passion conceived the *ascenseur* at Strépy-Thieu, and offered many a tip on the design of Milton Keynes Centre and the Oxford Business School. Jim does not like things that move beneath him, like boats and pontoons and lifts, but here we were at floor fifty-six in seconds, looking at Paris from the sky.

Just down there the Eiffel Tower, six feet high, and the métro with its stations every few inches. The little Arc de Triomphe a bit skew-whiff and Les Invalides a golden egg. The cellophane domes of Le Grand Palais and Le Petit Palais. The Seine does a lot of curling round and you can follow the line of trees to the LEGO blocks in the Défense, but we couldn't see the big arch because it was facing the wrong way.

There was the Bois de Boulogne where Monica and I were once ranked seventh man-and-wife cross-country team in Europe aged between forty and forty-two. Not every couple in Europe competed—perhaps they found something more pleasant to do first thing on a freezing Sunday than run around in the rain.

Lines of silver and grey roofs, little trees and lawns. All that mighty heart was lying still, in a blue and white light, softened by haze, in the bowl of the river.

THAT NIGHT WE SET OUT TO HAVE DINNER AT the restaurant where first we went, at the Bastille. As we arrived the restaurant was shutting, because it was Wednesday.

We went to another, but it had shut because it was dinner-time. On we walked and arrived at the Gare de Lyon, which was open. Where is the restaurant? I asked.

Up some stairs and past a neon sign, *Le Train Bleu*, and into a great room coloured like a tropical moth, with angels on the ceiling and statues of mermaids and yellow electric flowers in sprays and painted people in old-fashioned clothes having picnics up the walls. It was the sort of place the Queen would be taken on her birthday.

My mustard T-shirt said I was leader of the day in the Tour de France, and my shorts were held up by my hand in the pocket, and Monica was in her bush hat and baggy trousers. Only Jim was well turned out, in a close-cut velvet suit, a bandanna at his throat.

A tall man in a dinner jacket closed in–*Monsieur?* Do you accept dogs? I asked, thinking This will not take long. Why not, *monsieur*? said the head waiter. He showed us to a table by the window, where we could look out on the street scene and the lights, and in at the diners at the crowded tables: all pink, their linen white and their suits ironed, shouting and waving their knives and forks.

Monica had the best steak in Europe and I had pig's trotters in crumbs. To describe the pig's trotters would need the pen of a Wilhelm Albert Vladimir Alexandre Apollinaris de Kostrowitzki, to name but a few. For Jim the head waiter brought a plate of meat, and water in a silver bowl.

AT THE BASTILLE END OF THE MARINA, AWAY from the Seine, is the métro station and under this a tunnel. From time to time three hundred ton *péniches* came out, looking much taller than the tunnel. They had come down the Canal de Saint Martin, under the streets. Funny things happen in tunnels and Monica wanted us to go through that tunnel in the *Phyllis May* and Jim and I headed north to see if we could find a reason to stop her.

The canal was roofed over with the long gardens of the Avenue Richard Lenoir, where twice a week there was a riotous street market. Sometimes there were circular holes with a dome of railings leaning over them and down in the dark I could see water. We walked for a mile and the canal was open again to the sky and trees, and there was the Hôtel du Nord where Arletty lay in the arms of Jean Gabin and a lock with water surging in and a ruined houseboat trying to keep afloat as it rose.

I've come on tunnels that you won't believe, I said to Jim. I have been through the terrible Harecastle in Stoke. The water is orange-red like the blood of Daleks and as you go into the darkness they start a ventilation fan to scare you. It gets colder and wetter and narrower and lower until you are kneeling at the tiller, shuddering with fear. I have been through the Netherton tunnel near Dudley, which is cut through pearl and crystal, where the walls are flashed with black and crimson and you can hear music. But I have never been under a city. What happens if the road caves in? What happens if one of those big barges comes along against you? It says in the book that it takes ages to go through and nothing works and there are rats, and gongoozlers look at you through cracks.

Jim listened closely, waiting for the words pub or chips, and started eating something dreadful off the ground.

TO SAINT-GERMAIN-DES-PRÉS, DOWN THE RUE Guillaume Apollinaire. A century ago, when Paris was the centre of the world, the poet Wilhelm Albert Vladimir

Alexandre Apollinaris de Kostrowitzki was the centre of Paris. He was very good at fish. He did crayfish–Backing away, backing away. He did carp–You live so long, has death forgotten you, melancholy creatures? He said he was like an octopus, sucking the blood of his friends and squirting ink. He wrote about jellyfish with violet hair; dolphins playing merrily in the bitter sea. He didn't do dogs, but he did a cracker about a dromedary, and if you have no respect you can change the dromedary to a whippet–

> *With a narrow dog called Jim*
> *A certain Terry Darlington*
> *Sailed from Stone to Carcassonne.*
> *And I would do the same as him*
> *With a narrow dog like Jim.*

SAINT-GERMAIN-DES-PRÉS WAS FULL OF PEOPLE having a drink before dinner and then they all went home or to the Rue Mouffetard which is like Soho but with twice as many restaurants. After dinner I walked into a bollard that had been knocked horizontal by a car. While Monica looked for a taxi Jim and I went into a bar to sit down and watch my leg swell up.

In the bar were half a dozen fat slags–Oh isn't he lovely! Look at his ears, his cravat! Look at the little curls on his ass!

It's always dog, dog, dog, I said, no one notices me. When I was nineteen I was beautiful. I had curls too and I wore a cravat–young girls sought me out.

The fat slags were from Denver Colorado on a cookery training course. They had not been to Europe before and they thought Paris was much nicer than Denver Colorado. They were drunk and smoking and shouting and gorgeous. Monica came back as I was about to ask them all to crew for us to Carcassonne, though more than one would have sunk the *Phyllis May.*

Back at the boat I took an oral infusion of three fingers of whisky and the pain went and in the morning I was almost cured.

YOU'VE GOT TO SEE NOTRE-DAME FROM THE left bank, I said to Monica, and we did, and then we shouldered over the bridge through the tourists. When the tourists saw Jim they poked each other and called out sadly in Japanese.

Behind Notre-Dame, on the southern tip of the Ile de la Cité, is the Monument for the Deported. You can see nothing from the gate. We walked inside–Can we bring the dog? Yes, said the guardian, but you must leave him on the lawn here. I will look after him. He smiled. We walked down the steps and Jim started to cry. Jim is good at waiting but when we reached the bottom of the steps we could still hear him crying.

We were in a small court with a barred window looking down on the Seine. We couldn't see the sky; just the light on the river. Through an entrance and we were in a lobby with cells opening off and words on the heavy walls as if they had been scratched by prisoners. Louis Aragon, Jean-Paul Sartre: words of defiance and pity. In the centre a cell which went into the distance, a tunnel: millions of lights on walls and ceiling–the road to freedom. In the middle a tomb.

In the Second World War two hundred thousand people were deported from France and were worked to death, or starved, or gassed. Half were Jews, and twelve thousand were children. Children.

When we came up the steps Jim was still crying. Don't

worry, said the guardian. He saw you going down into the ground and he thought you would never come back.

YOU DON'T WANT YOUR BOAT LOOKING LIKE a tailor's dummy, Clive used to say. Indeed a sweet disorder shows that you are a friendly bang-about boater who is likely to come through with the gin and tonic as the questing vole seeks his rest. But white balloon fenders get dirty and hang off your boat like rotten fruit and are impossible to clean.

Together with their telephone numbers and pictures of themselves when young, Bruno, Guillaume and Bernard had given Monica a leaflet for the local chandlery. I looked at it over breakfast—*All your needs and repairs.* Let's smarten up for leaving Paris, I said—I'll pop out with Jim and get those black fenders, and come back and help tidy the boat.

We walked along the quay and started up the steps to the street but there was scaffolding, and a little man covered in white dust. *Monsieur,* you are blocked, blocked I say. He went into a hole in the ground. We had to walk all the way down to the lock on the Seine but it was a sunny morning and Who cares? We waited for a boat to drop into the river and I carried Jim across the gate and we went up the other side of the basin into the world.

At the address on the map there was a distributor of religious vestments, but after a while we found the chandlery, which was shut. We'll have a coffee, I thought, give it a chance.

In the café there was room for the Algerian *patron,* and me, and an Algerian drunk, with Jim in a corner being narrow. The drunk had come upon the secret of life. He was having trouble getting it across to Jim and me, but he was trying hard. The *patron* made a sign—he will not attack you.

I am desolated, I said, as I ordered a coffee, I have only a twenty-euro note. No problem, *monsieur*, said the *patron*, I beg of you. I gave him the twenty and he went into the street, and the drunk carried on explaining the secret of life. After half an hour the *patron* came back and handed me the note—It is too early *monsieur*, no one has any change. I will return, I said.

I went to another café and ordered a brandy. The French will take a brandy in the morning and it can help if things are starting to break loose. The barman took several bottles off the shelves and examined them, then lifted a trapdoor and went into a hole in the ground. After a long time he came up with a bottle. Alas, I said, I have but a twenty-euro note. *Monsieur*, he said, I beg of you, and took the note and brought me a brandy and turned to a bald customer with an eagle tattooed on his head. He bent over the counter with the bald customer, as if they were racing spiders. There was some confusion about the result of one of the races and I felt it was not wise to hurry a man with an eagle tattooed on his head and it was half an hour before I got my change.

We went back to the Algerian café and the *patron* took a euro and shook my hand and the drunk blocked the door and explained to Jim the concept he had not made clear before: the last piece in the jigsaw, the one that you knew all the time, revealing the beauty.

In the chandlery a thin man with white hair was curled at his desk behind an outboard motor, talking on the phone. He flickered his fingers at me. I looked around the shelves—one tenth of the stock in the chandlery in Stone. The French don't go inland boating. The concept has not entered their culture—rather as we are unable to conceive of tea dances or tripe sausages, or Valéry Giscard d'Estaing.

Well, good luck to you, the thin one was saying, waving

his hand, but my cousin lost his leg on the Rhône, so it didn't work for him, did it? You should see him hopping around—he wished he'd listened to me, didn't he? They never found his boat—crunched to bits, washed down the sink. He smiled and put the phone down—*Monsieur?*

I seek fenders, I said, black fenders, seventy millimetres. No problem, *monsieur*. He backed away among the shelves like a crayfish and returned with a fender and bounced it on the counter and tapped its belly with a feeler. It was dark blue. I ventured a joke—*C'est magnifique, mais ce n'est pas le noir.* He smiled thinly and lifted a trapdoor and went backwards into a hole in the ground. A long time later he came up out of the sand—*Non, monsieur.* He didn't seem sorry at all.

Jim and I walked back down to the lock and waited a long time while a boat came up into the basin and I carried Jim over the gate again and when we got back to the quay I chased him and put on his life jacket and handbagged him over the barge and on to the *Phyllis May.*

No fenders then, said Monica. And no help with cleaning, and you're late for lunch. And you smell of brandy—you are so greedy—self, self, self. The dog and you, you're the same. You're as bad as each other. It's the way he stares at you every night with his horrible slanty cunning eyes when he wants to go to the pub. He won't eat his dinner, he just stands there whining. All he wants is to go out with you and eat scratchings. Now you've started doing it in the morning. I don't know why I married you. It's your mother, she spoiled you, she thought you were marvellous, she never let you go.

You know, I said to Jim, I think we are missing the leisure opportunities in this boating lark. Some days we should try not getting up.

• • •

THE LAST PERSON I EXPECTED TO SEE IN THE Rue Daumesnil on a wet Sunday evening was my father. Jim and I looked along the long row of shops under the arches of the viaduct. I thought they would be artists' workshops but they were showrooms for rich people setting up home. I liked a few things but something would have to go from the *Phyllis May*–something like Jim, who was pulling and whining and being a bugger. He does this now and then. Monica says it's his hormones and the only solution is Off with his goolies, but you can't do that to your best friend and anyway he wouldn't look right.

We stopped outside a shop full of musical instruments and I thought of when my father had bought me my first clarinet. He knew I wanted to play jazz and he didn't warm to that and he had very little money but he bought the clarinet. It's cruel that sons have to reject their fathers to grow up. I suppose like a swan you have got to find your own territory–it's the only way it can work.

I could feel him standing by me in his old raincoat and I could see his shape in the window, in the rain, and I longed for him like a lover. I wanted him now, if only for half an hour, to say I know how you felt and I wish I could have been kinder and I'm sorry and I wanted to press my face against his rough air-force trousers, and smell the tobacco and feel his hands on my head.

Come on Jim, I said, let's go back to Mon. And stop pulling for God's sake.

AT LAST THE BIG NIGHT OUT—THE CRAZYSHO. It said in the listings it was *transformiste*, with *imitation* and *parodie*. Brigitte Bardot would appear, and Céline Dion, and

Charles Aznavour. Britney Spears would be there, and Whitney Houston, and Edith Piaf.

We walked east down an avenue of shops. It was dark, when you would expect shops to be closed, so they had opened, and the light bounced off the shoppers in a fine rain. Fire engines came past yelling like Grendel with his arm torn off and ambulances howled to the Saint Antoine hospital and birds fell dead from the trees. Then things got quiet and dark and there was the red neon sign for the Crazysho.

A huge queen was on the door with glitter on his eyelids and I couldn't think what to say. Tell me all, young man, he said encouragingly, so I did and he showed us in.

It was a dining room for about fifty people. It had been painted black, and there was a small stage. It was nearly full, and the trestle tables were laid and people were testing the weight of the knives and forks. There was music, and everyone was shouting. Food and noise—Welcome to France. This is going to be great, I said, no tourists here—this is the turtle, not the mock.

A man in black who looked like Frank Sinatra leaned over with the menu. The aperitif *maison*, he explained, came from his home area in the Auvergne. The berries from which it had been distilled were from bushes planted in Roman times. They were gathered by farmers who lived on the edge of starvation and they were ripened between the breasts of young girls. We ordered one each and Monica said it was not bad and I had a beer to forget the taste. The meal was all right and so was the wine and the service was good and soon the performance started.

The show rested unsteadily upon two pantomime dames, including the one who had welcomed us. They mimed and camped unknown songs and impenetrable comic routines from tapes. I don't think they actually spoke or sang a word all night. The loudspeakers convulsed, the tables shook, our ears rang, and the lights spun and strobed and blazed, usually straight at us. There was applause and laughter on the tapes in case we forgot. For each number the queens changed their clothes. The audience was good-humoured, and when Frank Sinatra sang he got a big hand because he was not a tape recorder. For the finale a couple of the waiters appeared in jockstraps and danced with the queens. We clapped the performers and our special enthusiasm was asked for the young lady who had shone strobe lights down our throats and we all clapped her too. Everyone who worked at the Crazysho was friendly and committed and the atmosphere was great but it was awful.

Our taxi driver was from Haiti, sending money home to his wife and family. I can't believe how good the taxis are these days, I said—Paris taxi-drivers all used to be criminals—lose themselves, steal your luggage. It has changed, he said, there is study of maps, there are examinations and controls. Monica explained where we wanted to go and he put us down by the Seine, further from the boat than when we started, and we walked back in the rain.

THE DOG DAYS HAD TIRED US AND IN Charleville-Mézières we had caught a bug that kept us down for a week. Hi folks, it's the bug again—I'm not what I was, but I will make a codswallop of all your plans for Paris.

How can I go to the tea dance? said Monica, I'm not right. Perhaps you could buy those shoes you were looking for, I said. No hamster went up its tube swifter than Monica up the steps to the street, with Jim and me in pursuit, along the Rue du Faubourg Saint Antoine.

Once in Birmingham Monica stayed in a branch of Monsoon for so long I reported her kidnapped. In Paris Jim and I went into a pavement café and I put my fleece on the floor and ordered a coffee and a brandy and settled down for the day and all Paris came by, three abreast.

You could divide them into men and women but that wasn't much of a start. Old and young, but most were neither. Black and white, but some were brown. Pretty and plain, but many were in between. Fast walkers and slow—that's more like it. Whether they were pushing to close a deal or meet a girl or whether they were just on the stroll. Whether they were on foot or on Rollerblades, brushing the walkers, *distrait*, feeling their balance. The pretty girls, dark, graceful, head to toe in one concept—student in jeans, African princess in bracelets, sophisticate in jacket and skirt, artist in black, gaol-bait with a ring in her belly button. The workman, the beggar, the drunk, the couples holding hands, all crowding by, knowing who they were, going somewhere.

How would Jim and I look to them? I wondered. The little yellow hound with the glossy coat and the bandanna, relaxed on his master's fleece, and the old man, red with sun and wind, in his crumpled trousers and his mustard Tour de France T-shirt. Unlike them I don't know who I am—I'm a mess, a foreigner, I don't have a concept. But they don't see me anyway when Jim is around. Like the man in the yellow jacket, I am invisible.

A lady came across to Jim, and looking hard, saw a disturbance in the air, and me, transparent, in the corner. *Monsieur*—I have one. A girl whippet. She is my love.

Jim knew Monica had decided to come back before Monica did, and went to the window, picking her from the crowd when she was a hundred yards away. The shoes, the shoes. They didn't cost much, said Monica sadly, drinking my brandy. Oh dear, I said—would you like me to go back and give them some more money? They're very nice, but they won't last, said Monica. Better get another pair, I said, for when these wear out. Don't be silly, said Monica, they'll be out of fashion.

THE CHINESE GENTLEMAN SMILED AT ME AND swung to the left and swung to the right, his hips in counter-rotation, his elbows following his shoulders. I thought, Shall I smile back?—he looked like a villain in a Bond movie, the sort of chap who might take offence and kill me. I tried to twist a grin that said Goodness how quaint that two obviously heterosexual males are dancing together. Oddjob moved towards me cha cha cha and I thought, He is seeking his balance and he will chop me down with the side of his hand, but he was grooving at my partner, the American friend from the Tjalk. She knew the right smile to give before turning away. You don't get to be blond and sixty in San Diego without learning to say No thanks, perhaps later but not now, no.

In the world of aquaria, in those rows of bright tanks with the streaming bubbles and the hair weeds there are darker tanks, and these contain the tetras. They are black but they shine with a cold light, brighter than the micro-organisms of the night sea: half an inch of neon blazing from their transparent hearts. In the tea dance the ultraviolet fired up shirts, blouses, cuffs, earrings. My partner smiled with luminous teeth, the whites of her eyes flashed and her hair glowed. We swam around slowly, under the glittering balls, under the woofers, in the disco dusk.

Everybody was there, the living and the dead, and as the

lights came up and the music fast-forwarded to 1975 you could see that you knew them all. There was Giscard d'Estaing, his jacket close on his snake hips, dancing with Margaret Thatcher. There was Ann-Margret—time had not been kind to Ann-Margret, but she still had her lion hair. There was the lady from the news-stand at Meaux, looking good in a suit, and with her Sacha Distel. Jean Gabin and Arletty had struggled out of bed and come across from the Hôtel du Nord, and goodness me, Sir Norman Wisdom was in, his face against the jacket of Sophia Loren. François Mitterrand was there twice—how can that be?—once in a grey suit and once in a smart black blazer. The hairdos were careful, men and women: not boater's punk but waved and sprayed and there was a chap in a full ponytail, and I'll swear he was older than me. Must be taking steroids. Sitting at a table was the lady in the flowered dress from Armentières, and Jean Marais drifted by, smiling sadly, clicking his fingers, his body hardly moving but you could see the rhythm flowing through.

Monica was delighted because a Frenchman had tried to pick her up on the way back to our table. The ladies explained that a lot of the people were singles, and the men were asking new partners to dance. Indeed on the floor no one was saying Wasn't it fun in the bath last night. It was chat-up time—After I sold my software business and bought my motorboat I decided all I want is a friend who will be sincere. It was the first pull, the shopfront, the big pitch, like when I talked to Monica about Baudelaire that night so many years ago.

Monica and I mounted the platform at the end of the disco and started to do the jitterbug, which we had learned before rock and roll. We forget about one step per decade, which science has proved to be the rate of loss. Across the floor, up the wall, over the ceiling. Rock me, sailor baby, shimmy my timbers.

As we were going to our table Charles Trenet asked Monica to dance. I am here with my husband, she said, right behind me. *Pardon, monsieur*, he said, flashing that music-hall smile. No problem, I said. No problem at all.

WHY IS YOUR DOG SHIVERING? ASKED THE Englishman. He was on a yacht, which had been modified for the canals. The mast was down, a red bandage tied to the end, and the boat was hung with planks and fenders. It looked humiliated, like Concorde turned into a restaurant. We are leaving tomorrow, I said, and he can tell by our brain waves. He is a coward, and he doesn't like boating.

This morning we are going up the Canal Saint Martin, I said, under the market of the Avenue Richard Lenoir, and across the north of Paris along the Canal de Saint Denis, and back on to the Seine twenty-five kilometres downriver. Then we will come back upriver all the way through Paris, round the Bois de Boulogne, past the Eiffel Tower, and away south to our winter mooring. I'll be lucky to get this lash-up to the Med, said the Englishman, without bothering about tunnels. I wish I had stayed out at sea.

It took a long time to say goodbye to Bernard and Bruno and Guillaume. After Jim and he had shared their last desperate kisses Bernard said—I have a Gryphon. It is a big one, very strong. He twisted his face and walked towards us, his arms hanging, like a monster.

My God, I said to Monica afterwards, he has a Gryphon. That's a cross between an eagle and a lion. I didn't think they existed. Perhaps he keeps it up the Saint Martin tunnel, and flies it over Paris after dark. It's a griffon, said Monica, a sort of dog.

After three weeks I enjoyed feeling the boat move again. Jim was in his kennel and Monica was at the sharp end and I switched on the tunnel light and the boiled-sweet navigation lights and the wand on top of the boat that had dazzled me out at sea and we went towards the Bastille métro station and as a train pulled in we slid under the platform and under the streets of Paris.

There was plenty of water in the tunnel, and now and then daylight fell in from the holes above us and plants trailed along the roof. There was no one around, no rats, no gongoozlers, no Gryphon, just walls and arches and vaults, usually a towpath. Then there were fancy floodlights for the trip boats and along the brickwork a black *Phyllis May* sailed through a rainbow.

After twenty minutes we reached a vault like a submarine pen and then we were in the open air, in a lock, and from a footbridge between the trees twenty gongoozlers stared at us rising in the foam. As we left I swept off my bush hat and waved it. The gongoozlers screamed and waved back, as if they had been watching a penguin in the zoo and it had asked them the time.

Seven more locks and we were in the Villette basin. Lunch by the great water—the restaurant looked like a seaside tea parlour but it was racketing full.

THE NEXT MORNING THE GREEN BRIDGE AT the end of the Villette basin rose horizontal into the air, grinding and flashing and cheeping, and we turned left on to the Canal Saint Denis, which goes through the garden shed of Paris. Piles of dust, rusty tools, broken doll's houses, all the things you couldn't quite throw away. Then the new model stadium, the Stade de France, hid among the debris ready for Christmas.

In the last lock we sank slowly to the level of the Seine then the man in the tower filled the lock again and asked for another twenty euros—he had noticed on his form that we were a *bateau spécial*. The navigation is run by the city of Paris, and the sharpest minds may be in other departments. I wanted to go back and be nasty but I thought of my good behaviour resolution and anyway we were out on the wide mirror and pushing upstream.

We were heading south, and after fifteen kilometres we would double under the *route périphérique* at the Quai d'Issy and head north towards the Eiffel Tower. Under the bridges of Paris with Jim.

The wind came downstream and turned the mirror into Flemish glass and then broke it into fragments and spots of spray and then the sun came out and set it all on fire. Soon on our right the skyscrapers of La Défense—*C'est magnifique, mais ce n'est pas Manhattan.* And where is the arch? Still facing the wrong way. One or two hulking barges churned by, but otherwise, as usual, we were alone.

Long islands divide the stream. On the Ile Seguin the thirties Renault factory: clothed in white concrete, endless, wonderful. With what passion, what clangour, those halls had rung. Now pigeons whirr under the roof, and nettles dance in the white courts.

Suburbs and offices and apartments and moored boats, the boaters waving. On the right couples and fishermen and people in suits eating sandwiches and now on the left cardboard villages: groups sitting around fires in the cold sun. Every kilometre a mighty bridge: decorated, scrolled, iron, concrete—take any arch you like, they're all free. Power it through–give those guys on top a wave. And a smile–might as well use the teeth, they cost enough. But can they see and do they care, who stand so far above?

A hot-air balloon rises in the blue, and with five play-bricks of thirty storeys standing guard in line, here comes the Eiffel Tower. But first the Statue of Liberty–are we so far out of our way?

Down on the right the Quai de Grenelle, where a stranger can moor. Monica climbed up on to the quay and we threw a rope round one leg of the Eiffel Tower and tied it off and had a cup of tea and a lie-down. We had been going for seven hours.

THE BOAT LIFTED THREE FEET IN THE AIR AND bellyflopped. I was asleep on the sofa and Jim was asleep on Monica. He sprang into the air and ran to the saloon and pressed himself to the floor with his legs out–I've got her, I've got her, but I can't hold her long. More bellyflops–*crash, crash, crash.*

It went on until after midnight, when the *bateaux-mouches* stopped running. They came long and they came very long, and they came very long indeed, lit in bright colours, and they came fast. In the night our back rope, an inch thick, snapped and only a line from our centre ring held us from waking up in Rouen.

We cast off and were gone early, before the tourists left their hotels and the *bateaux-mouches* started flailing by, and headed south.

PARIS STANDS BACK FROM THE RIVER, AS IF afraid it might fall in. The buildings are handsome but not tall compared with the great river, which is wider than the Thames, and there is always a road in front, and trees.

London stands on the water's edge, peering over, looking for dolphins—the Houses of Parliament right on the water, the London Eye with its feet wet, the offices and monuments hard on you as you sail by, even absurdities like the MI6 building saying Here I am, ships, water, looking right at you, on the scene—hi, how's the tide running? But Paris is too polite to make a fuss on the waterfront: too beautiful to wear its jewellery on its breast.

And so to Notre-Dame, from the north, past a notice—

On no account go down the right-hand side of this island. It is formally interdicted. It could be gravely hurtful to your health and that of your entourage. You will become incontinent and unable to put on your socks. Do you understand, don't do it. This is the Ile de la Cité, for Christ's sake.

I don't care, I said, I saw a *bateau-mouche* come down last week.

We went down the right-hand cut, under the cathedral, through the little stone bridges, unchallenged.

And then I was sitting in my study at home, officer, and these three men with guns broke in and shot my dog and said we saw you go down the wrong side of the Ile de la Cité—we saw you and now you will have to fill in this form—any more argument and we will pump you full of lead.

On to the broad Seine again, blue, chopping, deserted, leaving behind the moored cathedral and the window just above the water where behind the bars two hundred thousand ghosts looked out, and in the wind the voices of the children—*We only wanted to be free like you, we only wanted to grow old like you.*

Past the ruined open-air sculpture museum, past the runway of The Albatross, past the lock opening into the Bastille basin, then under the knitted Austerlitz viaduct and the Charles de Gaulle javelin. On the right again the South Goodwin light vessel, nodding, nodding, just watch out, just watch out.

Next door a floating chandlery. The gentleman on board let down a ladder. That will be a euro a litre, *madame*, he said. And it is the end of the season and we have only one fender left, and it is white, and I am over eighty years of age, and what do you think of that?

On the boat the phone rang–the lady we had met in Namur, whose husband had told us about the eleven sunken narrowboats. She had fallen down a hatch and had been in hospital for a month. A thousand miles, said Monica–we have come far enough and we have pushed our luck far enough. I want to go home and see the grandchildren and the kids and my friends. It's late October and I'm tired and I'm fed up. Jim is fed up–he wants to run on grass again and eat scratchings.

I want to go home too, I said. I want to drink beer in Langtry's with Clifford and my sons-in-law. I want to jog with Jim on the common. I want to go down the running club and see my mates. I want to watch television and try to find something interesting in the Sunday papers and open Christmas parcels with the grandchildren. We'll come back in April when the canals open again and we'll tackle the terrible Rhône. And we'll get down the Rhône, one way or another, to many-towered Carcassonne.

I leaned on the throttle handle and the engine clamoured and we splashed south, between the piles of sand, towards our winter boatyard seventy miles away: into a cold wind, in a silver light.

Nine

JACK THE DISEMBOWELLER

The River Yonne

The weather shrugged—his coat let fall:
The wind, the frost, the needling rain.
In his embroidery again,
Dressed in sunlight overall.

No beast, no bird, that does not call,
Singing or crying, sweet or plain.
The weather shrugged—his coat let fall:
The wind, the frost, the needling rain.

River, fountain, waterfall
All their livery regain.
See the drops of silver shine,
The jewels, and the bright crystal.
The weather shrugged—his coat let fall.

Charles d'Orléans lived seven hundred years ago, I said. We captured him at Agincourt but the king was his uncle so we sold him back to the French. In the Middle Ages a toff could fornicate with his best friend's wife, kill a man in a swordfight, and turn a reasonable *rondeau*, all before breakfast. Our princes can still fornicate, said Monica.

It was Easter Sunday. We had collected the *Phyllis May* from her winter quarters and were moored in Sens, by the bridge.

It must have been a spring day like today when Charlie wrote his *rondeau*, I said. But the cathedral wasn't finished, and Sens would have been small, and all over this side of the river, because the Yonne would have been too wide for a bridge. No stone quay, just wood. I suppose they had rowing boats, said Monica—look at the green current, and the fish rising.

Although Jim can fly we have to lift him off the boat. Once he jumped out when he was tied up so you can't blame him. He stands shivering, his eyes fathomless with reproach— Now you want me to hang myself?

Across the stone quay, past the flower beds, over the road and up the main street. The shops were shut but there were plenty of people around. At the top of the hill someone was throwing narrowboats out of a window, like doors slamming in hell. We expected the main square to be full of twisted iron, but the concussion came from the cathedral. A narrowboat weighs about sixteen tons, and it says in the book that the cathedral has two bells, one weighing fourteen tons and one sixteen. So I wasn't far out–a couple of octaves below middle C, I would say.

People in the cathedral door collecting euros. Monica slipped inside. Give them something, I said, it will be for the fabric. They were beggars, she said, they smelt of drink.

Many in the Easter crowds asked if they could stroke Jim. *Oh le toutou! Et son foulard! Toutou* is the French for pussy-cat, but for a dog. We don't have a word like that in English, thank heaven. But translation is impossible even when words and phrases seem to match. The only way is to walk briskly into the topic through a French doorway and wave your arms.

Excuse me again *monsieur*–a small brown old man with a wife and a dog the same. When we met just now, he said, you told me the race of your dog but we have forgotten. A whippet, I said. *Un wee pet*, repeated the small brown old man. *Un wee pet*, repeated his wife, *un wee pet*–the accent as ever on the last syllable. What is the race of your dog? I asked. He is a *péniche*, said the brown old man. *Un péniche*, I repeated. Exactly, said the wife, *un péniche. Bonjour, m'sieur 'dame*, we all said and walked on. Damn funny, I said to Monica, a dog called a barge. Must be some sort of boat dog. *Caniche*, said Monica, a poodle.

We walked back down to the river. He's not fat, said a child, looking at Jim. He's all thin, said another. Oh *Maman*, it's the same dog, said another–that's the one that jumped me on the way up.

DOWNSTREAM NEAR THE BOATYARD THE BIG retail sheds, among car parks and bad roads and nettles and desolation–shops that have ten thousand of everything. We had to buy provisions, and paint and varnish and thinners and Brasso and brushes. We had allowed a fortnight for re-stocking, and for freshening up the *Phyllis May*.

In England shops are normally open, and in France they are normally shut. When they are open the lights may be out and you bang on the door to get in. Market stalls close like oysters as you draw near. The brass plates of doctors and lawyers have a piece of paper with yellowing tape saying that no opinion will be offered until ten to three Thursday fort-night. Outside a restaurant in Sens the list of closing times is longer than the menu. There are supermarkets the size of a city that seem to be open from time to time, but they are not–they are going round behind you making faces.

Leclerc supermarket is open but turn up with your films and the photo shop is shuttered. The restaurant is open but All we have this evening, *monsieur*, is a cold tripe sausage and a glass of milk. The bar is open, with pumps, and rows of bottles and tables and chairs and a man in a pinafore and a moustache–selling soft drinks only. The restaurant sells wine by the gallon, but that bit is shut.

Don't try to understand these things–every nation has its private parts, where no light falls and reason takes a holiday. Think of the Financial Services Authority, or Prince Michael of Kent.

Monica was at the other end of the Leclerc fresh fruit sec-tion but there was a slight mist so I couldn't see her. We re-united joyfully by the fifty yards of soup in boxes, and by asking directions worked our way to the checkout just before Jim died of grief in our camper van outside.

Foir' Fouille was not so big–the size of Hampton Court maze. It was closing in ten minutes. Acres of plastic flowers and wrapping paper and china fish and pictures that light up and buckets and coloured glass plates and socks with French names on. A discount store.

One Saturday in November I took my mother out in the Black Country. We parked off a red-brick main street that was nearly all discount stores. My mother wasn't walking much but we went along every gondola. I bought a red Porsche 911 cabriolet for a pound and an antique Chinese vase for fifty pence and some postcards of Alan Ladd as Jay Gatsby. The sunlight was horizontal. We had a sit-down in a baker's and a cup of orange tea the same colour as the sunlight.

I have looked for that street since but I can't find it. You can't find these places again.

TERRY AND MONICA DARLINGTON
AND JIM THE NARROW DOG
INVITE TOUT LE MONDE
CHEZ EVANS MARINE FOR

DRINKS AND NUTS AT SIX

BEFORE THEY LEAVE FOR CARCASSONNE

JUST TURN UP. OR DON'T TURN UP—
PLEASE YOURSELVES—
SEE IF WE CARE

Before the party I decided to touch up the paint on the radiator. When she heard this Monica went back to bed. Jim greeted the day as he always does—his head and shoulders in Monica's lap under the quilt and his bum sticking out.

That didn't take long, I said, as I carried the paint and the brush back towards the engine-room, another job done, ho ho. Then the lid came off the can and the black paint went on to the carpet, into the bathroom, and over the bed. You can get radiator paint off most things with acetone but it takes all morning. You can't get it off beds.

The radiator dried with streaks down it. I hadn't read the instructions. Monica put a chair against the radiator, and the coal-box that says *Phyllis May* on the front side. They won't notice, she said, they wouldn't have noticed anyway. Then she turned the coal-box round so it said *Kiss Me Again* on the backside.

No one's going to come, said Monica. It's no good just telling the boatyard and putting up a notice. We'll be disgraced. How can we be disgraced? I asked, we don't know anyone to be disgraced with. If I stand here I can see the boatyard, said Monica. There's no one coming and it's half past six. And if they come they'll be awful or they won't like us. Another of your lunatic schemes has gone wrong. It was just another excuse for you to find drinking cronies.

We'll eat the cashews, I said, and drink the beer, and put on Bananarama, and get a garlic sausage out of the fridge, and have a party—you and me and Jim.

But people were walking up from the yard. One arrived with a Starsky screech in an old red Mercedes, and one bumped alongside in a clinker boat. About twenty people turned out.

A narrowboat is a fine place for a party. Out on the bow round the well-deck sit the smokers, who bend forward and talk about lung disease. Inside are the standers, holding close to the cashews. They tell stories about boating or about the country where they were born and where they spend the winter and which is a most remarkable place. Music sounds good on a narrowboat and past the stove there is a place to dance, as long as you don't move about. The galley makes a good bar, and in the cabin there may be a gentleman asleep on the bed, deceived by a large Ricard. If the young people get bored they can always go into the engine-room and have sex.

He can see hardly at all, said the lady in the suit, and he's Welsh. Her husband was small with a pointed face and looked straight ahead. I wish he wouldn't do so much engine maintenance, said Simon from the boatyard—he'll kill himself on the electrics. He was in the Navy, said the lady in the suit, he was a lieutenant, he's eighty-four.

Were you in the war? I asked. Yes, said the blind lieutenant, on the motor gunboats, the MGBs. We had three Rolls-Royce Merlin Spitfire engines, each eleven hundred horsepower. I was the engineer officer—it was my job to make sure the engines worked. We are forty-three horsepower, I said, here on the *Phyllis May*. What speed could you do?

We were wood, said the blind lieutenant, seventy feet long, and we went up on the plane and we could do forty-four knots. If we went over a mine, by the time it went off we were gone. Our territory was E-boat Alley, where the convoys went past Dover and the mouth of the Thames. We were there to kill the German E-boats. They were steel with diesel engines and we were full of petrol. We were out every night. We had an Oerlikon 20mm gun—there was a lot of shooting. I can't say it was very nice.

We went along E-boat Alley, I said, in the *Phyllis May*, but it's quieter now. I think we got most of the buggers, said the blind lieutenant.

Simon's mother accepted a plush frog from Jim and he wouldn't let it go so they pulled each other back and forth the length of the boat until Jim won, as Mrs. Evans is old and not very big. But Jim always wins anyway. We left England in the eighties, said Mrs. Evans, to start a boatyard business in Greece. When we got to Sens people kept asking us to stay a bit longer and we never finished our journey. My husband has gone and now the yard is run by my son Simon.

How did you enjoy your voyage from Paris last year, she

asked, down the Seine and the Yonne? Saint-Mammès was nice, I said, with the barges at the canal junction. It was October and in the market they were selling winter coats like they wear in Canada. But when I had the films of the journey developed it was an old roll of film and everything was muddy and grey. We were tired, and that's how I remember the journey too.

A thin man in jeans explained he was Den from the next boat and though he was sixty and on his own and not pretty or well off he was a bit of a lad. He had spent the whole winter in the Bastille marina because Bruno and Guillaume and Bernard had forgotten he was there. Over Christmas he had met one or two ladies and had spent three days with them. He couldn't remember anything about the three days and his audience fell back into the cashews.

Monica had invited a reporter who had interviewed us the day before—no more than a student, all in black, too tall for the saloon. When he spoke he did not smile. What is your paper called? I asked. *Le Senonais Libéré,* he said—the *Liberated Person of Sens.* I imagined the first issue of the little paper, sixty years ago, handed out in the street by young men like the reporter, their eyes wild.

Next morning Simon took us to see three boats in his yard that had been across at Dunkirk. They were wooden boats, about thirty feet. They were loaded to the gunwales, said Simon, with water over the back deck—it must have been awful.

One boat was afloat, looking good in white with woodwork and brass, and the other two were in the weeds, held up by stakes, their paint peeling, their windows blank. Across the yard we could hear the blind lieutenant working on his engine.

· · ·

THE FLOWER BEDS WERE BRIGHT AND THE lawns cut, and the trees dressed in sunlight overall. The Yonne was green and blue, like the Channel. We had been in Sens three weeks already, and this should be our last day, but I was in trouble. I left Jim, betrayed, on the boat, and struggled over the bridge. A man was polishing the rails.

I need both your feet, said the *podologue*, so I can see if they are in any way similar. Ah, you have a corn. In France we do not do much of the jogging–we believe one should not exaggerate. I will cure your corn but it may come back and then you must come and see me again. You are not leaving soon?

I went to a bar to celebrate the loss of my limp. *Madame*, I said, I have seen the French drinking in the morning and in England that is not normal. But out of respect for your culture I am prepared to have a brandy and a coffee after breakfast on occasions of importance. Is this behaviour correct?

You must be the gentleman from the long boat with the little wife and the thin dog, said the lady. Of course, *monsieur*, you are correct. But it is even more correct in the morning to have a café and a marc, or a café and a calvados–*un café calva*. That sounds nice, I said, a *café calva*–what is marc? It is an alcohol, said the lady. It is made from the residue after the grapes have been pressed. It is very strong. A Frenchman might drink many *cafés* in the morning but he will drink only one glass of spirits.

It was a fishing bar: a fishing shop with a beer pump and a coffee machine and two stools. On the shelves were jars of plastic worms. What is the water like in the Yonne? I asked. Here upstream it is clean, *monsieur*. There are trout, which are sensitive.

Prescott came at me and took the lower part of my face into his mouth. Prescott was the size of a brown cow, and as affable. He is *un dogue allemand*, said the lady. Prescott went behind the bar and the lady turned on the tap and he reached up and sucked down a gallon of water and the lady wiped his chops. You must return when you are accompanied by your thin dog, said the lady, it will be *un contraste saisissant*, and Prescott likes small dogs. We do hope we will see you again, *monsieur*, Prescott and I.

Back on the boat Jim and I could hear the roar of battle up in the town as Monica and France Telecom fought over the commissioning of a French mobile phone. A fortnight, they had said—just wait in Sens and all will be arranged. If not *quinze jours*, a few weeks at the most. Then you must go to Orléans to buy the cables to complete the connection to your laptop. But if you stay here until the summer all will certainly be arranged, if we can get the parts.

On the quay an old man stopped us. My whippet died seven years ago, he said, he was fourteen. He was the same colour as your whippet—sand. When I see your whippet of sand I weep. He wept. I hope you will not go soon, he said, then I can see your Sheem again.

It was the first time Sens had been open—the pedestrian street up from the river with its flower shops, pavement cafés, patisseries, *traiteurs* with feasts of pâté: windows full of painted robots, oriental bracelets, pancakes, lacy underwear, children's clothes, futile gifts in royal blue—everything different from home, often nicer. I looked through the window of the phone shop but Monica and France Telecom were well matched and this one would go the distance. I am not at my best with the public sector so Jim and I went across the cathedral square and through the indoor market. Banded brick and beams and light from great triangular windows up high. Meats and fishes and cheeses, and vegetables you could devour raw.

And so to a bar–I hooded my eyes, and said *Un gafé galva*, in a very deep voice, trying to sound like Jean Gabin, a gangster, *un mec, un maquereau*. To my surprise I got served. Next to us a couple of old chaps looking at the colour pictures in the *Liberated Person of Sens*. It's you, isn't it? they said. No, I said, I am I–the man in the photograph is an impostor and I have never seen the woman or the boat. Pardon, *monsieur*, they said, my God, we are desolated, we are not polite–but *monsieur*, excuse us, there on the floor is the very dog, the thin dog, *le chien étroit*, with the big ears, looking at us. I took my Breton sailor's hat off the table and put it on. We hope you will stay, they said, and your thin dog. Tomorrow is the annual fair.

Jim and I walked back down the shopping street and everyone was reading the *Liberated Person of Sens*, and poking each other and pointing. Three police came up towards us, one a woman, in bright blue. They touched their weapons and looked at each other.

I waited for Monica in our favourite bar by the bridge–It's you, shouted the waiter, and so did the chaps at the bar, on their fifth calvados of the morning. No, I said, the man in the newspaper is my cousin. You are not going today? they asked–tomorrow is the annual fair. And you are famous, and your thin boat looks nice on the quay. There is a man who will come and help you polish it.

Jim put up his ears and went to look out of the window and ten minutes later Monica came in. There is something going on here, I said. You know Ulysses, whom I so closely resemble–when he reached the Sirens, they tried to keep him and his crew for ever. The liberated people of Sens have decided they don't want us to go. France Telecom is in on it, and the police and the *podologue*. The mayor wants to put notices along the motorway–*Sens–sa cathédrale: son narrowboat fleuri: sa petite anglaise: son toutou étroit.* If we are not careful we will run aground on the Yonne like the Evans family. Tomorrow you and Jim must put your hands over your ears and I will tie myself to the generator pole and we will go full speed for the south. Another day here and we'll never get to Carcassonne.

Next morning the thunder and wheedling of the annual fair rolled down to the river, and the sweet anguish of the lady mayoress spilled out of the speakers and coiled round our prop. But we held our course upriver and the music fell behind us and was gone.

WE SAILED INTO A FALSE AUTUMN, WITH branches bare, or yellow leaves uncharged with chlorophyll and the leaf-cases of the poplars gold and red, unrolling and floating into the stream. The spring sun came round low and the trees shone orange and I pulled down the peak of my cap. Over all before us lay the Plateau de Langres and six hundred miles away the sea.

When we woke, Villeneuve-sur-Yonne had swept its stone quay and turned its pansies to the sun and picked up its litter and checked that its free electricity was pure sine wave, clean enough for our laptops, strong enough for our fan heater and our kettle.

A man came by with a dog. It was a small dog with a grey muzzle and a kind face. What race is your dog, *monsieur*? I asked. He has no race, said the gentleman—my Socrates is a dog. I found him by the side of the road. I was driving my car and I saw him staggering and falling down. He had been tied up and left and his collar had bitten into his neck and he was bloody all down one side. The vet said he had not eaten for a month. It was more than a year before he was well. How can anyone do such a thing, *monsieur?*

Another man came up. He had a long head and short muscular legs and a wide smile and he shook our hands. There may be another boat later today, he said, though probably not, and if you are leaving I will go and open the lock. He went back to his white van with VNF on the side.

The lock was two hundred yards long. It had sloping sides, and a little pontoon for pleasure boats. As the lock fills the pontoon runs up the side on rails, with occasional jerks to throw into the water anyone standing on it holding a rope. The lock-keeper closed the gates behind us and walked to open the upstream paddles; then he walked back to the pontoon. Ah *madame*, I started to learn English but the lessons cost four hundred francs an hour. England is such an interesting place. I have the cards of many English who come through. This lady wants me to find her a cottage by a lock.

I am reading a book now about England, he went on. It is called *Jack the Disemboweller.* It is written by a lady who has been many times to England and is a specialist. She knows all about your country—all about the fogs and the gas lamps and the prostitutes. It was once believed, *madame*, that Jack the Disemboweller was the Queen's physician, then that he was a member of the royal family, but now it is revealed that he was Walter Sickert, a painter. He suffered from an abnormality in his genitals—the lock-keeper made a large gesture below his waist—which caused him much grief and as a child he was ill-treated.

The pontoon tried to throw Monica into the lock. My husband is writing a book called *Narrow Dog to Carcassonne*, she said, and pointed at Jim on the roof. A gripping coincidence, said the lock-keeper—I too am writing my memoirs. As we left the lock he waved to Monica. *Bonne chance*, he called to me, and he made a scribbling sign like one calling for the bill, and we exchanged a salute.

The Yonne has crystal water like the Lys, and a broad valley like the Trent and Mersey. It has hills like the Thames south of Oxford. It is as wide as the Seine, and bluer than the Marne. I suppose there is a more beautiful river, but hardly in this world. There is a particularity about the Yonne—thousands upon thousands of poplars in woods and groves. They are planted in rows and the low sun made lamps of their new foliage and their trunks crossed and recrossed in lanes and you could see the hills and the yellow rape fields behind.

PAST THE PERFUMED BUSHES, PAST THE HOTEL that was shut because it was Sunday evening. Monica and I walked on wet cherry flowers, and Jim drifted above them. Over the bridge and into the town on the hill. Joigny had been disembowelled by excavators, its entrails exposed through the pavements. There are wood-framed and carved houses hundreds of years old but the narrow streets of Joigny were full of gravel and the town was sad and dirty.

A Moroccan restaurant was open. I asked for a half-litre of beer. Fifty centilitres, I explained, a big one, *un demi*. The waiter smiled and said *Monsieur*, here in The France one does not find glasses that size. But the steak was good and the African wine was a beaker full of the warm south, much needed in draughty Burgundy.

There were not many chips with the steak. Jim was too lazy to sit up so he turned his head round and gave us the stare upside down. Better watch out, said Monica, or he will report us to the RSPCW. They will come in the narrow vans with the brindled paint-work and staring headlights, their straight sixes throbbing. I gave Jim some chips and he ate them backwards.

NEXT DAY I NOTICED THE RIVER WAS FULL OF thin green fish the size of sardines. I could ask someone what they were but what's the use? They would say something like *Monsieur*, those are *les norberts dentressangles*, and you forget what they said and are none the wiser. Or maybe they call the creatures *theen green feesh*. With such empty thoughts rattling in my head I set out with Jim for a quick one. Monica stayed on the boat for the latest round with France Telecom. When we left Sens they had disabled our e-mail.

Central Casting had worked hard in the bar by the bridge. It was full of gangsters from Marseilles—*mecs*, pimps, *maquereaux*: swarthy, dwarfish, skinny, misshapen. As usual they had overdone it a little—one chap had a ponytail to his waist like an unravelled mooring rope and a T-shirt with the device of the Goat of Bentès—the Devil himself. And the women need not have been so menacing, so dirty, so small.

A group was gambling at the far end of the bar, banging down cards and shouting words I did not understand. At our end two men in distressed black: shirts and boots. They were normal, even well-built—leading players. One was the hero type, a decent man at heart, who had lately drifted into murdering people, while his friend had been at it for some time. They were unshaven and wore gold, some of it in the ears. Jim went up to them.

My girlfriend had one of these, said the hero. *Un wee Pete*—they are racers and can run at sixty-five kilometres an hour. And you hunt rabbits with them, with a torch. Yes, I said—indeed one has some sport. He looks feeble, said the hero, he looks delicate, but he is solid, he is robust. They turned Jim over and squeezed his thighs and frowned and drummed their fingers on his chest and pulled open his mouth to see his four rows of teeth and spanned his loins with their fingers. Jim didn't mind at all.

Monsieur? asked the *patron.* A large beer, a half-litre, I said defiantly—fifty centilitres—*un demi*—a big one, and do you have some sheep? Of course, *monsieur.* The glass he brought me contained forty centilitres. No crisps. You can't take on a whole culture, I thought.

I told the assassins that I reckoned Jim could run at forty miles an hour and we tried to work out if that was the same as sixty-five kilometres and failed, but we agreed he could run very fast. I was hungry and asked myself how can it be that a French *tabac* is full of drink and cigarettes but the only food is chewing gum?

Crackle crackle behind me and the Goat of Bentès—the Devil himself—hurried in from the street, under his arm a green bag half a metre long. The *patron* came to my table with seven crisps in a saucer. I offered one to Jim and he turned it down. To show appreciation I ordered another forty centilitres. It all came to nearly ten euros, but think of the size of the cast.

I WOKE AND PULLED BACK THE CURTAIN AND over the other side of the Yonne a grebe made a splash landing in the rain. You have got to like grebes. They have crowns on their heads and rust-coloured cheeks and they sit low in the saddle, though not as low as a cormorant. They let you come close and then they dive and come up in Avignon. One day on Tixall Wide near Stone a pair of grebes was teaching its brood to fish alongside our boat. The youngsters rushed around just below the surface, accomplishing nothing. They were striped like bull's-eyes. The adults dived and came up with fish which they gave to the juveniles.

Another grebe arrived on the Yonne and the pair looked at each other and dived. When they came up a long way away they were together.

A walk by the river. Jim's first countryside, his first chance of a burn-up since we came back from England. The path between the trees was bordered by new grass, with constellations of buttercups. Bird's-eyes looked at us and we were children again. Once when I was ill, said Monica, I went for a walk and the bird's-eyes were out and I said to myself everything was fine when I was a little girl and it will be fine again.

The chestnuts and the rowan and the rape and the bird's-eye speedwell and the fume of the may—by the Yonne you can be a child again.

THE NIVERNAIS CANAL IS CLOSED, SAID Monica. The VNF have just told me on the phone. A lock has gone at Auxerre. We'll have to go down the Burgundy Canal. It comes out on to the Saône at St. Jean de Losne.

But no one goes down the Burgundy Canal, I said. It climbs to twelve hundred feet. It's as far as Stone to London, with two hundred locks. We won't see anybody for months, just each other and Jim. There won't be any radio or newspapers and our phones won't work and the locals probably hunt each other with dogs.

Do we want to get to Carcassonne or not? asked Monica.

We waited in the pretty stone basin and sailed into the fifteen-foot lock and up on to the Burgundy Canal.

Ten

THEIR SEVERAL GREENS

The Burgundy Canal

At the quay stood Den. Won't talk, he said—bit of a session last night—an Englishman, a Frenchman and a Dutchman. He tied off our rope and went back to bed. We were in the town square of Migennes, with the first game of *boules* of the year tapping outside our window. A hire fleet owned by an Englishman lay immaculate, like the twenty swans that drifted around the basin, wings over their heads, asleep. Across the basin the railway and the sewage works and a boatyard, owned by an Englishman.

I had rung the Englishman at the boatyard before we left for France and mentioned that I was hoping to sail the Channel and he said I've done a lot of boating and yachting—I've been across, I know. If you are writing a book and you want to finish it go over on a lorry—you can lose your boat or your lives. I thought we should look at his yard and give him the news of our success, which with any luck would cause him great unhappiness.

The Englishman came out from under a boat and looked almost pleased—like Jim a master of the dramatic art. Crossing the Channel is no joke, he said. Quite right, I said, we did eighteen months' research. We would have waited a year for the weather. We mustn't have too many people trying to do it, he said—would you do it again? No, I said, we are glad we did it once but we were lucky. So much could have gone wrong.

THERE ARE A HUNDRED SYSTEMS ON A BOAT, and some of them are always broken, so every voyage is a disaster more or less under control. The two hundred gallons of water in the bedroom at Watten would not have helped our trim off the North Foreland. Going to London we broke a belt and seized up in a laundry of steam. Once the *Phyllis May* sank at her mooring because the propeller shaft leaked. Here in Migennes the shower pump stopped working.

It's only a switch, I said to Monica. The principle of the switch has been established for centuries. Attack is needed and the appreciation of first principles—don't walk away, Renée. I took an *haricots verts* can and drained the beans off and put them in a cup. Then I took the tin-scissors and cut the lid of the can in half. I screwed the two semicircles to the side of the bath, trapping each of the wires from the switch.

Watch, I said to Monica, this will hold until the end of the summer. We must be prepared to look after ourselves, to be resourceful. I rotated one semicircle on to the other. The shower pump hiccuped and there was a hissing and the bathroom filled with sparks.

The electrician from the boatyard said he had heard you cannot electrocute yourself from a twelve-volt system, but he had never really believed it until now.

New-washed we headed down the empty avenues. Straights five kilometres long, lined with poplars and lit by chestnut candles, with mown paths along each side. Green water, light with a hint of blue. Cowslips as single spies and in battalions; margins where you can moor. The locks were forty-five yards long, always empty, ready for us to sail in. Get the rope up round a bollard quick and wind it round the grab-rail and hang on and *bang bang bang* as the lock fills and slip off the rope and out through the gate with a salute. I am not a regular lock-keeper, said the young lady. I am not surprised, I thought—the speed you filled the lock, silly little bugger, could have done for the lot of us. Ah, I said, you are perhaps a student. Yes, *monsieur*, a student of psychology. Perhaps you could have a look at my dog, I said.

For the first time we felt we were going somewhere, not conducting trials or trying to be brave or rambling round in the sun. We were on our way to Carcassonne. A lock-keeper gave Monica a bunch of lily-of-the-valley, which is offered, not for luck, or for good health, but for happiness.

WE HAD REACHED TONNERRE, AND I WAS ILL. Now it has been revealed how it is going to be, I said. No appetite, wanting nothing of life, no lust for drink, or girls, or sport, or green fields or friends or success or fighting: just sickness, tiredness, just what the hell. Lurching towards death, my incontinence pants rustling. Don't be silly, said Monica, you'll be better in a couple of days.

I sought comfort in a French inland waterways magazine. The world will not end in conflagration, it said, it will expire in coldness and emptiness as the galaxies rush apart. The French like to put things in perspective. The editor of the magazine, with three lines left, had reached the attempt by Charlemagne to reunite the Rhine and the Rhône, but I had to go.

When I returned, I looked at Monica's vase of flowers–lady orchid, a hundred little dolls; Solomon's seal, pearls for the livery of a duke; star of Bethlehem, bringing the news. In Stone we had one or two Solomon's seal in the garden, Monica said–here they are on the bank in sheets.

A text message came through *peep peep*–friends we had asked on the boat had not been given a date and do you want us or not? We printed out the e-mail traffic and realized it was all our fault and I blamed Monica and Monica blamed me and Jim sat in the corner and cried. I said Shut up Jim I've got a problem here and I'm not well and if you don't bloody shut up I'll strangle you and he cried more because we were upset and it was the only way he could help.

A knock on the door–Michel from the boatyard. I have excellent news–your engine need no longer sound like a German bomber. I have found a new alternator and it will be here tomorrow. But alas it is a special alternator and it will cost not two hundred euros but five hundred euros. Would you like me to order it? If you do not replace your alternator your batteries will die.

I don't mind the money so much, I said to Monica when he had gone, it's just that it's wrong to support crime. And I'm ill; what can I do to defend myself? They are gathering round me like vultures. This could be the final curtain. And all my friends hate me because I have offended them.

Jim started to cry again, as if he had realized the world was going to die in cold and emptiness. Jim, I said, I am a sick man and you are driving me nuts. One more sob and it's into a sack and over the side. Jim started to howl.

Monica sent a text to our friends and they said it was all their fault and they were coming to stay and I rang the engineers of Bordeaux about the alternator. My God, they said, you are the English *monsieur* who crossed the Channel—we have your picture on the wall. Is the gentleman giving you a good service? It is not an enormous price for an alternator.

I said to Monica I think I could face a bit of bread and cheese. Jim had gone to sleep.

IT MUST BE WONDERFUL TO TRAVEL, SAID THE lady on the towpath, but you need money. There are no jobs in Tonnerre—all the industry has gone. I am lucky—I have a job for two hours each afternoon.

Monica went into the town. You stay in bed, she said when she came back, you haven't missed anything. It's all gaps and boards and dust.

On one side of the canal basin an empty silo and sad conifers, the other side majestic with trees, and underneath a satellite office of the Chamber of Commerce, open four hours a day. The windows were polished, the brochures in rows. At the desk a lady in a suit, fully made up, with brooches and a gilt watch. No one came to ask her anything.

Alongside us knocked an empty dinghy. It had drifted off its mooring. Apart from the *Phyllis May* and Michel's small hire fleet it was the only craft in the basin. Its sail bore the name of the Tonnerre Philatelic Society and the image of a stamp. The sun came out and the little plastic boat flared with red and orange paper flowers.

We went to see the lady with the brooches. It is the

Nautical Festival of Tonnerre, she said—three days of intense sensations. There is a demonstration by *les godilleurs de France*, who scull a boat along with the single oar: there is music, there is a monster. She gave us a newspaper which explained that the monster was the creation of the carnival committee, and when it came to astonishing the public with its monsters the carnival committee of Tonnerre knew no rival.

We dressed the *Phyllis May* overall in bunting and hung out the big French and English flags and the one with the Welsh dragon. A snail four feet high, covered with red and yellow paper flowers, floated past our windows.

On Friday empty stalls appeared on the lawns and a merry-go-round arose, and some houses near the basin were covered with paper flowers. Bunting was strung between the trees. On Saturday morning the stalls were furnished and at two o'clock the music started. There was Gerry Rafferty, Bill Haley, UB40, Tom Jones, Bananarama, Dexy's Midnight Runners, Shirley Bassey. How strange, I said to Monica, their music is so like our own.

A lady with a clipboard passed and thanked us for decorating the boat. Two German professors waved through the window and we asked them inside. Jim jumped them and rushed off and got his frog of plush, which he offered and would not let go. After a while the German professors got the hang of his game, and seemed to enjoy it *Ho ho ho braver Hund Mein Gott.* They went and then they came back and gave us a bottle of German wine.

The festival had been advertised down through Burgundy and half a dozen English people had been caught in its toils. They came on board. There was a circuit judge and he was most interesting, especially if you know nothing of circuit judges. He said being a judge was a holiday compared to being a barrister, where he had nearly killed himself with worry and overwork, and yes, he nearly always knew straight away if the defendant had done it or not.

One of the visitors was on his narrowboat on the Yonne. We always wanted to go down the Rhône, he said, but we bought the wrong engine. We looked into it afterwards and found out it's just not possible and we can't afford to change our engine again. My wife has been in tears. It's the gas barges–they are huge and they go like hell. The currents would sweep us under them and their props mince us into scrap. Like a leaf in the tide–our engine is only forty-three horse.

Oh, hard luck, I said–have you seen our log-box? It has *Phyllis May* on the front side and *Kiss Me Again* on the backside. It is based on a joke I heard Ted Ray make in the Stoll Theatre in 1947. Sometimes I sit in my chair with my feet up on the log-box and say it over to myself and laugh. Like a leaf in the tide, said the narrowboat skipper.

A couple of months ago I met your friends Beryl and Clive, he said. They were asking where you were–they came across on a lorry. Very sensible, I said.

MONICA AND I WALKED WITH JIM BETWEEN the festival stalls and tents. There were not many people around. The voice of the mayor came from the trees, thanking the high school, the single-oar scullers of France, the rugby club, the kung fu fighters, the graffiti sprayers, the town band. The biggest tent was the philatelic society. Please please come in, said the old gentleman outside, there are many nautical pictures. In the tent there were hundreds of postcards pinned on boards, showing canals long ago, but you could not see them because it was dark. Monica tried to buy some stamped cards to send home—But *madame*, that is for collection, you must not put it in the mail.

There was a tent celebrating the Canal du Nivernais, with models of boats and locks and a relief map, and T-shirts, but the Nivernais is another canal. There was a junk stall with a pretty plate from Verdun. Hello, sailor—a life-size plastic *matelot* outside a tent filled with pictures of war machinery and model ships, with a recruitment video playing inside. A stall sold sausages and onion jam.

On a platform a musical group. Five trumpets, played by children. On the floor lay five adults, holding the legs of the music stands so they didn't fall over in the breeze. The children played slowly, in harmony, in strictest time, hitting the notes cleanly, keeping the pitch. They played 'Rock Around the Clock' and then 'YMCA', making both numbers sound like chamber music. Monica and I started doing the actions to 'YMCA' but stopped. We went and bought some onion jam.

The Tonnerre Noise Society came down from the town. There were twenty members, in cruel blue, each holding a drum. They played one two-bar figure over and over, hitting the drums as hard as they could. The world will end, I thought, not in ice but in noise, and maybe this evening.

Behind the drummers was the monster. This was a decorated tool-shed on wheels, on it the giant head of a frog. A dozen men with dirty faces and nets and tridents came before, and a dozen children came after dressed as frogs: then a young woman in green in a motorized wheelchair, and a bespectacled lady of a certain age in green and yellow frills and flukes and fins, waving her arms. They processed to the bridge and turned back and started walking into one another. In the head of the monster a loudspeaker thumped out a tune, and from its mouth there reached a bloody hand.

The lady of the brooches was in the Chamber of Commerce booth. Your boat looks nice with the flags, she said. It is a pity you are the only boat to visit us. We try very hard but there are few private boats on the Burgundy Canal and hirers won't stop at Tonnerre. The hotel boats with the Americans don't come through much since the Twin Towers. Then the canal has been closed the last two summers because there has been no water. This afternoon is the graffiti, and the hip-hop, and *les godilleurs*, who scull a boat along with the single oar.

IT'S THE SMELLS, MAINLY, THAT YOU REMEMber from the Burgundy Canal. The bass notes are from the locks and the banks. You feel them in your guts, not your nose—heavy, muddy, headachy, as when you first looked over a bridge and longed for a fish or bathed in a stream. The middle registers are cut grass, with its sweet breath, and the may flowers, which say relax, it's OK, it's warm, there's no problem, don't rush, stay here and let's all get drunk. Over all, the floral tunes of rape and chestnut and lime.

Then the scale of the cut, its boldness. The Oxford Canal writhes like a scotched snake; the Trent and Mersey squeezes through necks of reeds; the Kennet and Avon struggles across the West Country like a cripple; but Old Father Burgundy Canal keeps rolling along down broad straights, with ash and willow and alder and rowan and beech and laburnum in royal proportion, and avenues of poplars that would honour Cleopatra. Grassy ways and verges; ten feet below through the trees the river Armançon, and on both sides titanic breasts and bellies of hills in their several greens. *La France profonde, la France vaste.* Sometimes a tufted water meadow and white cattle. No machinery, no workers in the fields. No trees undressed–the leaves are darkening and the candles of the chestnuts gutter and burn out.

Tanlay, Lézinnes, Ancy-le-Franc–little pale towns, mostly shut. You must not miss the frog's legs in Tanlay, the judge had said. At the restaurant there was a notice–***Open Every Day***. In the courtyard a couple sharing a bottle of wine–*Oui, monsieur*, we are open every day, but not today.

In Cusy, which was the shut part of Ancy-le-Franc, which was shut anyway, there were four deceased cafés. But here and there often enough among the dust and glare of the narrow towns a house of wedding-cake perfection, or behind a gate a court with a green lawn, a tree, a table, a wall with the new leaves of the vine. And as you sail on you will sometimes see a chateau between the trees–and even a chateau pup in Renaissance style, dreaming in the middle of a lake.

Overhead the fast jets soar, under Mach 1 in respect for the stillness of the water. Below, the bream, in their dozens, a pound in weight, climb and fall away, their dark bodies and fins an echo of the jets: the same sense of power held back for fitness to the time of day, and the season, and the Burgundy Canal.

WE WERE IN A BACK YARD, WHICH THE RESTAU-rant probably called its *terrasse*, in Ravières. The Bourgogne Aligoté was dead right for the snails, I said–never heard of it before. And I thought the red burgundies were heavy, but the ones from round here are fine and light and you can sort of taste the soil they grow in. I will give up beer and steeplechase my way burgundy by burgundy from Chablis to Mâcon. You'll kill yourself, said Monica. The canal is only the start of the wine region, and we're not halfway along it. There are four thousand vineyards in Burgundy.

Hello, are you the people on the English boat? We are from Denmark—that's our cruiser over there. You are going down the Rhône? You have a big engine? Can't complain, I said. We are two hundred horsepower, said the Dane—we can get down and we can get back up. We winter in the south—the weather is good apart from the wind. There is a community of boaters in Aigues Mortes, many English. They spend their time grumbling about France. Aigues Mortes is a tourist place. We went to Sète to stay—that is a real town. In Sète they fish and grow oysters. There is an inland sea down there, a big one.

There are a lot of locks ahead of you at Vénarey—forty, close together, continued the Dane. They give you your own lock-keeper and he goes home and then he comes back for the second day. It's sixty kilometres and eighty locks from here to the tunnel at Pouilly, and after that it's seven hundred kilometres downhill to the sea. The tunnel is three and a half kilometres long and has no lights. It carried away our canopy. But you'll be OK with your low-air draught and your narrow hull. They are strict about life jackets and lights and horns since a lady got drowned there. Nice to meet you—drop in on the way back to your boat.

It must have been dreadful for the lady in the tunnel, I said to Monica. Think of the darkness. One move, one step, and it's end of adventure or worse. Our engine is too small for the Rhône and even if we get down it what will the south be like? We have to get across that inland sea place, the Etang de Thau—it says in the book there are gales and it's full of oyster beds. The French probably lay mines in the oyster beds—remember Churchill sank their navy in the war. But what is the Midi? What is the Camargue? You can read books but it means nothing. It could be awful. All I know is something about white horses, from television in the sixties.

And flamingos–in *Alice in Wonderland* they seem rather unpleasant. Perhaps they attack whippets. We don't know anything about Carcassonne–we chose it because the name sounded nice. In the pictures it has castles, but I bet they are not real castles like we had in Wales, with walls twenty feet thick. It's probably all fake, and full of Irish pubs. Everyone we know has been to Carcassonne already, and some of them are there now, sending us e-mails saying Ho ho we got here first.

Very true, said Monica, it was all a bloody silly idea and a waste of three years. But if we survive the Vénarey locks and the Pouilly tunnel we will pour a glass of burgundy in the canal. It will find its way down between the Massif Central and the Alps all the way to the Mediterranean, and so will we. You're depressed after being ill. Let's go and try some of that Danish hospitality–perhaps it will cheer you up. I hear they give you the bottle and let you get on with it.

WE MOORED IN THE BIG BASIN AT MONTBARD and in the morning Monica went to the launderette. She put on her determined expression and as she walked by children burst into tears. I carried the bags and left her hammering and kicking the machines and Jim and I wandered about the poor town, all sideways and up a hill–and behold, a cinema.

I used to take my mother to the Showcase in Walsall. We went early, and often we were alone. The best bit was the popcorn and the coffee and the Brazil nuts with chocolate on them. One day as we were going through the barrier my mother said loudly–Are you sure you have been to the lavatory, Terry? Mother, I said, I am sixty years of age and a company chairman. But resistance is futile–if I had held my ground she would have told the girl on the turnstile about when I was a baby and she took me down into Pembroke Dock and had me circumcised.

The last film we saw was *Quiz Show*, with Paul Scofield playing Mark Van Doren, who must have been a very boring man. If I had known I could have taken her to a proper film, with the Borg, and Klingons.

It's called the Phoenix, I said to Monica. It's sort of twenties style; it's concrete and it's small and it's lovely, and it's showing an American film at eight o'clock about people murdering each other and at five o'clock a French comedy. Let's go to the French one. We owe it to their culture—after all we are their guests. I thought of Jean Gabin at daybreak finishing his last cigarette and reaching for his revolver. I thought of Jean Marais walking through the melting mirror and down the corridors of hell to rescue his wife. I thought of Paul the student, the dominant male, destroyed by his weakling cousin. I thought of Stéphane Audran, as one does, and I thought of Anna Karina, and Catherine Deneuve, and I thought of popcorn and Brazils and big paper cups of coffee and fat cashews in tins.

Monica had forced the washing machines to submit and was in a good mood so she said she would come to the pictures with me. To my joy the Phoenix was open as advertised, though it was Sunday. Two old folk sold us the tickets and hurried round to take us inside.

The cinema had been refitted in a steep rake with a hundred blue airline seats for children. A few people of our age sat in the middle, quite close together, the ladies holding handbags in their laps, the men in white shirts and brown jackets. We sat down and I realized that there had been no snacks for sale.

The advertisements began. There were glass slides of each shop in Montbard—the florist, the *podologue*, the launderette, the *tabac*, the *traiteur*, the baker, the dog hairdresser. Each was shown for ten seconds, while a Sidney Bechet track was played. You couldn't see the slides properly because someone had left the door open. Then there was a filmed commercial with flashing lights. This ice-cream bar, said a commanding voice, is not just chocolate, but double chocolate, and also caramel. I think mention was made of nuts. A spotlight came up and the old chap from the ticket office came through a door with a tray at his middle. He moved at a steady five knots to another door a few yards away and went out. No one in the auditorium had moved. My hand was still in my pocket for change.

The screen moved its sides in and out a few times and the film began. It was about a bunch of middle-class French people who go to a wedding and it was based on the idea that if you sleep with your brother's wife this can cause disarray. The bride's mother wasn't very nice and the best man lost the ring. There was a large cast and a lot of shouting. The story was set in the Rhône-Alpes and would make you want to go there as long as you could be sure never to meet any of these people. The audience did not laugh and the actors were all the wrong ages. A lot of actors have got old and died and perhaps there aren't so many to choose from any more.

FROM BEHIND A GATE SOME DONKEYS LOOKED across at the lock. You know that poem called 'Prayer to Go to Heaven with the Donkeys', I said, by Francis Jammes. Yes, said Monica, it's in all the anthologies. He was younger than Arthur Rimbaud, I said, and he was around when Louis Aragon was around. He could have been a surrealist, or a communist and written about politics, but he didn't. It's a Catholic country as well.

When I must come to you, My Lord, let it be a day in spring when the dust shines in the sun. I would like to choose my own way, as I did on earth, to go to Paradise, where the stars shine by day.

I shall take up my staff and set out on the great road and I shall say to the donkeys, my friends—I am Francis Jammes and I am going to Paradise, because there is no hell in the land of the Good Lord.

I will say to them, come, dear friends of heaven, poor dear creatures who with a brisk movement brush away the dull flies, and blows, and stings . . .

Let me come to you, Lord, in the midst of these creatures that I love so much, because they lower their heads gently, and stop: putting their little feet together in a sweet way, which makes you pity them.

I shall arrive followed by thousands of ears; followed by some with crows on their backs, some who drag carts of acrobats or carriages with white feathers and silver, some with barrels hunched on their sides, by she-asses full as a leather bottle, with broken steps; by some with little trousers because of the seeping wounds made by the stubborn flies that crowd around.

Lord, let it be that I come to you with these asses. Let angels lead us in peace to wooded streams where cherries tremble, smooth as the joyful flesh of young girls, and may I, leaning over your heavenly waters in this dwelling place of souls, be like the donkeys, whose humble and sweet poverty reflects the clarity of eternal love.

The bit about the feet, said Monica—Jim does that. Yes, I said, the poem makes you wonder what other creatures might be feeling. Look at the herons—they wait until you are nearly on them and then they sail ahead and then they fly around behind and settle again. They must have some sort of feelings. Even the black and green dragonflies must have some speck of awareness–even the spider in the engine-room.

I started the motor and climbed out on to the back counter and took the tiller. A carp as big as a haversack had come in between the boat and the rocks and now it was trapped and the propeller was hammering and the boat was moving. The fish heaved itself free and bolted away down the side of the boat as if in great fear.

IN ENGLAND THE PIGEONS ARE NOT ALWAYS polite, but in France they say *Là-bas au fond, là-bas au fond*– down there at the bottom, down there at the bottom. Then there is a bird that says *Kiss kiss* with a French accent. All rather encouraging. In Vénarey something was going *Cricky cricky croo* and its friend would answer from over the basin *Cricky cricky croo.* What bird is that? I asked. It's frogs, said Monica, this is France–there are frogs, they eat them. They haven't eaten these, I said. Lots more frogs started saying *Cricky cricky croo*, louder and louder, and then as night fell they started to neigh. It was important that we slept well that night, but the frogs neighed until midnight, and started again when the sun came up.

We cleared out the well-deck at the front of the *Phyllis May* so we could jump in and out safely and moved the diesel reserves from the engine-room in case there was a fire and set out in a thin mist. A buzz-bike arrived. I am your lock-keeper, said the rider, taking off his helmet. He was small and brown, with a round face and round glasses and muscular legs. How many locks do you wish to do today? he asked. I thought of the twenty-nine locks of the Caen flight in four and a half hours. All of them, I said. No, *monsieur.* Twenty today and twenty tomorrow. Afterwards I thought That's funny, we did not shake hands. In France you shake hands with everybody, including the chap next to you at the checkout.

The sun came out and the poplars took us round bends between the green hills and one of us was on the tiller and one of us walked the towpath with a boathook and Jim trotted along behind. As we left each lock our keeper stayed behind and closed the gates and emptied the lock and opened the bottom gates, which is how they like it on the Burgundy Canal. While this was going on we sailed to the next lock and opened it and went in. Then we had to wait for the lock-keeper to buzz up and fill it, because he was the guy with the key. It was much slower than doing it ourselves. When he opened the gates we sailed past him with a cheery word but he did not reply or he pretended not to understand.

What's the matter with him? I asked. No one goes up the Burgundy Canal so the VNF can't afford a lock-keeper on each of the locks, said Monica, and the lock cottages are falling into ruin and I think they let people live in them free if they will take boats up and down. We are taking two days out of his farming.

He's not a farmer, I said. Look at him. Look at the people he stops and talks to. They're all short and fat and brown and none of them says hello to us. And have you seen their ears? The VNF have come to an arrangement with the local trolls. Ours has stolen a pair of spectacles to look more like us.

How do trolls live? asked Monica. They hunt and eat other primitive creatures, I said, mainly gnomes, but they will tackle a goblin, and they keep goats. They hate us but are frightened of us because we are bigger than them and have guns and dogs and fire. They piss on us from holes in empty locks. They do crop circles for whisky. They live near bridges and locks and passes and threaten travellers. From the garden of a lock cottage a couple of brown goats looked at us.

Our lock-keeper was joined by a female. She was four feet tall, nut-brown, spherical. I had seen her face before, in British Columbia, on a totem pole. She didn't say hello. She talked to the lock-keeper all the time so things went much slower and she opened the paddles before we were roped up so we banged about and our cupboards fell open.

That evening at dinner a bottle of Marsannay, from the Côte d'Or. I suppose we'll give the troll bloke a tip, said Monica—I mean he is at our service for two days. We'll put a note in an envelope with a card and put *merci* on it and his name. But we don't know his name, I said. There is no personal relationship, he is not even polite—no tip for him. It's a matter of principle. If anyone wants a tip from me they have to grovel. I was a waiter as a student. I know the rules—I grovelled.

The Burgundy Canal is beautiful even when you are slogging up locks in the sun in the company of hostile life forms. We were climbing on to the roof of Burgundy, the Langres plateau, not looking up at the hills any more but looking across at them. The avenues of poplars had lost twenty feet in height; there were more oaks and some conifers. Always the smell of cut grass. The machine that mowed the towpath had left flowers here and there in islands.

No towns, no villages, no passers-by, no boats. At every lock a ruined cottage. One or two were occupied, though still ruined, and then our companions had loud discussions with the tenants, or vanished inside with a gesture, leaving us hanging on our ropes in the sun. At one cottage there was a heap in

the garden–the remains of dozens of gnomes–disembowelled, red hats scattered, arms torn off. Bastards, I thought.

Before lunch Jim lay down by a lock and would not get
up, so we picked him up and put him in the boat, where he
slept for three days. After lunch I fell over some gate gear.
The secret of falling on concrete is to hit the ground with as
much of yourself as possible, but I knew I would be stiff for
days. Oh Lord I can hardly move to reach for the rope. Only
ten locks to go, only five, only two. Just keep moving.

The French do a low-alcohol beer which is not bad if you
mix it with one of their strong lagers. Two or three of those
make a reliable isotonic drink. Did you give him a tip? asked
Monica. Yes, I said. He took it all right but hardly thanked
me. I thought you were going to make a stand against rude-
ness, she said.

Their job was to get us up the locks and they did it, I said.
We are fifty miles from anywhere and these guys control
the canals and they all know each other. Remember what
happened to Jon Voight and Burt Reynolds in that film.
Remember what happened to Ned Beatty, poor devil. You
don't mess about with the guys from the forks of the creeks.
But he got no envelope from me, no card with his name on
it–I gave him the money straight in his hand. I didn't want to
be hard on him, but it's the only language they understand.

THE POUILLY TUNNEL IS THREE KILOMETRES
long and very boring. Before you go in you can see the point
of light at the other end and you watch that all the way. After
about twenty minutes you get mesmerized and nearly fall off
the back of the boat. But we were through, into a fine stone
cutting with moss and overhanging trees and a thin rain, and

into a basin. We poured a glass of Marsannay into the water and crossed to the lock, where the A-team waited for us, moving from foot to foot.

Four chaps in fluorescent waistcoats, smiling and jogging and buzzing up and down the towpath. The A-team were under the control of Dijon, not Tonnerre, and big rich Dijon had not come to an accommodation with the local primitives. All eleven locks were open and full when we arrived and we were down the lot in an hour and a half and into the next basin, to be welcomed by the deadly embrace of the Spider Woman.

I'll take Jim for a walk, I said. This was no news to Jim, who had known for some time. Under the bridge a notice— *Grocer, Wines*—and a cave with provisions on shelves. I tied Jim up and went into the cave and a bell rang.

A big woman with a white face appeared beside me. She was wearing a loose black dress. She smiled—*Monsieur?* Do you have any burgundies of the region? I asked—I am doing a little research. Ah, *monsieur,* yes, of this very town, only five euros. I'll have a couple of those, I said, and do you have any marc? The marc, yes indeed, *monsieur,* the marc—she reached one of her arms out of her dress and took down a bottle and handed it to me.

How much is the marc? I asked. Thirty euros, she said, and smiled, and moved closer. It was dark but I could see her lipstick was red. Oh well, I thought, it must be a very good marc.

The wine is *ordinaire,* said Monica back at the boat, brushing cobwebs off my jacket. It should have been one euro fifty. And the marc is not even a full-size bottle. You've been had. Thank God I only gave you forty euros. I should never give you money—someone always takes it off you.

A knocking on the roof—the Englishman from a big steel

cruiser above the lock. Did I see you going to the grocer under the bridge? he asked. I should have told you. She's very
good, I said, it was an experience. Oh, she's good, said the
Englishman, she smiles. I was afraid she was going to eat me,
I said.

The marc was packaged with transcendent vulgarity in a
narrow bottle inside a moulded transparent box. It had a
copper spring around the neck and a cork with a brass top. It
said on the bottle it had been aged for ten years in oak casks.
It was excellent. The wine was not worth five euros, but it
was not bad, not bad at all.

I AM DEVELOPING TERRY DARLINGTON'S TIPS
for successful boating, I said, as tested on the canals of
England and France and Belgium, and on the surging main.
No top-up-your-diesel or black-your-bottom stuff—this will be
a broad perspective from a guileless mind. It could change
the culture of boating. What do you think of this?

> *Before a tunnel wear sunglasses for a couple of days and take
>   them off as you enter*
> *When you walk on a beach, look out for rope and string and
>   collect it*
> *If you are fending off another boat, don't use a boathook or a
>   bargepole—use a broom*
> *When you clean the glass on your stove, finish with a used
>   teabag. When you light up, the boat will be full of perfume*
> *If you come upon pine cones on the ground, gather them to
>   light your stove*
> *To get rid of a gongoozler, stare at him through binoculars*
> *Make sure your dog is always wearing his collar—then if he
>   goes over the side you have something to catch hold of*

If you have your water tank cleaned out and painted with
pitch, your tea will taste like Earl Grey for six months

Is that all? asked Monica. I can't think of anything else at the moment, I said. The sunglasses were my idea, said Monica.

Another thing, I said—it isn't fair to put Jim in his kennel every night. Why not? said Monica—he's a dog. It's a lovely comfortable kennel. He goes there a lot on his own. But if we give him his freedom at night, I said, he can sleep in my chair, or on the sofa, according to his whim. That dog is all whim, said Monica. The creature is ruined. He outwits you at everything. Whippets are supposed to have a gentle nature, not be following you round staring and yipping and hustling for treats and walks all day and listening for words so you have to spell things out like the country singer singing 'D.I.V.O.R.C.E.'. He's cunning, and passive-aggressive, and thieving and disrespectful.

But we've got this lovely boat, I said. And on a narrow-boat everything must be used all the time. We must share our blessings. Why shouldn't the poor creature sleep where he wishes? Because he'll finish up on the bed, said Monica, and we'll finish up in the kennel. Oh no, I said, oh no, that battle is won. He comes on the bed by invitation only and never at night. He's accepted that. Animals are very sensitive about hierarchy, and about space: about where they are allowed to lie—they never challenge the space of the alpha male. Which one is the alpha male? asked Monica. Me, I said—don't worry about Jim, he knows how far he can go.

Jim went to his kennel in the bow towards the end of the evening and when we were going to bed he came down the boat a little and quietly occupied my chair and curled up.

There you are, I said, how sweet. When I got up in the night for a pee he was a bit nearer, on the sofa, fast asleep. When I woke up in the morning he was lying on my chest, looking down my throat.

I SLOWED FOR A LOCK, PAST A YELLOW AMERI-can machine, one of those backhoe loaders mowers pruners diggers that is without shape because it seems to be folded into itself, all but the one arm or set of teeth that is doing the damage, as its tracks heave it back and forth and its engine makes the air shimmy like jelly. At the lock was an old chap. Aha, he shouted, the noise, the machines, the boats–the English are coming. And the Americans, and the Canadians. It is the big day today–D-Day–the day of the landings in Normandy.

When we moored up there was an e-mail from Georges Berger in Nogent–Georges the poet, Georges my fellow albatross. He wanted to tell us about his day exactly sixty years ago–

It was Madame Dubus our neighbour from above who told us the great news of the disembarkation of the Allies on 6 June 1944. My stepfather was the concierge and many tenants found themselves at our apartment just to talk about it. I can see them now, the seven or eight crowded in our little room between the bed with its red embroidered counterpane and the sideboard with two shell-cases engraved with a country scene. On the wall the photograph of my solemn communion. This had been delayed because one of the little girls in my catechism group had been killed by an Allied bomb in an apartment block in Letort Street.

What spontaneity in the celebration at 145 Rue Marcadet! No one doubted the Anglo-American soldiers would succeed. Everyone was making strategy and calculating when the Yanks would arrive in Paris. From time to time someone tried to get Radio Londres.

Under the bed we had a treasure, a bottle of sparkling wine and six bottles of red wine laid out carefully and wrapped in newspaper. Full litres, without labels, which the wine merchant across the road, next door to the tabac of Monsieur Pons (where my mother got her fags), had sold us, in more or less unlawful circumstances. Camus, my stepfather, considered the occasion too fine to ignore and we had to have a toast. We drank one bottle of the wine and the bottle of sparkling wine. Almost everyone in the apartment block came by, just to say a word or two and drink a glass. Even I drank a little glass, because this was an occasion which I must remember.

WE WERE IN THE DIJON BASIN: PARKLIKE, TREES a hundred feet high, a few boats. A heron landed in his nest in the sky. I walked to the station and picked up some English papers—our first since Sens. Dijon did not look much—cramped, beggars, shapeless. It is the capital of Burgundy and may be a fine city indeed—it depends how you feel, and we were feeling that six weeks on the Burgundy Canal was a long time.

The herons hardly troubled to peer down as we left the next morning. They looked comfortable up in the sun, as if they had enjoyed their coffee and croissants and were having a quiet hour or two before slipping out for the fish for lunch.

Brickyards and silos until our canal became once more the most royal and rural of waterways. Only thirty kilometres to go—dead straight. At the end of each kilometre, in the haze, a lock, with a cottage with roses and a garden fully gnomed. Lock-keepers, smiling by the open gates, once or twice a gamine lock-keeper so slim and tanned that it was hard to drive out of the lock without hitting something.

The barley just browning, crops strong after rain, the cut grass, the trees, the avenues of poplars, the royal avenues. A constant neighing, or the cries of a duck caught in a mowing machine. It is the frogs, *monsieur*, said a lady lock-keeper. At night they sing most strongly. They are singing most strongly now, I said—I wish I could see them. I saw them, said Monica. They were green and yellow like in children's books. When I was on the tiller they were sitting on lily pads looking at me; they were swimming round in a ring. It's *Dive dive dive* when I come along, I said, and for you they put on a variety act.

A plain with no hedges and crops changing as we passed and the roofs of cars speeding half a kilometre away. Three jet fighters alongside, their tails up—they took off with less noise than we expected: silver bats and then pinpricks. They headed south and returned ten minutes later, having buzzed the topless towers of Carcassonne. When they landed the angle of attack was so great that they seemed to be on their hind legs. One flew right over us, clothed in white metal: riveted, shivering, roaring.

We were closing on the last lock of the Burgundy Canal. In the water, red stems and green hair, and clouds and inverted trees. I tried to look through the reflections. I knew there were forests of weed beneath the glassy cool translucent wave, and green herds that swim through rainbows from the skies. But I could not visit the forests, to see where the carp slept or the crayfish laid their plans. The *Phyllis May* was an airship passing through the clouds, forbidden to land, though her captain longed for the streams and woods below.

• • •

THE BASIN AT ST. JEAN DE LOSNE WAS FULL OF steel cruisers with relentless bows. There were hundreds, and they had all been polished that morning. Many were too big for the canal and must have come up the Saône. A chap in overalls waved us to a narrow slot on a pontoon, deep among the cruisers. A couple of dozen boaters came up on to their fly-decks, hoping to divert from their craft some of the destruction to come, and to have a good laugh.

The tiller on the *Phyllis May* has a brass frog sitting on a brass arm, with a long white tassel hanging under him. The tiller arm goes back horizontal for three feet and then bends down like a flamingo's neck, and is welded to the rudder, which is crimson and heavy.

A narrowboat tiller has considerable decorative value, and is something to lean on in time of trouble, but its effect on the direction of a boat is small. When you go forward the propeller winds your stern round to the right, and drives water from under you, sucking you into the bank. When you reverse you swing the other way. The current or the wind can always take you over. Some narrowboats have thrusters, which push jets of water from either side of the bow, but the *Phyllis May* does not. Except in extreme conditions it is usually possible to steer a narrowboat without a bow thruster, and in extreme conditions the thrusters are not much use anyway.

I felt the wind on my cheek. First a three-point turn so I can sail between the rows of boats. Now reverse, to stop and pull the stern to the left. Now a forward burst with the tiller hard left to swing me some more. Try to miss that cruiser. My bow was sixty feet away but I had hit things often enough to know where it was. Now the clever bit. Stand there, look bored, do nothing, scratch yourself. Leave it to the wind—here it comes, slow man slow, sixteen tons kissing the pontoon. Want to see it again?

The audience went down, cheated, to polish their woodwork and drink gin. I don't know what lieth ahead on the Saône and the Rhône, said Monica, but the fat old cross-eyed geezer sure plays a mean pinball. You never said anything nice like that to me before, I said.

And for us the Burgundy Canal was over—its locks, its trolls, its hills, its frogs. We would not pass above it again, forbidden to land, visitors in the sky.

Eleven
BATTLES IN THE CLOUDS

The Saône

The evening before we left St. Jean de Losne we had dinner out and when we came back to the marina there were flashing lights and vehicles and people on the quay. What's happening? I asked a man in a blue uniform. Have a good night's sleep, he said.

In the morning we went to pay our bill and in the office they told us that the lady in the cruiser next to the *Phyllis May* had killed herself. We knew her—she had come on board for drinks with her husband, Harry. They were long-time boaters, very friendly. They knew a lot about the Rhône and had given us a list of moorings.

As we were getting ready to leave the marina Harry came out on deck. He was a tall chap with thick grey hair. Did you hear anything last night? he asked. No, I said.

I barely heard it from the galley, said Harry. The gun was legal, a double-barrelled one, that we used for vandals. It fires rubber bullets or real bullets. It had rubber bullets last night, but she put it to her head.

It had rained in the night and the sun was shining and the air was soft, and there were white clouds. She used to get depressed at times, said Harry, but why do that? Why do that? We had been married for thirty-three years. She was clever, good-looking, we never left a row unsettled. Look at our boat, our cars, our life—going where we pleased. She would never tell me but I knew when she got depressed: she held her hands differently, with the thumbs like that. She had lovely hands. Don't say anything, Darlington, I said to myself, just shut up. I will help you get out like I promised, said Harry, I must keep doing things—give me your rope.

Captain Bob, the retired aviator who lived in the marina, took a rope as well and he and Harry pulled the *Phyllis May* from her slot and set her up to sail through the ranks of cruisers.

Captain Bob came along the gunwale. We've all been there, he said. Anyone that says he hasn't is a liar.

I thought of Bob the angel hovering by the carriers to rescue any guy who went in and how he waited for Virgil Grissom to ditch his space capsule in the sea and I thought of his photograph with John Glenn and I thought No one is safe: not the brave, not the young, not the virtuous, not the kind, not the mother with a baby on her breast—no one is safe from this enemy, this killer who will not show his face.

Harry was crying now and I thought Let it go, Harry. God bless you mate, I said, and shook his hand and Harry went back into his boat, into the steel hull, the woodwork, the brass, the instruments, the sofa, the death. *Why, this is hell, nor am I out of it.*

We sailed down the Saône, with its wide plain and the sunflowers and the poplars. Georgia's baby, our new grandchild, had been born. He's early, said Monica, but he'll be all right. Poor Harry, poor, poor Harry.

Above us red kites wheeled, like risen souls.

THE CLOS DE VOUGEOT IS A CHATEAU SURrounded by vineyards. It is the sort of place you are supposed to visit. In reception there were a few maps and corkscrews—no, we don't sell wine but in forty minutes there is a tour—four euros each please. Don't give the lady a tip—it is formally interdicted.

A vineyard is a good place for a walk—there are lanes between the rows of vines, and the vines were fresh like lettuce and the grapes were small and green and the sun shone and the leaves were giving off oxygen and you could feel it in your lungs. Jim walked with us and sometimes he jumped into the air and lingered a moment, then turned round and made a four-point landing, and shook himself and looked at us sideways so we could see the whites of his eyes, making sure we had noticed. The vines ran away up the slope of the Côte d'Or. It is called the Golden Slope because in the autumn it turns to gold, but this was July.

There were four of us on the tour—Monica and I and a Frenchman of a certain age with the young wife of one of his friends. When he thought we weren't looking he would squeeze her.

The lady who did the tour was small and pretty. She took us under the ski-slope roofs to where the monks had first pressed the grapes eight hundred years ago. The presses looked like siege engines and lay under a cavern of rafters.

There is a particularity about the roof, said the lady. I know, said Monica, putting up her hand. I know, it is the chestnut, which will not abide the spider. You are right about the properties of the chestnut, *madame*, said the lady, and about the importance of denying the spider, but these rafters are oak because of the size and strength and for the spider we have another particularity. We have *les chauves-souris*, the bald-mice, the bats, which eat the spider. Ah, said Monica, the bald-mice.

Up the stairs in the building next door, said the lady, is a *son et lumière* that will astonish you, and afterwards please pass through into the auditorium where there is a presentation of importance about the burgundy.

We went up the stairs in the building next door and the lights went out. Floods shone on the rafters and a deep voice, with music, explained that since man first drew himself erect and walked out of the valleys of Africa on to the Mediterranean shore, rafters have been important to hold up his roof. There are rafters that go sideways, said the voice, and told us all about them. There are rafters that go up, the voice continued, and explained about the rafters that go up. The picture was completed with a short address about the rafters that went off at an angle. We passed through into the auditorium, where there were a hundred seats.

The slide-and-sound presentation was about an organization of fat old men who said they ran the burgundy wine industry. They wore dark suits, and red hats like inflated berets. They gave banquets and stood on platforms and hung medals round each other's necks, with the Tonnerre Noise

Society in full support. At one of the banquets was Catherine Deneuve, looking desperate. Nothing was said about the burgundy wine or why we should buy it or where we might buy it or what was in it for the customer.

Monica and I laughed at the old men, and the Frenchman and his friend's young wife laughed at them too. They are so far up their own arses, I said to Monica, they should have worn the red hats on their feet.

IF SWANS WERE RARE, PEOPLE WOULD TRAVEL the world to see them. They pass across the sky like angels singing. They are powered by discreet rubber paddles, and asleep they are lilies—

> *His breast is moulded in a globe*
> *They say that white camellias glow*
> *But the white satin of this robe*
> *Is like the sun on morning snow*

The only trouble with swans is they are not very nice.

At Seurre Jim and I went for our walk before breakfast and when we returned to the boat a family of swans had arrived. There was Mum and Dad and four youngsters the size of ducks. The youngsters had been stitched together roughly from that woolly grey fabric they used for sofas in the fifties, and then they had been stuffed, but not well, because there were lumps and rough bits and their back ends were wrong.

Dad Swan saw Jim and opened his mouth, showing a fat pink tongue with pie-crust edges. He began to make a noise like the pressure cooker before it sprays your dinner on the ceiling. Jim crouched and pressed down his tail to cover his rear. Go and get some bread, darling, I said to Monica, and throw it up the other end, so Jim and I can get on board. Dad moved closer. He had plans for Jim, including using his skin to line his nest.

The family was very hungry. Dad managed to get a few pieces of bread while still blocking the way on to the boat, and I had to smuggle Jim across the bow. He went below and hid. It took a long time to empty the *Phyllis May* of spare food and persuade the swans to Please please go away it's all over and then we sat down to breakfast.

After ten minutes there was a knocking and a thumping and a splashing against the boat. Dad Swan had come back for Jim. He attacked the boat for half an hour, pecking and beating with his wings. Jim lay in his kennel, in no hurry to come out.

THE SAÔNE WAS THE WIDEST INLAND WATER we had sailed. My God, what will the Rhône be like? They say that on the Rhône you can see the curvature of the earth.

The valley still flat—welcoming margins, fields and lawns and occasional trees. On the waterline a heron on a branch, and just below him another heron, upside down. Forty-two kilometres—a marathon day.

Push down the Morse handle, a diesel likes to work; get it up to six knots, never mind the noise, sit and watch the clouds, let the wind dry the sweat off you like a hot towel. The sun, the spray from the prop: the jewels, the bright crystal. Every quarter of an hour a boat comes by, always with a wave of the hand, even the hire-boaters, who don't need a licence and know nothing. But their plastic dish-boats hung with fenders are pretty and practical and why shouldn't they have a mess-about holiday? That's how Monica and I started, forty years ago—across the sky on the Pontcysyllte

Aqueduct, the family of grass snakes swimming by, the old couple on a narrowboat, the pub like Granny's front room. And now we are an old couple on a narrowboat. It was the family of grass snakes that did it.

A two-hundred-yard lock, gates open, over it a tower, too high to see anyone. A noise over the Tannoy–*Life jacket please*. I put on my life jacket and twenty thousand tons of water were emptied just for us. When a lock empties it is quieter than when it is filling, and we did not bang around. It was downhill now until the sea.

Monica did an hour on the tiller and then I took the *Phyllis May* towards Chalon-sur-Saône. An island, a display of flowers only a big town could afford, lots of boats. A man waving his arms–You can't come in here. Yes I can, I shouted, plenty of room. We have five boats to come, reserved, he said, but look on the old pontoon. An English couple beckoned– Breast up, breast up. But we would overlap their cruiser and block the boats both sides. I waved thanks and we sailed past.

A chap with a German accent leaned off his boat–Do not go that way–go behind the pontoon. Why? I shouted, there is space in front. Do what I say, shouted the chap, do what you are told–no argue, do not discuss, what I say you do, do not discuss, you understand? Better go behind the pontoon, called Monica, I think the first chap said it was safer.

We moored up and walked around to thank the English couple. They were very old–We have a narrowboat back home, they said. I said Excuse me a minute. Along the pontoon there was a big chap in blue shorts. Are you the gentleman who shouted instructions just now? I asked. Yes, he said. Well, I said, I found you to be rude. If you are to shout in English you should know the language better. I leaned forward and put a foot behind so I would stay upright as I was being pushed into the river but the German made no response and I walked back to my group.

I knew you were going to do that, said Monica, you are so weak, you have no self-control, what about your resolution? You said you were going to be nice.

Thank you, said the old lady, for putting him straight. He shouted at us yesterday. All we were doing was going down the one-way system the wrong way. He is just a hire-boater passing through and he is throwing his weight about because he knows a little English.

Perhaps he doesn't know we won the war, said the old chap. They never stood a chance, I said—how can you win a war if you can't go the wrong way down a one-way street?

Both sides of the pontoon filled up with boaters during the day. It was the holiday season and all the hire fleets that had lain at anchor were on the move.

SOMEONE HAD DROPPED A BOMB ON GENEVA. We could see the mushroom rim up in the night fifty miles away and the fires reflected under it. The other side of Chalon-sur-Saône was in flames. Nuits Saint Georges exploded and then Beaune and then Oh my God they got Mâcon. Sheet lightning, forked lightning, battles in the clouds.

You have chosen? Yes, I said, for both of us the snails. And for *madame* the zander, and for me the frogs, *les grenouilles.* I spoke without expression, as if in Stone, Staffordshire, we ate little but frogs. *Pardon?* said the waitress. You said it wrong, said Monica, you made it sound like Granville, which is a town by the seaside.

We were sitting at our table in the middle of the road, as were all the tourists in Chalon-sur-Saône and most of the population. It was eight o'clock and the town had fulfilled the destiny of all French towns and turned itself into a restaurant. Jim panted under the table and sweat ran down my neck and a bolt hit Châteauneuf, leaving not one stone on another.

I had never eaten frogs before. I'll eat cows and pigs and ducks and fish because they are neutrals in life's struggle but frogs are on our side. There is something in my blood that draws insects for miles, and a single bite will give me misery for a week. This season the boat is barbed with machinery: blue-light zappers, poisonous lamps, and whistles that imitate the sound of a mosquito saying Let's get out of here. Meanwhile in the engine-room and on the roof the spiders work with patience and cunning and in the waters around us the frogs hunt in posses—the fastest tongues in the West. Three-quarters of all living things are insects, and the only reason they do not grow bigger than us is that they breathe through holes in their skin and the air can't get in deep enough, and if the spiders and frogs weren't hassling them they would have solved that one long ago.

It started to rain and then it stopped and then another storm passed along the horizon and Jim panted and I sweated. Then more rain came and the staff in the restaurant came out and in eight seconds moved everyone indoors and all the furniture and Jim.

You have such bad weather here, *madame*, Monica said to the manageress, how smoothly you all move, you must be doing that all the time. We have done it once, said the manageress, in twenty years. *Après nous le déluge*, I said to Monica—I hope they don't find out we bring impossible weather wherever we go.

The frogs tasted of nothing and were full of little bones. As I lay in bed the frogs in the Chalon basin went *Cricky cricky croo* and I thought I ate your uncle tonight har har, but I didn't feel good about it.

TOURNUS IS NOT A BIG PLACE BUT IT IS ON THE railway and on the main road so the toffs used to stop on their way to Cannes and Nice. Now the motorway has passed it by but there is still a four-star hotel and some restaurants, and gift shops around the abbey. The waterfront is run down. Sewage enters the Saône by the pontoons, so it is best to moor upstream and upwind, where trout prowl the margins and the *norberts dentressangles* flicker along your windows.

In the abbey, music lingered loath to die as a group of musicians practised at the end of the nave. My gaze lingered loath to die on the balance and proportions of the pillars and arches and on the balance and proportions of the lady lead violin as she swayed in her long *pantalon*. There were some abstract modern windows–avocado and taupe, inspired by the landing window in a general practitioner's house in Milton Keynes.

Dinner in a square. As we left, the English couple at a nearby table spoke to Jim, who pulled across to try his luck. Would you take offence if I gave your Jim a piece of my steak? asked the gentleman. Sit Jim, said Monica. Does he hold out his paw and say please? asked the lady. No, I said, but if you give him a bit of your steak, he'll sing 'Moon River'. The gentleman gave Jim a large piece of steak and then he gave him two more pieces and there was a small piece left and he ate that himself.

They were so nice, said Monica. They were from Rochdale, I said. It's like the Potteries. Remember when I asked the girl at the sweets counter in the pictures in Stoke-on-Trent for some chewing gum? Yes, said Monica, she said We can't sell it because they spit it all over the pavement but here have a bit of mine. It's a pity the southerners aren't like that, I said, but they have to go to work by train so they get tired and there are so many of them and if they had to be nice to each other it would drive them mad. But come on we have a date.

Fritz had been stalking the *Phyllis May* down the river with his camera since we left St. Jean de Losne and the Burgundy Canal and we had asked him on board and now we were invited for a drink on his motor cruiser, of which he was very proud. *Siegfried* was blue and smooth and made of steel and fitted in walnut inside. It was fifty-two feet long–shorter than the *Phyllis May* but twice as wide and three times as deep. It had two engines, a generator, four storeys, two bathrooms, a terrace, a basement, a laundry and a games room. It cost three grand to fill with diesel and you could drive it to Norfolk, Virginia, without drawing breath.

Fritz was a surgeon from Hamburg and Marlene had been a patient. They didn't speak much English or French but Monica speaks a bit of German and Fritz had a big face that showed what he was thinking all the time anyway. Fritz and Marlene kept *Siegfried* very tidy and were very friendly and not slow with the wine and the cashews, and those little footballs full of cheese you used to have at parties fifty years ago and can't find any more.

It's a nice boat, said Monica later, but if Fritz filled it with diesel and tied it with a bow and put in a hundred cases of Gevrey-Chambertin I still wouldn't swop the *Phyllis May* for it. Perhaps he would throw in Marlene, I said, and an unlimited supply of cheese footballs.

• • •

IT SAYS HERE IN THE *GUIDE NAVICARTE* THAT there are scenes of unusual animation in Mâcon on the quay, said Monica. Mustn't miss those, I said. It's men, said Monica, in shorts and moustaches–Hello sailor. We are not going to moor there. I know you, you'll get knifed. Look what you were like with that German.

We moored in the marina three kilometres upriver and the next morning walked into town along the riverside parks in the sun. On the way we played The Game. Monica walks on nearly out of sight and Jim stays back with me, on the lead, whining. After a time he starts to scream and people turn round to look and he screams and screams until Monica stops walking. You fool, you fool, Jim is yelling–she'll escape. Look what happened to Clive and Beryl, you let them escape, you fool, you sailed away and left them, and look what happened at Watten–I had to get Monica back myself. You are incompetent, oh God I wish I was bigger than you. Look, here's a thought–why don't you let me take over and be captain? I can run fast and see for miles and smell for miles and I can take responsibility and I am very intelligent. You could still be president or something and wear the Breton hat.

Don't be silly, Jim, I say. You walk the other side of a lamp-post when you are on a lead and then look at me and say What is going on? You piss on yourself. I'm in charge here–go boy, go.

Mâcon hugs the river like a sailor and there is the Restaurant Lamartine. Alphonse de Lamartine was born in Mâcon, though to the best of my belief he was as straight as a die. As well as writing boring poetry Lamartine put his restaurant too near the waterfront traffic so we went and looked over the bridge at the trout and the bream and the chub and the norberts, and had lunch somewhere else.

This did not stop us eating out again that evening on a terrace next to the marina, with a bottle of Pouilly-Vinzelles, which was four years old. It was very nice but beginning to go a bit yellow and taste of toffee. Thank God, I said to Monica, we got here just in time. On the menu was Fry-up of Saône.

What is this Fry-up of Saône, *monsieur?* I asked. It is the *ablettes*, said the waiter, and when they arrived it was the norberts, the theen green feesh themselves, in a light batter. The owner came up–These are impeccable, said Monica. They are not frozen, said *madame*–they are caught from the river in nets. There is a gentleman who catches them–sometimes he catches only two kilos, sometimes ten. He cannot live from the hunt of the *ablettes*, so he has another job. Every little fish is emptied here in the restaurant, so they are light and fine. There are crayfish too, *là-bas au fond*, down there at the bottom, under the bridge.

After dinner I will go and see the crayfish, I said. Jim and I will stun them with the light from our kitchen torch and then we will catch some and have them for lunch tomorrow. Alas, *monsieur*, said *madame*, they are fearful, they back away. She backed away from our table, *à reculons, à reculons*, and with a twitch of her tail she was gone.

I'M FRIGHTENED, SAID MONICA, ABOUT THE Rhône. They don't allow hire boats on the Rhône–there must be a reason. But we must have faith, I said–we have sailed past the Houses of Parliament, we have sailed up the Severn, we have crossed the Channel. Yes, but you organized those, said Monica. I didn't have the responsibility. I am organizing the Rhône and I am frightened. Fritz said the Rhône runs *whoosh whoosh ha ha Mein Gott*, and Captain Bob said he would rather try to make landfall on a Pacific island in a Catalina running out of fuel with an engine out and a compass off a box of cereal than find moorings on the Rhône.

I'm not frightened myself at the moment, I said, but I usually am frightened, and we have been OK, so probably I should be frightened and because I'm not something awful will happen.

Wherever you looked there was Saône, and on it floated islands loaded with trees. You would not know where to go but you followed the stakes driven into the water about half a kilometre apart, and as they were fifteen feet high and a foot wide and striped in red and white that was OK.

Monica came along the gunwale. I can smell burning, she said. You've been going flat out. The river is too warm so the skin tanks along the hull are not losing the heat and you will blow up the engine. The cooling fluid has expanded—it should be only halfway up that tube and now it's right up the top. You are getting careless—you think you are Captain Jesus Christ but you will do for us all. Typical—you're either scared stiff or going like a madman. Take over, Mon, I said.

I found the temperature gauge, which I had a feeling was somewhere on the control panel because I thought I had noticed it when we had the new engine fitted. It's OK, I said—it's eighty centigrade—I think it said in the book that's the best temperature—on the canals we run a bit cool, at seventy. Monica slowed down to eighteen hundred and we ran a bit cool, at seventy.

Nearer to Lyon Jet Skis, speedboats, waterskiers, one or two pleasure launches, a few barges, two eighty-seven-metre barges locked together end on end with a pusher unit behind them. The speedboats buzz you and try to turn you over with their wash, or play chicken across your bow. I wave to them and they wave back. Why not?–they have a right to their waterway. Bloody prats.

We can moor here, or somewhere else, said Monica. OK, which? I asked. I don't know, it's always questions, said Monica. You expect me to find moorings but how do I know if they will be full and it will be worse on the Rhône. I turned and headed upstream to the Rhône Yacht Club. It said in the book that the Rhône Yacht Club used to be the most prestigious club in Lyon.

The clubhouse was a shed and there were seven plastic chairs and a broken yacht trailer and a barbecue. A young lady ran out along the pontoon and took our rope with a brownskin grin. The rigging of the yachts whipped and rattled and the water drove up into foam and we could have been out at sea.

We are at the start of the funnel between the Massif Central and the Jura, said Monica. This is the north wind that comes down the funnel, except in the winter it blows twice as hard and people go mad with the noise and the cold drops them dead in the streets. It's the mistral.

WE HAD SEEN MANY FINE BUILDINGS FROM the waterways–the houses and boathouses up the Thames, Canary Wharf, the Grand Hôtel Régnier, the Renault factory, the chateau pup in the lake at Ancy. But my favourite of all was on the Saône right next to the Rhône Yacht Club.

A dirt car park with rusty knitted fencing, and convolvulus. No cars. Two black dogs bellowing behind a gate. Jim gave a quiet bark, saying If I were as big as you I would be quite short with you, but since I'm not I rather hope you can't hear me. A menu on the wall, patched with rain, chipped concrete steps up to the first floor, and through a glass door.

The room did not seem to have walls—there was the river running to Lyon, the trees on the banks, sky, white clouds. Inside the long rooms the Art Deco shapes and proportions were unspoiled—low ceilings, curves, pillars. And much of the detail—flecked concrete floors with red and black lines, metal window fittings, even the apple-green paint.

We'll both have the pizza with anchovies, I said, and a bottle of Beaune. That's near here, isn't it? The waitress was not young, heavily painted, dark, with a smile. I don't know, *monsieur*, she said. My father will know. Yes, he called from the bar, it's just up the road.

On the way out I spoke with Father. We use this floor, he said—the rest is empty. We can do two hundred covers. We have been here eight years. Nineteen thirty-seven it was built—the original clubhouse of the Rhône Yacht Club. Look at the balconies. It is a ship, you know, *monsieur*, a ship.

As we sailed for Lyon next morning I looked back from the tiller and could see the whole building—the curves and balconies and the flat roof and the windows holding a mile of river. It was Fred and Gingerland, Craven A, the Schneider Trophy, the sigh of trains, the *Normandie* with all the gulls around her. An ocean liner taking me back to my parents' dream world, the world that rose from the depression, brought a glimpse of foxtrot heaven, and was torn apart.

TO LYON DOWN THE SAÔNE IS FLAT AND FACTO-ried, at its wharves barges filling with sand, and on the right beyond the Beaujolais hills, the first outcrops of the Massif Central. Dull apartment blocks. A green hill ahead, with houses, and behind it another, and a cathedral with four minarets, attended by a withered Eiffel Tower.

We had been told Lyon did not welcome boaters. But walls in cream stone made one long wharf for miles into the city, double- and treble-ringed, and the wharves and rings were empty. A theek white feesh a couple of feet long threw itself into the air—it was frolicking. Under a footbridge. Look—some other boats under willow trees—and we moored next to Fritz.

On our bank Paris, with its waterfront avenues, tall stone buildings, squares and spires, on the other bank ramparts climbing two hundred feet to the cathedral. You must go to the top of the hill, said Fritz. There is a funicular, there are parks for Jim, there is a rose garden.

The funicular would not accept whippets, in fact they were formally interdicted, so we walked up the parks, which were vertical. Not much good for Jim to run, said Monica, too steep. We could throw him off the path, I said, he can fly. He'd need a hang-glider, said Monica.

It was hot and I climbed at survival speed, that is just this side of a heart attack. This includes long periods of static sweating. Monica and Jim were waiting at the basilica. I thought there was a rose garden, I said. That was Fritz, not me, said Monica—I beg your pardon.

I have been nervous about tying Jim outside churches since I hitched him to the gate of Gloucester Cathedral on the way back to Stone from Sharpness. A chap came out— How dare your dog piss on my cathedral, he said. That's a fine Christian welcome, I said, for a visitor to your city and his little dog. We were about to settle the matter by combat but some more Christians came along and I moved Jim back to unhallowed ground.

The Notre-Dame Basilica was built in the late nineteenth

century to thank God for keeping the Prussians out of Lyon, and it did that job until November 1942. Outside it looks like an elephantine Star of Delhi, with two poppadoms and ladies' fingers, and the interior is a trip inside the skull of a religious madman. It curls, it swerves, it flows, it glows. It bulges, it effulges, it thrusts, it protrudes, it retreats into vaults and domes. It is silvered, rouged, gilded, azure. The heads of drowning Turks, fully turbaned, sweep across the walls in mosaic, or crowds of people with big hats and haloes surround pious popes, their sermons endless.

When we came out we had managed to make Jim disappear. Masters of illusion, we had come out of another entrance. They have stolen him and gilded him and put him in one of the niches, I said. No one will notice.

LYON IS THE SECOND CITY OF FRANCE. PARIS has ten million people, and Lyon fewer than a million and a half, and so Lyon is in some ways nicer. It is built where the Saône flows into the Rhône, making a narrow triangle, and both rivers are wide and there is a lot of light around, as in a seaside town. We walked through the little squares and the big Place Bellecour, past the fountains through the wide pedestrian avenues of same-as-everywhere-else shops and up the side streets with the I've-never-seen-one-of-those-before shops.

We walked to the Rhône, which was much wider than the Saône. They never told me it was blue, said Monica, and it's not running very fast. Fast enough, I said, thinking of drowning in turquoise, like the poor Turks in the basilica.

In Lyon we ate out more than usual. How can they do it, asked Monica, slicing her roast rabbit, with so much brilliance and for less than the cost of a meal in England? I poured another glass of Chiroubles and picked up a lamb chop. To get the taste of Chiroubles say the name twice slowly and roll your eyes and think of blackberries and rain, and if you are a bloke the taste of the mouth of the girl you kissed by the privet hedge when you were sixteen and you hoped her mother wasn't watching through the window.

It's a cultural thing, I explained, when I had stopped thinking about the girl. It's what people have got good at over the centuries. In Lyon it's food. But there are things we do better in Stone. There are only two footraces in Lyon all summer and I bet that lots of the guys you see on the streets, even the young ones, would have trouble running ten miles in seventy minutes. And very few Lyonnais could sit in Langtry's and drink eight pints of Pedigree and hardly say a word all night, like any decent fellow from our town.

WE ARE IN VICHY NOW, I SAID, IN PÉTAIN'S FREE France that was not free. We have been in Vichy since we left Chalon-sur-Saône, after the storm. The boundary went across nearly to Tours, and down to the Spanish border. Vichy was most of southern France, with the Germans hold-ing the flanks round Bordeaux and Grenoble. How could Pétain agree to an armistice? How could he sell out his country?

Did you expect them to fight the panzers town by town? asked Monica—would you have fought? I don't know, I said, but my family fought, and so did yours. Churchill was going to spray the invasion barges with mustard gas. The Queen had a pistol so she could take a German with her when she went. Four French boys, children, paddled across the Channel in a canoe to join De Gaulle—Churchill thanked them himself and so did his wife, Clementine. Jean Moulin, the prefect of

Chartres, tried to kill himself rather than sign a document he felt to be dishonourable. But the French National Assembly supported Pétain by five hundred and sixty-nine votes to eighty and signed away half their country to thieves and murderers.

What Pétain did wasn't so wrong, said Monica. Think of the lives it saved. No, I said, it wasn't evil, it was absence of virtue—and before long he was signing the edicts against the Jews.

THE GERMANS OCCUPIED VICHY FRANCE ANY-way in November 1942 and SS First Lieutenant Klaus Barbie was sent to Lyon as a member of the Office of Reich Security, which included the Gestapo. As well as deport-ing Jews, Barbie's job was to help destroy the Maquis. Lyon is not far from Switzerland and was the capital of the Resistance. We saw the Gestapo headquarters, where thou-sands were tortured. It is now the Museum of the Resistance and Deportations.

> *I will betray tomorrow, not today.*
> *Today, tear out my fingernails,*
> *I will not betray.*
>
> *You don't know the end of my courage.*
> *But I do.*
> *You are five hard hands with rings.*
> *You have shoes on your feet*
> *With nails.*
>
> *I will betray tomorrow, not today,*
> *Tomorrow.*

I need the night to make up my mind,
I need at least a night
To reject, to dishonour, to betray.

To deny my friends,
To put aside the bread and the wine,
To betray life,
To die.

I will betray tomorrow, not today.
The file is under the flagstone—
The file that they have missed.
It's not for the bars or the hangman.
The file is for my wrist.

Today I have nothing to say.
I will betray tomorrow.

Marianne Cohn was arrested on 31 May 1944 while leading twenty-eight Jewish children across the Swiss frontier. She was murdered on 8 July. She was twenty-two. One of the children saved the poem.

Some years ago Monica and I visited the Vercors plateau, a hundred miles south of Lyon. It is thirty miles long and fifteen miles wide, and reaches three thousand feet into the clouds, almost to the height of Snowdon. With the trial and imprisonment of Klaus Barbie and the founding of the Museum of the Resistance the evil that fouled the air in Lyon has been metabolized, municipalized, wept over and added to history. This had not happened in the Vercors when Monica and I were there and I don't think it will have happened yet. The Vercors Museum of the Resistance that looks out over the snows of the lost plateau is not talking about history. It happened yesterday and it happened here and it happened to us, and we are angry and our hearts are breaking.

After the Normandy landings in June 1944 four thousand Maquis declared a Free France on the Vercors plateau and waited for reinforcement from the Allies. The Germans sent in the Milice, the French traitor police, and then attacked with twenty thousand troops, tanks and mountain guns. The German troops were under the command of General Karl Pflaum. In the Maquis field hospital in the Grotte de la Luire cavern they murdered the wounded on their stretchers and then they murdered the doctors and the chaplain. In the valleys they flattened the houses with the people inside or dragged them out and murdered them in scenes of great horror. Fifty years later in the market square of La Chapelle-en-Vercors Monica and I could still smell the blood and the fear.

In the Vercors and in Lyon the flowers of evil grew rank, but their roots had struck long before. All that evil requires is an absence of virtue, where somebody didn't make a stand.

Twelve

THE DESTROYER
OF WORLDS

The Rhône

*I*t was your mother, said Monica—why did she appear to me and not to you? It's because you were in the saloon, I said. She always appears in the saloon. That's where her photograph is on the wall, and there isn't enough room for her to appear anywhere else. She wouldn't be able to stand up in the engine-room or on the end of the bed and you can't make an appearance in the bath.

Why does she come back? asked Monica. It's a bit like the Queen, I said—the right to be consulted, the right to encourage, the right to warn. So she can't actually do anything? asked Monica. People say they can chuck things around, I said, but in my experience they just hang about and look sad.

I woke up knowing something was wrong, said Monica. I got up and she appeared at the front door—she had her hat on and her green winter coat. She started walking down the boat towards me, holding out her hand. Then Jim came out of his kennel behind her and ran through her, yelping, up to the engine-room and banged against the door and then he ran back and kept running back and forth shouting Abandon ship and she was gone. Then the heaving started, and the bucking. I was so frightened, and when I woke you up you just sat there.

I was fast asleep, I said, and I didn't know my mother had turned up and I had finished that bottle of Côtes du Rhône at dinner. I knew I had tied us securely and I thought it was only the wake from a barge. You sat there like a dick, said Monica, saying It's all right Monnie, it will die down. It did die down, I said. Yes, said Monica, but it was ages and we could have been smashed up and sunk.

I realized we were in trouble, I said, when I looked out of the window and I saw the torrent. It was black, with white foam. It was throwing the boat up and the boat couldn't move because I had tied the fenders tight to the pontoon. I used those ropes I bought in Dunkirk. They weren't very thick but they were ocean strength and it was a fixed pontoon. So the boat was going up in the air and it was snatching and going up again and snatching and it was like being in a pepper pot.

The next morning we looked at the ropes and they were frayed. Where they were tied to the steel handrail the rail was bent. Perhaps it was a weir opening, said Monica, or there is a power station upriver and maybe it was that. But it must have been millions of tons of water, I said.

We looked out at the morning Rhône flowing through Vienne: blue, peaceful, harmless—come on, I'll carry you to the Med, let it be. It's at night-time, I said, it turns into a raving lunatic. It's Dr. Jekyll and Mr. Rhône.

THE RHÔNE HAD JOINED THE SAÔNE JUST south of Lyon. The blue water merged with the green water and the banks went away left and right and it wasn't like a river any more, it was like being at sea. You held a bit to the right because that's what you do but you couldn't crawl along the banks because of creeks and islands and you were out in the stream and it was like walking a tightrope because there was nothing but air and water on both sides for half a kilometre: the sun heating the steel boat and a hot wind blowing in your face. It said in *Le Monde* that this was the hottest spot in Europe—thirty-five degrees.

What's that further down? It's a big barge but too far away for the binoculars. That white dot you thought was a buoy was a motor launch. Better give them a wave, though they pass hundreds of yards away. Here comes the big barge—we can handle the wash, we can handle a Sea Cat. Oh, look, they are taking pictures of us.

Dots and blurred chalky lines ahead. Every fifteen miles the river goes over a weir, and if you choose the right line and don't go over with it, you carry on down a lock cut. At the end of the cut you can sail into the jaws of a hydroelectric station, which is several hundred yards long and a few storeys high over the stream, or you can sail towards the lock and try and get in. It is easy to make the wrong choices, because the map on top of the boat is the other way round, and there is also carelessness and incompetence and weariness with living because it is early August and so damn hot and you made a fool of yourself last night with a slab of Roquefort and a bottle of Côtes du Rhône.

Monica points from the bow—Left left. Ahead are signs, none of which I understand. Left, shouts Monica, the lock. We enter the canal leading to the lock and stop at a red and green light. What does that mean? I shouted. I was answered by a great voice from the sky.

Do not go through the red and green lights, you yachts, just stay where you bloody well are.

Then it said something similar in seven languages one after the other.

The light went green and I moved into the canal and I could see the lock tower and a gate far ahead. Behind me a grinding, and a gate arose from the deep. We weren't in the canal leading to the lock. This was the lock.

We tied to a bollard in the wall and sank twelve metres. As we sank the bollards along each wall sank too, groaning like cows in a slaughterhouse. We were the only car in Oxford Street and the road had descended beneath us, until we could hardly see the sky. Silence. A klaxon sounded *Kraak kraak kraak*—My God, they have lost control like those guys in Paris. We'll be washed into the sluices and they'll have to send the divers down. *What's this red and black collar, Alphonse, and this ear?*

The gate at the end of Oxford Street raised itself a crack: a guillotine winding up for the next drop. Then an opening, then a cave mouth and outside France was green and sunlit. As we passed fifty metres under him the *horla* in the centre of the arch looked out and waved.

Whenever I think of the Rhône, whatever happens to us, said Monica, I'll think of the nice *horla* and the wave.

NEXT MORNING IT WAS COOLER, THIRTY DE-grees, humid, no sun, no wind. No real clouds either, just a dark haze. The lock cut was twice the width of the canals in Belgium and ten kilometres long. It went straight between banks of heaped stones while the river wandered off and would no doubt join us later.

The Rhône had been transformed after the Second World War by the Compagnie Nationale du Rhône from a raving lunatic to Dr. Jekyll and Mr. Rhône, with twelve locks between Lyon and the sea. I tried to work out the amount of earth and rock that had been moved to make this lock cut and couldn't.

Ahead a city of tubes and fractionation towers and a dozen stacks with the smoke rising straight two hundred feet and blossoming and fading. A fire in the sky. It's only a burn-off, why was it making me afraid? I pressed on, and the fire took a long time to get nearer.

The roof of the boat seemed to buckle and I felt sick. I couldn't see properly, and I held on to the grab-rail to keep my balance. My God, I said to myself, it's the poison gas, like the dick said we would get in Belgium—in Charleroi it was windy but today the gas is going straight up and coming straight down.

Monica came out on the bow and shouted OK? Fine, I said. What are you supposed to say—I am being poisoned and I want you to come up here and be poisoned too? I thought If I faint we will run into the bank and Monica and I have our life jackets on and all dogs are supposed to swim. But all dogs are supposed to wag their tails and eat their dinner. Now just breathe normally, try to stay conscious, don't make a fuss. I held on, the air swimming and stinking of sulphur.

We passed through the smoke and the fire and sailed into clean air, straight into a lock on the green light. We were lock veterans now, we knew about the moaning cows, the voice from the sky, the klaxon, the gates rising like Triton. We had been waved at by the *horla*.

Sixty feet away on the bow Monica was talking into the FM radio. That should have been me, the skipper, with manly repartee—*Péniche de plaisance étroite, bandits at three o'clock, pan pan medico, seelonce feenee, Roger the lodger, over and out*. But to get our certificates Monica had promised the captain with a beard that she would never let me use the FM radio. As we left the lock the keeper came through *Squawk squawk*. That's nice, said Monica, he said Happy voyage, little ship.

On to Andancette, under the half bald half green hill with tall crosses near the summit. Two girls had thrown themselves off the cliff when their fiancés did not come back from the Crusades. Maybe they came back late from a Saracen gaol—Sorry lads, but see those crosses?

IN ENGLAND WE HAVE PAVEMENTS. IN FRANCE if you have a row of broken stones six inches wide for yourself, your dog, your pushchair and your grandmother you are lucky and if you don't like it go to the next village which has been there a thousand years and there are no pavements at all.

In Andancette there is a bridge, connecting it to Andance. The Rhône is not wide there so it's the same place, really. We went to walk over the bridge but little cars were rushing across and there was no pavement so we gave up and said Sod you, Andance.

We walked down the river and picked ripe figs and wondered at the locust trees with their many-fingered leaves and brown pods. We are in a different climate, I said. Of course we are, said Monica, it's the start of the Midi. Then it rained and rained and thundered and the river was exploding in blue and grey and then it stopped and the trout came up and the perch and the norberts and the chub and cruised along our windows, looking in.

Why go into Andance—stay here and watch us. Later we will do you a bit of synchronized splashing, a few colour changes, some jumps, nothing too grand.

MONICA ON THE TILLER, ANOTHER BLUE DAY. When not driving I stretch out and read, getting up now and then to look back along the boat from the bow and exchange a thumbs-up. Or just look out of the window—the dry hills of the Côtes du Rhône and the scrub and the little rows of vines hanging on. But I was restless and walked around and found things to tidy away and fell over Jim. Was it Dr. Jekyll or Mr. Rhône today?

The *Phyllis May* skidded sideways as if doing wheelies on ice and Jim ran out on to the bow. We were too far from the bank to jump so he ran back into the saloon—We are done for, *sauve qui peut*, every man for himself. The boat surged into the air and again swung sideways and took Jim's legs from under him and dumped me on to the sofa. Jim lay still, hoping for a merciful death.

It was as if the front of the boat had become detached from the back and none of the movements had any rhythm or sense. I crawled out on to the bow and stood hanging on to the roof over the door. I could see Monica on the tiller, her face white, and passing us from behind and very near a gas barge, a hundred yards of stainless steel and piping, low in the water. Ahead of it a glassy cool translucent wave a metre high and behind it a maelstrom. Accelerate, I shouted, accelerate, but we were pointing into the bank and Monica had throttled back on to tick-over and the *Phyllis May* was twisting like a leaf in the tide. As the barge passed, Monica turned away from the bank and revved up and the boat stabilized and the tumult died and Jim looked at me—Are you quite sure, sir, this is wise?

I knew he was coming up on me, said Monica. I held hard right but the navigation channel is narrow so he was coming across and pushing me into the bank. I was so near the side I had to go into tick-over, then the wake hit me and right on top of it the echo wave from the bank, then everything at once.

Give me a Sea Cat any time, I said, at least you are staring death in the face. The bloody Rhône comes up behind you and hits you over the head.

FOR LOCAL WINES, SAID THE LADY VINTNER IN Tournon, we have the St. Joseph, and then the Hermitage. Those are the Hermitage hills over the river. The rosé does not start until further south, but this is a good one. We bought two bottles of each and I noticed five steel barrels in the room behind the counter, each of them a ton. Yes, that is the wine *en vrac* said the lady, two euros a litre, or one euro twenty. Would you like to taste it *monsieur*?—I have some plastic bottles. The red wine at one euro twenty was good, so we had five litres and a litre of rosé.

I have a theory about wine in France, I said to Monica. There is the wine for drinking, which costs nothing and they drink it like water with their meals, then there is the wine that costs a lot of money and they drink that in a different way and taste it and talk about it. Yes, said Monica, and then of course there is the wine in the middle.

Tournon, like Lagny before Paris, is a river holiday town. There is a wide square by the river, then a row of shops with many restaurants, not expensive. Under the trees thirty camper vans and caravans. By the *Phyllis May* three young men in trunks were washing themselves with a brush on the end of a hose. A gentleman was cleaning his teeth at the water tap. People were eating breakfast at tables under the trees.

By the boat was a Max with a fishing rod. All yesterday afternoon he had been talking. He would say something loudly and people would laugh then there would be a pause for six and a half seconds, and he would say something loudly again and people would laugh again. We thought we would go mad, and shut the front door despite the heat.

This morning he was on his own. Did you catch anything, *monsieur*? I asked. Goodness me yes, said Max. He made a gesture suggesting a fish two feet long. A barbel, he explained. Can you eat them? I asked. Yes, he said, but I put him back. Are you in your caravan? I asked. Yes, he said, I am passing through. I spend a couple of days and then I go to the Midi. We all have to go by Saturday—there is a market in the square. I thought this was the Midi, I said. No, not really, said Max, the Midi is on the sea.

Monica and I had a cup of coffee in the boat and there was shouting and we looked out and Max's rod was bending and the line was moving around the basin. The barbel was about four pounds, and had short whiskers under its chin. The underside of its body was silver, and its sides were gold, with scales the size of five-penny pieces. The scales were not just golden gold, they were textured gold, with grades and lights that made ordinary gold look boring. On the back of the barbel the gold darkened almost to bronze.

The most cunning smiths could not have worked the gold that clothed this fish. No supermodel, no rich man's whore, was arrayed like one of these. Would you like it, *monsieur?* asked Max.

I took the barbel into the boat. It was trying to breathe but it was tired. Monica cried to see it suffer and I hit it on the skull with a wine bottle. Monica began to prepare it for dinner and I went out to thank Max. When I came back I had another fish.

We took a photograph of Max and his hangers-on and the two barbel on a tray and sailed away from Tournon hooting, and Max and his hangers-on waved from the quay.

The barbel is a bottom feeder and we expected a muddy dinner but the fish was delicious poached, and the rosé *en vrac* is just the thing for your barbel.

IN THE MARINA AT VALENCE DINNER WAS BARbel once more, this time fried in butter, with St. Joseph white wine. This is not the best region for white wine, but their barbel are the finest in the land. Along the pontoon two couples—Hello we are English and this is our friend Sacha and we heard there was a narrowboat. They were all in their fifties and looked fit and young, and Sacha had shaved his head and wore black.

An hour later we were in the roof garden of Sacha's forty-five-foot cruiser. During the war everyone in France was *Pétainiste*, said Sacha. Everyone wanted to keep things going, everyone wanted to get paid. But you just said your father fought with De Gaulle, I said. These matters were complicated, said Sacha. But in the north, I said, it was not complicated—it was the French, and the Allies, and *les boches*.

When the Germans came the people from the north ran away into Free France, said Sacha, but after the armistice they all went back. There is much you do not understand. In Croatia they hate Churchill.

Sacha told us why in Croatia they hate Churchill and the sun went down. Sacha shone a torch into the marina and the fish jumped. They do not jump for the light, he explained, they jump to avoid the pike, who can see them when the light shines—it is complicated.

The English couple spoke of Carcassonne. Alas, said Sacha, you will not be able to get to Carcassonne. The canals have been closed for repairs.

Where are you mooring tomorrow? asked Sacha. La Voulte-sur-Rhône, we said, by the bridge. This is most serious, said Sacha, please follow me. We all went down a couple of floors to the inside wheelhouse. This is where Sacha sits when it's raining and he doesn't want to perch twenty feet up on the fly-deck like a pigeon on a shithouse roof. The inside wheelhouse was full of dials. The wheel was a yard across and next to it there was a computer screen the same size. The dead, said Sacha, ah, the dead. How little you understand.

First the hotel boats, said Sacha. They are a hundred yards long. There were two the same. One is the *Camargue*, which is still on the Rhône. This picture shows the other one caught under the bridge at La Voulte-sur-Rhône. They got the people off and for ten days it agonized, being torn to bits, then it was swept away. See, it is half gone. They start slowly then it speeds up. It's like growing old.

Then the barge, this January. Two one-hundred-metre units and a pusher, coming up against the stream. He touched the bridge and the whole thing was swept back into the pillar. Folded like a knife. Look at that picture–that current, like madness. Took these on my digital camera, not bad, don't you think? There were four people on deck. She hit so hard they were thrown off the deck into the water. Never found the bodies. Those are the barges wrapped round the bridge and that's the pusher unit as it was going under.

If you try to moor at La Voulte-sur-Rhône you will have to cross the current, like these boats. These were long boats, like yours. Long boats don't work on the big rivers. They are too long, too slow, the currents turn them over. Tomorrow you must not moor at La Voulte-sur-Rhône. You must go on to Viviers. There you will be able to get a mooring without turning over.

Sacha, I said, for us it would be eight hours to get to Viviers and we stand on the back on top of the engine and it's hot. It's too far, it's impossible. Your engine, said Sacha, how much does it use? Two litres an hour, I said. Mine uses fifteen, said Sacha. Now I will show you my new video camera. I will let you look through it. Do you understand video cameras?

WE STOOD ON THE BACK OF THE BOAT AS IT filled with diesel. I couldn't sleep last night, said Monica. There's nowhere to moor and I don't want to drown. I want to be there at my funeral, not in another country bumping along the bottom of a river. And they've shut the canals to Carcassonne. It's all going wrong. It's the Rhône. It's all smiles and blue water and nice lock-keepers and then it's torrents in the night and poison gas and madmen with gas barges and people getting drowned.

I didn't sleep either, I said. I was thinking about it all, and I've made up my mind. We have had gongoozlers, and we have had Jeremiahs and vandals and dicks and now we have had Superdick, the destroyer of worlds. Sacha is a nice guy in his way and he was trying to help but I've got the measure of him and I've got the measure of this river and sod him and it. Today we will moor at La Voulte-sur-Rhône. It's August now, the current is down. And if we can't take the *Phyllis May* up the Canal du Midi we'll bloody well walk to Carcassonne and camp along the towpaths.

As we left we could see our English friends on their pretty Dutch barge, and we waved and came out of the mouth of the marina, and the Rhône leaped on us like a tiger.

The hot wind off the Sahara, the sirocco, was straight against us and nearly had my Breton hat and nearly blew Monica off the gunwale. Rows of white horses galloped up the French-blue river and smashed into our bow, throwing spray. I'm frightened, shouted Monica, turn back! But there was no swell under the waves and the propeller didn't leave the water and the *Phyllis May* roared on towards La Voulte-sur-Rhône, at the helm the King of Rock and Roll.

HOTEL BOATS ARE FULL OF DEAD PEOPLE. IF you pass a cruiser the skipper and crew will always wave and when it is an English cruiser they keep on waving. If you pass a working barge they will hold up the dog to see you and if you pass a fisherman he will often say *nice boat* in sign language, because you have slowed down for him and he sees the red ensign and he may not have seen a narrowboat before. But hotel boats are like the walls of a fort lined with dummies and with the bodies of the guys who got an arrow in them yesterday afternoon.

At La Voulte-sur-Rhône the current ran no more quickly than anywhere else. I headed for the bridge wondering what festers in the mind of a Superdick, and saw through the arch the hotel boat *Camargue*. It's OK, it's a long way away—look at the size of that—look how fast it's going—oh God it's coming straight for us—no it isn't the profile is changing—yes it is, we are done for—it's miles away—it's nearly on me. I turned away left and revved up and the *Camargue* missed us and moored up where we wanted to be, the only mooring for so many hours, at the death bridge of La Voulte-sur-Rhône, leaving us in the middle of the stream. I found a space behind the monster and crept in and we drove in stakes as the hotel boat roped itself to the bollards.

When that boat moves, said Monica, it will crush us like a beetle. It's right up on the bridge and it has got to reverse before it can get out and we are behind it and it's twelve yards wide.

I walked the hundred yards along the length of the hotel boat, past the rows of windows and the dummies propped up with a gin and tonic. Up the gangplank, into the varnished teak, the chrome, the tables with white linen and three wine glasses at each place. A young man in shorts and a white shirt with gold stripes on the shoulders danced down a flight of open wooden stairs between the potted palms, like Fred Astaire about to face the music.

I wonder, *monsieur*, I said, if it would help you if I moved my boat? If you are leaving soon I may be blocking you and I would not for the world wish to cause you difficulty. The young man smiled—No, *monsieur*, there is no problem. I am leaving in half an hour. Have a nice afternoon.

I tell you he can't get out, said Monica—we'll be crushed. He said everything was OK, I said—he said have a nice afternoon. He didn't understand your French, said Monica. He thought you had come with the bread for lunch. He still doesn't know we are here. We have two alternatives—straight out into the river or abandon ship. I will get the passports and your camera, you fetch the floppy disk of the book and the dog. We'll sit on the bank. And don't forget the money, I said, and the mobile phone. Who will we ring? asked Monica, and what do you say?

The *Camargue* began to tremble and with two smooth chassis steps to the right slipped from the bank on side thrusters and into the stream, going neither forward nor back. Then, foaming from the stern, she gathered forward speed and went under the arch of the bridge at La Voulte-sur-Rhône, where in January her sister had been torn to pieces and swept away, like growing old.

WE SAT DOWN TO LUNCH AND A BARGE CAME by and the *Phyllis May* went up in the air and her sixteen tons came down on a ledge underneath her hull. Jim made for the door and I rugby-tackled him and shut him in his kennel. We can't stay here, said Monica, we'll be knocked full of holes. It says in my notes there is a quay, a high wall, an hour away. It's still early—we might get on it.

The sun beat on the top of the boat and it was like driving an electric iron plugged into the mains.

The quay was much higher than the roof of the boat. Overhead a car with a chap inside having a sit-down. Monica summoned him from his driving seat and he put a rope round a bollard, and another rope round the other bollard. He got back into his car and drove away before Monica could ask him to cut some sandwiches. The waves banged us against the wall. The *Phyllis May* took up all but the last ten feet of the quay.

We're trapped, I said. This is a barge quay–the wall is too high. It's not like Belgium–they had ladders there. Here there is nothing. We must get to Viviers–we can't stop here. Jim has to get out.

But we would have to leave now to get through the last lock before it shuts, said Monica. It's six hours and we are tired already–we'll have an accident–Jim can pee on the front deck, on the *Figaro*. He won't, I said. He'll burst, he's very fussy. I might be able to climb up somehow, said Monica, and we can haul him up on a rope.

A gas barge went by and the boat rose and crashed and re-crashed against the wall and Jim started to cry. A transport barge was coming upstream and seemed to be getting very close. We went to the window and the thousand-ton barge was coming straight for us.

Sometimes you feel there is no point trying to think of something–if Tonbridge rugby team has decided to take off your clothes and cover parts of you with black boot polish there is not much point developing plans of your own. The monster came closer and closer and halfway past and turned and bumped us smartly on the stern with its own stern, like hands knees and bumps-a-daisy. The collision had been more a slap on the bum than a blow. It was much less than when our daughter Georgia hit the bridge at Aston and ran away over the fields yelling I never wanted to come on your bloody boat anyway.

A boy ran down the side of the barge and shouted–We are parking our car, or We are not parking our car, or You are parking our car, or Let's all have a banana. However good your French is you will never understand advice shouted from a boat on the river, particularly when it is fifteen feet high and weighs a thousand tons and seems to have chosen your craft as a sexual partner.

The barge was holding itself six inches away from us and whirring. A little car parked on it near the stern rose into the air like a Harrier jump jet and spun once and dropped on to the quay and the lady in a flowered dress and forties hair, first seen playing the guitar in Armentières, jumped six feet down on to the quay with a shopping basket and drove away.

The barge detached its stern from the *Phyllis May* and headed upstream. I gave a wave and the boy waved and his dad waved from the controls. I think we had better stay here for a bit, I said, and have a cup of tea and a sit-down.

Monica and Jim got up on to the quay before nightfall. Monica proved that she had come from country folk who would climb the highest tree to steal eggs and apples and Jim dangled from a rope in his life jacket as he had never dangled before. I am proud of you both, I said. The waves dropped at dark and the river traffic stopped and we had the quietest night for weeks.

VIVIERS HAS BEEN THERE FOR A LONG TIME, and the streets are very narrow. From the cathedral we looked down on red-tiled roofs and away down the Rhône. We were in the deep Midi now.

Lucy, our eldest, rang at breakfast. Where are you? On the Rhône, down towards Avignon, I said. We are just getting ready to go through the Bollène lock, the second deepest in Europe. I am nervous, and your mother is nervous and we are being nasty to each other and we have made Jim nervous and he's whining. These locks are so big that one false step and you would never be found. Awful things happen on the Rhône. You don't know what has been going on here. We never know what to expect.

You know I just can't understand you, said Lucy. I was talking to Clifford about it and we really don't think it's good enough. I mean Cliff and I and Georgia gave you the best years of our lives. Whenever you needed us we were there. When you wanted advice we gave it, when your friends let you down we would comfort you. If you had bad luck in business or sport we would remind you what mattered was your own integrity, that bit of you inside that you know is good and no one can take away. We didn't ask for anything in return, only your love. And now we are getting old you leave us, you go off and do things against our advice. You don't care what we think any more. People ask Where are you, they have heard you are in trouble, and we say, We don't know, they probably are, they usually are. Grandmothers have evolved over millions of years so they can be backup mothers, and grandfathers so they can put up shelves and build barbecues and give people money. Other grandparents babysit and tile their daughters' bathrooms but all you do is wander around and risk your lives and lavish your affection on a wretched dog that looks like a skeleton and steals things. You sit up drinking with people we don't know, dropouts and expats and bums, and your little grandchildren say Where are Granny and Grandad Why can't they come to the pictures with us or take us to Chester Zoo and we say Last we heard they were being swept away down the bloody Rhône in a boat that was made for two feet of water with a dog that should be under the table in the Star or running around on the common chasing rabbits.

It was Lucy, I said, wishing us luck with the Bollène lock.

• • •

THE RIVER WAS SMOOTH, AND WE THRASHED between chalk and green hills, under bridges, and down the lock cut, the Train à Grande Vitesse overtaking us every half an hour at just under the speed of sound. I've got him, said Monica, waving the VHF, I've got the lock-keeper. I can understand what he is saying. He knows we are coming down the Rhône—he says he is expecting us—*Le narrowboat anglais* Phyllis May *avec ses géraniums.* Isn't that nice?—look, the gates are open, there's no one else, go in.

What is the drop in this lock? I shouted to Monica. Twenty-three metres, she said. Listen, I said, tell him on that VHF thing what Mad Mozza said—click click, let the water out click by click, what's the hurry, and all that. Go on, tell him—click click.

The water began to move down the walls. Down and down we went, bollards groaning, alone, into a void six hundred feet long and thirty-six feet wide and seventy-five feet deep: Gloucester Cathedral, with green and black and yellow walls, mud and weed, armoured gates, water falling down. Two hundred million gallons. It took only ten minutes.

Did you tell him what Mad Mozza said? I shouted—click click? Watch out, shouted Monica, the gate is going up, the light is green—let's get out of here—let's boogie.

SAINT ETIENNE-DES-SORTS IS ONE OF THE VILlages where the Côtes du Rhône Villages wine comes from. It is old and narrow and built along a quay and the Rhône is so wide that you think you are by the sea. All the men wore swimming trunks. As we left Saint Etienne the church rang like Debussy's underwater cathedral.

The August wind was hard against us and you could smell the Sahara. When we entered a lock it was a blessing to fall down the wall into the shade. Out on to the stream again we were chopping through the white horses and the swell and the Rhône was getting broader and broader.

Then we were in a bay kilometres wide and far away a wall where there should be mooring rings. A smudge turned into a big Dutch barge but we saw room behind it and came in against the current, as you should. But the wind and the swell were behind us and it took half an hour to rope up. We lay down, our clothes dark with sweat, Jim panting and pressing hard to the floor, and went to sleep.

Look, said Monica, the wind has changed. The clouds were still moving from the south but now the wind was from the north. The swell was still running upstream but the ripples were running downstream. It started to rain and the Dutchman from the barge came on deck and so did I and we danced around and waved our arms and shouted. It rained hard for ten minutes and there was hail and the air was cooler.

On the towpath fourteen chaps with Fartblasters ranted down and back again, and a chap with a Jet Ski came alongside so that we would know he had a girl on the back, and would be sure to enjoy a night of love, so furious was his exhaust. Two heads floated by—the Dutchman and his wife, who had thrown themselves into the water. An ancient castle on the other bank, far away when we had arrived, was now half a kilometre nearer. By my troth, quoth Lancelot, this is a funny place.

> *Sur le pont d'Avignon*
> *Lonnie Donegan, Lonnie Donegan*
> *Sur le pont d'Avignon*
> *Lonnie Donegan still plays on.*

What rubbish is that? asked Monica. I just made it up, I said. But he's not playing on really—the Rock Island Line came and took him away. We're all waiting at the station, you know.

We won't have to wait very long the way you are steering, said Monica. You've got to get across the path of that barge before it runs us down and go hard left up the Avignon branch and all the signs are reversed because you are going upstream, but you don't understand the signs anyway so it doesn't matter.

Going into Avignon I was pushing against the Rhône for the first time and on our right in the sunlight over the hill a gold Virgin. Half an old bridge and people on it taking pictures. Don't go through the arch, said Monica, there's no depth. See all those big poles?—that was the marina. The French invented aluminium so they made the marina at Avignon out of aluminium. It's not there any more, the Rhône got it. A chap on the stone quay waved and showed us to a space.

We were outside the city walls and to get inside we had to cross a main road and go up Death Alley. To go up Death Alley you hold hands and keep the dog's lead short and do some stretching and some deep breathing and then you rush down the middle of the street, which is five feet wide with three-inch pavements, before the little cars realize you are there and come after you. If they catch you up you have one chance—there is a doorway and you can press into it. They have the same arrangement in train tunnels—I know, I was caught in one as a boy, but it was not as bad as Death Alley. As the cars brushed by they gave us a wave—one sportsman to another.

Steps up to the viewpoint by the cathedral and a gate and a notice—*No dogs.* Jim will wait outside a shop but he is not good at waiting on steps and we could hear him howl as we looked over Avignon, east to the mountains and down at the *Phyllis May* an inch long, holding her parasol like a white postage stamp over the front deck.

On Saturday evening the sun hit the cream walls of the Pope's Palace and shone in our eyes and the square dissolved into black and shadow. Cooler under the trees—the crowds, the tables and chairs, the roundabout horses, the whippet. He's called Nelson, *madame*, said the stallholder. He went grey when he was four. I mean he went white round the muzzle—he's grey anyway. There are not many whippets in France, said Monica. Oh yes, said the stallholder, there are many whippets. We have seen two of them, said Monica. Nelson wagged his tail and Jim looked at him as if he was mad.

When we awoke we were tired and nervous. The Rhône was terrible but at least you knew where it was going. Now we were turning right—across the bottom of south-west France, into Languedoc-Roussillon, leaving Provence on our left. It was the Petit Rhône for a while then a canal that seemed to go straight across the middle of lakes and then an inland sea and then the Canal du Midi. It would be all corners and decisions and hire-boaters and locks and Superdick had said the Canal du Midi was shut so we might have to walk. And there was a mistral for the next few days, said the chap on the next boat. The wind whined and whispered and shook the boat.

The weather had changed—it was twenty-two degrees and we shuddered with cold. I put on my life jacket and a woolly scarf and steered around the old bridge and the *Phyllis May* headed south for Vallabrègues.

• • •

HELLO–DUBOIS? THIS IS YOUR PRESIDENT. THE president of the Compagnie Nationale du Rhône, you fool. Who were you expecting, the President of the Republic?

Look, have you got rid of that damn toy barge yet? Didn't I make it clear? If all the private narrowboats came over from England we would have to find another hundred kilometres of wharf. Getting in the way of our gas barges, wearing out our locks, ruining our economy.

The water—did you let the water out in Vienne as I suggested? All four million tons? And they were still there in the morning? God, they must have steel hawsers. What about the poison gas—he sailed through it? Some sort of English robot with rubber lungs if you ask me. The gas barge? She headed for the bank? Those damn narrowboats only draw two feet and if they head for the bank they get away—it's happened before.

What about the lock-keepers? Always been my favourite—whoosh, whoosh, it's all over. Crane up what's left of the boat, send the divers down, mail home the bits in a plastic bag. What do you mean the lock-keepers say they like the boat, and she speaks French, and there is a dog? A dog? They said they would go on strike? For a woman in a hat, and a bloody dog? When we tamed the Rhône we had real men. All we get these days is pansies and pederasts.

Did you say Superdick? Ah nice one Dubois—I thought he had been put away. Superdick has never failed—the destroyer of worlds. What?—he failed? And he showed them the photos? He must have lost his edge after the electrical treatment. Dubois, if you sent in Superdick no man could do more.

Look, go home to your wife, lovely girl, leave it to me. Give her my regards, by the way. Tell her Hoochie Coochie Prezzie Boots was thinking about her—you're a lucky man, Dubois. And not a word about this business, or I'll make sure she hears about the lady in the flowered dress.

Once they get out on to the Rhône to Sète Canal it's outside my territory. The lads on the Rhône to Sète will help out, of course, but I owe them one already.

Dubois, we have very little time. I know, I'll ring the Air Ministry. I hear that fat oaf Darlington has been disrespectful in bars about our jet pilots. After what I tell them the air force will want to nuke the buggers.

Very soon afterwards four airplanes, fighter-bomber-size, came down the Rhône straight towards the *Phyllis May* on its pontoon at Vallabrègues, in a line, at a hundred and fifty miles an hour, six inches above the water.

Thirteen
THE WINE-DARK SEA

Languedoc-Roussillon

$\mathcal{B}$lue flowers like bells, and yellow stars, between the towpath and the canal. A hot wet wind from the south. No one about. Monica on the tiller and Jim on the towpath with me. The Rhône to Sète Canal is straight like the Gloucester to Sharpness Canal, and broad enough for the transport barges that come through now and then. Fish splashing and twisting near the banks, red and silver. In Paris it's the dancing dead, I thought, and here it's the dancing fish. Monica brought the boat into the bank–Your turn–and joined Jim on the towpath. After five weeks trembling on the rivers, Jim was free. We were at sea level, and would be on brackish water until we entered the Canal du Midi, a hundred kilometres away.

Over the bank a jingling and two curved horns, then the heads of half a dozen black bulls. Now a man's head at twenty miles an hour and there he was on a horse. Then in a gap a herd of white horses. One or two had egrets on their backs. We have had no egrets, I said to Monica. Egrets, she said, I've had a few.

We could see the Tower of Constance a long way ahead. This is a lighthouse standing on top of a castle keep, like a fag end on a tin of beans. It is on the corner of the walled city of Aigues Mortes, which means Dead Waters. Aigues Mortes is a castle but they lost the plans and it ran away and finished up half a kilometre square. They began to fill it with restaurants and gift shops in the thirteenth century and are making good progress. We reached it before lunch and went for a walk inside the walls.

Why is the local wine called sand wine, *madame*? Because it is grown on sand, *monsieur*. We have no *appellations contrôlées* wines, but these are wines of the area. No, *monsieur*, this weather is not normal. We have hot weather here, but not heavy like this with no sun. I tasted the wine—it was thin from the sand and strong from the sun.

WHILE MONICA IS IN THE FOOD SHOP I STAND in the wet wind in the square holding a case of wine and a carton of wine and some shopping bags and Jim and my haversack and I am trying to pull my arm up to eat my ice cream and Jim is pulling it down and crowds of people are pushing by covered in sweat and sand and my T-shirt is soaked and the mosquito bites on my legs and wrists are itching and Jim decides to squat in the square and I put everything down in the road and get out a plastic bag and clear up and then I give him the end of my ice cream and two other dogs come along to try to steal it and the dog lead wraps round my legs and the bags wrap round my arms and the sweat runs into my eyes and I wish I was in Stone and it was freezing and raining and Jim was pulling me into Langtry's and they were serving Timothy Taylor's Landlord's Bitter and Clifford was coming in for a pint and I wish I had never thought of this voyage and I want to go home.

DRINKS ON THE *PHYLLIS MAY* WITH A COUPLE we had met in Namur in Belgium. We wintered here in Aigues Mortes, they said. The weather is nice, windy now and then, but usually warm. There were five English boats— many Dutch, Germans, Swiss; and sixty people would come to a barbecue.

How did you cope with the Rhône? they asked. They threw the lot at us, I said—gas barges, floods, dicks, gales, poison gas—in the end we were attacked by fighter-bombers. We were on the outside pontoon and four of them came at us roaring. They stayed six inches above the water and got nearer and nearer and bigger and bigger and louder and louder. We thought we were done for. Piston-engine planes, looked a bit like lorries—they had square wings. Three of them were yellow and one of them was brown. They were almost on us and we were standing on the pontoon frozen like rabbits. Then one of them touched the river. Then the others did too and there was a lot of spray and a lot of noise and a wake that chucked the pontoon into the air. Then they swept away with a great racket, missing us by six feet.

We realized they were picking up water. We heard later there have been fires round Avignon and the planes dump the water on the flames. We thought they had come for us— you can get like that on the Rhône.

• • •

IT WAS TWENTY-FIVE DEGREES AS WE LEFT Aigues Mortes, and I shivered. Overhead a flamingo, its breast condensing the dawn, its legs trailing, its head forward like a swan, not back like a heron, its neck interminable.

The banks of the Rhône to Sète Canal were sandy, with desert scrub down to the water. We were sailing across the middle of blue lakes. Sometimes the canal was defined by banks and dunes, sometimes by rows of stones. Often currents poured through gaps to the southern waters on our left and down to the Mediterranean. There was a lightness in the air and a smell of salt.

Over the lakes the cream towers of a city–the island-valley of Avillion–

> *Deep-meadowed, happy, fair with orchard*
> *   lawns*
> *And bowery hollows crowned with summer sea*

Further the blue mountains, and the sky, and the clouds more pink than the flamingo. We came on Floridas you won't believe.

Smoke across the cut far ahead and a helicopter the size of a wasp and here come the fighter-bombers to drop their silver blankets and the fire went out and the planes went away with a noise rising in pitch–There you are, there you are, there you are.

AN ENGLISH HACK NARROWBOATER DOES NOT expect rivers to flow straight across canals without an aqueduct or proper written notification, and he is not used to winds that knock you down. When I turned left off the Rhône to Sète Canal towards the seaside town of Palavas-les-Flots the wind and current gripped me under the elbows and hustled me towards the Mediterranean, a kilometre away.

Turn, turn, shouted the captain on the quay as I swept by and I turned across the current so now I was heading for the sea sideways. I rammed the throttle forward and back to avoid the boats on either bank, and tried to turn right round, but each time a boat would come downriver at ten knots and block me. There was a lot of noise and smoke and spray, and crowds of gongoozlers. One chap was selling tickets. My hope was to get the bow caught in one of the wooden quays—if I failed I would finish up in Morocco. This one, *monsieur*, yelled the captain. All right, this one; oh well, this one.

I caught the last quay with the rope fender on the bow and the boat swung round and I beat back to a mooring. The captain, a young chap, shook my hand. I think it was the shared jeopardy.

Palavas-les-Flots is going to be like Blackpool, I said to Monica that evening. Down both sides of the river where I had roared crabwise into town were restaurants and gift shops and lots of people. One side of the river in hot shadow, one in the smouldering sun. We walked along and Jim looked for dropped sandwiches and Monica looked for a restaurant and I looked for a hat with *Kiss Me Again on the Backside* in French but there was none of that and no Palavas rock. There were no drunks. There was a good dinner and a bottle of local wine which was awful but Palavas-les-Flots on the Mediterranean made me think of Blackpool and I loved it.

Next night a wild mooring. Jim and I walked down the sandy path between the canal and the lake. Half the sky was dawn. A flock of flamingos was standing in the lake, all facing the same way. Their breasts were moulded like a globe and were as the wild rose. Some had blood-red on their wings. Most were asleep on one leg with their heads tucked underneath their arms and the rest were foraging under the water.

We walked on and here was a flock with heads, set on waving necks, having a chat—*Wricky wricky wroo, wricky wricky wroo.* Two of them dipped their beaks and raised them in perfect time. Jim followed me down the bank, close behind so the birds could not see him. The flamingos moved further into the lake, *Wricky wricky wroo, wricky wricky wroo.*

PAUL VALÉRY IS BURIED IN SÈTE, SAID MONICA. I didn't realize, I said. I understand his poetry better now— the heat, the light. But he does go on so. It's all life and death and the universe and exclamation marks. I'd rather Théophile Gautier and his white swans or Apollinaire and his crayfish any day. The best thing Valéry did was 'The Cemetery by the Sea'—

> *There is a coolness breathed out by the sea*
> *A salty power gives back my soul to me!*
> *Let's run down to the main, leap out alive!*

And while we are on the topic, I said. No, said Monica, we are not going out on to the Mediterranean in the *Phyllis May*, and that's final. The French have got different rules about going to sea, and we don't know anything about the access, and we haven't done any planning. We planned the Channel for years. We'll finish up in gaol or sunk and never get to Carcassonne. Why do you want to go out on the Med? Just another notch on the bedpost? We never said we were going out on to the Med. We are going to Carcassonne. We get so near and then you throw it all away because you want to boast to your drinking cronies. And you are frightened of the Etang de Thau. You are trying to prove to yourself you are brave and if we are put in gaol or they take the boat off us or we sink you will not have to cross the Etang de Thau. I can read you like a book.

We are on salt water already, I said. And people will say Did you go to Carcassonne and we'll say Yes and they will ask Did you go on the Med and I don't want to say Yes well we did in a way. I want to say Yes next question. But I'll leave it to you, I promise. I would never do anything to upset my Mon.

Before Sète there is a bridge, and it would not open until nine o'clock so we had an hour to wait. To the left, to the south, a broad channel, with a notice saying *No Pleasure Boats*. Monica came along the gunwale. I suppose that's the Med, she said. I turned left. No, she said, you mustn't. Just under the first bridge, I said. Just a look-see, just a reconnoitre— trust me.

It was calm and there was no wind. No craft around, every twenty yards a fisherman, looking at the *Phyllis May* as if he had slipped down a time warp or the Ricard had got him at last.

Under the first bridge the estuary widened, but the water was still calm and I went on. Stop you fool, said Monica, there's a notice—*No Houseboats*. The French call us a house-boat. Just a recce, I said. Monica went down to have a cry with Jim and prepare to abandon ship and I sailed on.

Now we could see the exit to the sea, between a little light-house and a breakwater. Through it a freighter. My heart beat faster—My God, a narrowboat on the Med. Will I, can I actually make it? If the coastguards come out they might take away the *Phyllis May*. Oh dear, what's that? A black boat heading for us fast, and I got that feeling you get when you see the lights of the police car in the mirror.

The boat went by about its business and we sailed on, past the lighthouse and the breakwater and on to Homer's wine-dark sea. It wasn't wine-dark, though, it was silver and smooth with a swell, and the early sun in his glory.

The freighter was heading west. There were fishing boats in the mist over towards the edge of the world. I couldn't see any other narrowboats. I turned and went back past the lighthouse and after a couple of days things were fine with Monica again.

THE ETANG DE THAU IS AN INLAND SEA SEVEN-teen miles long and five miles wide. To get to the Canal du Midi and to Carcassonne you have to sail the length of the Etang, and the idea was scaring me stiff.

First we had to leave the Rhône to Sète Canal and cover a mile to Sète harbour across the corner of the Etang. The sea was fairly calm and very blue. As we came near the harbour entrance two girdered bridges reared up together like man-tises. Nice of them, I thought, we could have passed under-neath, no problem.

There was a Sunday afternoon crowd in Sète and the streets along the river were furnished with stands and two white boats were rowing towards each other to the scream and thump of a bugle band. The crew were in white and at the back of each boat on a tower ten feet high a chap was holding a bargepole and looking determined. The boats passed and the jousters pushed each other with their poles. One fell spreadeagled, pausing before he hit the water.

Sète is a real town with boats on the quay that looked a bit like Fritz's cruiser but many times bigger and had winches on the back and smelt of fish. Tall buildings along the water, restaurants down to the harbour, an old town, leafy squares. A businesslike place—noisy, friendly, untidy, *en fête*.

Monica had some telephoning to do so we went back to the boat. The Canal du Midi is open, she said. There have been repairs which slowed things down but it is fine. I thought so, I said, to hell with Superdick. But, said Monica, there are force four to six gales on the Etang de Thau all week and the bloke I rang at the port said he had no information about when it would calm down. We are stuck and we can't get on to the Canal du Midi and we have to be there in ten days because we promised our friends who are coming to meet us in Carcassonne.

We can't sit here for weeks ringing some fool in the port who won't commit himself about the weather, I said, the waiting would send me bonkers. We'll set the alarm for six o'clock and if there is no wind we'll chance it. If there is wind we'll put the storm deck on and go the next morning. A large marc from the Spider Woman is indicated and an early night. Thank you doctor, said Monica, but it says in the book that the Etang de Thau cannot be crossed in a high wind.

Four o'clock in the morning is the time when people die and although I was not dead I was a long way away, dreaming about something very refreshing which made everything all right. It is painful to be untimely ripped from such a state just because a woman has started to scream.

Look, shrieked Monica, look, look, look, and out of the window I saw a boat, in full flower of flames, coming hard towards us. On the quay opposite another boat on fire. There was shouting and sirens and flashing lights and a fountain rose from the other side of the quay and fell on to the fire ship, driving it nearer to us and it had almost reached us when it went out. It's Hoochie Coochie Prezzie Boots, I said, sending in the fire ships. Do you think you and Jim could finish this trip on your own? asked Monica.

AT SIX O'CLOCK THE WIND WAS ROCKING THE remains of the fire ship and its prey. At eight I rang the man at the port and he said it was entirely up to me if I wanted to cross the Etang–he could not advise, but there were gales four to six and he could not say when they would end or if they would ever end. He's being sensible, said Monica–he would not want to commit himself and put you in danger. Very professional, I said, the prick.

A beautiful woman looked through the window and smiled and waved–I am the *capitaine*, that will be fifty euros. That is my *capitainerie–là-bas au fond.*

You'll make it, said the *capitaine*, in smoke-broken English, taking our money and drinking her coffee and punching in the weather forecast on her computer and arranging a friend's wedding on the phone, all at the same time. It's better in the early morning, but you'll make it if you go now. You crossed the Channel, you'll be all right. No, you don't need your storm deck. But remember it's a sea. It's too big to see the other side. Cross the Etang and follow the oyster beds to the west and then go for the lighthouse. The lighthouse is the entrance to the Canal du Midi. Don't let the wind blow you into the oyster beds, the fishermen don't like it. What horsepower is your engine? Forty-three? That's enough to keep you off. If you get into trouble drop the anchor and give me a ring and I'll come and get you. White, she's insisting on it, cheeky devil, and a tiara, and she wants some of those cheese footballs for the buffet.

As we sailed out of Sète the Etang de Thau was pouring grey waves from the south-east. They raised the bridges again, and I realized it was ten o'clock and that it had been ten o'clock when we had come in the day before.

ON THE TILLER OF THE *PHYLLIS MAY* I WAS treading the line between exhilaration and panic. The wind was strong and the waves were coming from behind, the colour of lead, row on row, and some were white at the crests. There was a noisy breaker over my left shoulder, as if it were chasing us.

The boat drove on, holding steady, not pitching or rolling, and the propeller was staying under, not grinding air and water. The waves were fearful, but the Etang de Thau is shallow, and there was no swell, and unlike the Channel, there were no hidden tides to carry us away.

The first job was to get across to the north side of the sea. A couple of windsurfers came across our course, and one fell off and got back on just in time. I headed for the oyster beds. There were many miles of oyster beds. They were marked by metal stakes in rows, joined by wires—all very tidy, and between the stakes a farmer tended his crop in a pram dinghy, which sprang into the air each time a wave passed.

We sailed along the beds for an hour, sideways so we were not swept into them. I felt in control, my weight forcing the tiller to the right and my arms and body taking the smashes on the rudder. Would we run out of diesel? Monica would never let that happen. Would the sea get up some more? The *capitaine* had looked at the weather forecast and would not have let us go. My God, what is that?—a block of oyster beds reaching half a kilometre out into the middle of the Etang.

They are not on the map but here they jolly well are looking at me and I have to turn left to go round them, and the sea is getting worse.

As I turned left across the wind the back of the boat began to skid to the right and the waves were breaking under her *Crash crash.* There were more white horses now and the sea had gone dark as wine. I wish I hadn't told the *capitaine* we had sailed the Channel. She must be some sort of transatlantic adventure hero and thought we were too. But all we are is a couple of pensioners and a canal boat and a wretched dog.

We are being pushed sideways—we are going into the oyster beds. I felt OK a moment ago, now everything has changed—I don't like being frightened like this. We must get round that corner, we must, or it's into the stakes and turned over and we're done for. All my weight to get the tiller right across, the waves smashing against the left side of the boat and the wind cuffing my shoulder and my face and shouting and hissing and driving us into the beds and our wave following to swallow us up and the counter swinging away under my feet. Jam my arm into the side of the hatch and keep the tiller locked. Just hang on, just hang on.

We missed the corner of the beds by six feet and turned round them and the wind came behind us and the boat settled. My coffee had wandered away over the roof and got stuck under the grab-rail and it was cold.

I COULDN'T DO ANYTHING, SAID MONICA, IT was awful. It was worse than we had ever seen and we were on our own and there was no pilot or anything. It was too rough to go on top with you. When the waves hit us sideways they came up to the windows and I could see the rows and rows for miles all grey and white all coming at us and the wind was howling like a horror film. Jim was marvellous, I mean usually he's a coward. I held on to him on the sofa and he licked my face. I think he knew we would get through—after all he can see into the future, although perhaps he was saying goodbye. Once or twice when it was quieter he would go to the engine-room to see if your legs were still there. I put on my life jacket and Jim's life jacket and on the table I put the floppy disk of the book and the passports and the *Book of Common Prayer.*

The Lord is my Shepherd, I shall not want. He maketh me to lie down in green pastures, he leadeth me beside the still waters. Yea, though I walk through the valley of the shadow of death, I shall fear no evil.

I said the bit about the still waters a lot. Then I prayed. Then after an hour and a half I started looking through the telescope and I could see the lighthouse and we got nearer very slowly and I saw two people surfing with kites and a crowd of yachts and I cuddled Jim and had a cry and I came up on the gunwale and put Jim on the roof and we sailed past the lighthouse into the waters of comfort.

THE CANAL DU MIDI HAD PLANE TREES EVERY ten metres. It was dusty and there were boats rotting and hirers who went as fast as they could. No views, just a tunnel of green—we were still at sea level. The first lock was a famous historical round lock—one of those places that people visit, to see the German hire-boaters, and hear their savage cries.

Agde runs into Cap Agde, which is on the sea and is probably posh, because Agde isn't. Roads you can't cross and squares and little streets with shops selling bracelets and pottery and postcards. We went to the riverfront, which is a row of restaurants. A lady of a certain age stopped us and explained that the fishing boat right there belonged to her family so our only rational course was to buy our dinner from her as it was caught by that very boat. We sat down and put a fleece on the floor for Jim.

As interpreted by this family, bouillabaisse–the dish of the Mediterranean–was dozens of fish of all sorts in a pan, covered with oil and saffron and boiled. With it came thin fish soup, and pieces of stale bread. To add to the soup there were small pieces of even staler bread and a little dish of oily orange *rouille.* There was a dubious bottle of wine. The meal was cheap and the fish was very good.

Under our window multitudinous mullet, the grey scavengers of the estuaries, fought for scraps with the ducks, and as there were only three ducks and the mullet were bigger than the ducks, the mullet came off better. There was a lot of splashing and I feared that the grey ones might leap from the river and seize my dinner off my fork.

On the way back it was dark. I fell behind and heard a guitar ringing like a bell and when I caught up Monica was dancing with Jim in an empty square to 'Johnny B. Goode'. Jim was beginning to get the rhythm, but rather like the albatross, his giant's muscles wouldn't let him dance. I tapped him on the shoulder and excused him and he lay down under a table. The French rock and roll band the Blue Shadows played 'Willie and the Hand Jive' well, though I am not sure they had seen anyone do the hand jive before. And now another number from fifty years ago, said the lead singer.

A lady came down from an apartment and said that she once had a whippet and how it warmed her heart to see a lady dancing with her whippet to the tunes we used to know.

Jim went to sleep under the table, and Monica and I danced on, alone in the shadowy square.

IN THE ARMY, SAID OWEN ON THE PHONE, there are eleven officially recognized types of fucking idiot, and you are eight of them. You ran out of diesel–two hours after crossing the Etang de Thau? Men have died for less. The fuel pipe goes into the bottom of the diesel tank–one bubble of air in that pipe and you stop. And you were out at sea and it was rough and chucking the boat about and there was a wind driving you into the oyster beds. Society would probably not miss you or your thieving hound but it would be a shame about Monica.

Monica has gone along the bank to hang herself, I said. Monica was in charge of the diesel.

Your fuel system is full of air, said Owen, because you are a prat. Now on top of the engine, on your fuel filter, is a small hexagonal nut. Undo that and go down to the left to a little lever on the side of the fuel pump and pump it until air stops coming out where the nut was and diesel starts coming out instead. Then turn the engine over on the starter.

Two hours later Owen rang. I pumped a little lever, I said, for half an hour, but then I found out it is not connected to anything, and my thumb has stopped working and I can't find the fuel pump. It's a miracle you can get your socks on in the morning, said Owen. I will come and help if I have to, but I am two hours away.

Monica and I sat in the saloon and listened to the man from the Citroën garage turn the engine over. He'll run down the battery, I thought, and we are half a mile from a road and on the wrong side of the cut. I have been rocking the lever, said the man from the Citroën garage, but it is not connected to anything and my thumb has stopped working and I can't find the fuel pump. Now I must go and have my lunch. There is no charge.

The Englishman from the hire fleet said This is a lovely engine—we use nothing else. But there is a funny thing about this engine—the little hand lever for the fuel will pump in only one position of the camshaft—come and see. I watched him inch round the big wheel at the front of the engine and work a little lever that I had not seen before. After a dozen tries diesel came out from under the hexagonal nut and he tightened it and turned over the engine for a long time on the starter battery and it fired.

My name is Greg, said the Englishman from the hire fleet. That's my real name. I usually give a false name because some of the English hirers try to get a free holiday and they will write reports about everything you say. The Germans don't do that, or the Swiss. If things go wrong the Germans are quite reasonable and the Swiss say There is no fire on the lake. But in England the papers are full of articles telling people how to cheat the holiday company.

BÉZIERS HAS TWO FAMOUS SONS—ONE IS JEAN Moulin. He was the prefect of Reims, the man who attempted suicide to defy the Germans. He went on to unite and lead the Resistance, but he was betrayed, and murdered by Klaus Barbie. In a clearing in the park a memorial asks you to remember Jean Moulin and the heroes and heroines and the martyrs who fought with him.

The other son of Béziers is Pierre Paul de Riquet, an entrepreneur who decided late in life against informed advice to link the Atlantic with the Mediterranean. He died in 1681, just before the first vessel passed along the Canal du Midi, from Bordeaux to the wine-dark sea. He now stands, green and fifteen feet high, in the main avenue.

Pierre Paul de Riquet would not have been pleased with the port at Béziers. A sunken cruiser, no services, poor access to the city. Béziers looks as if it was important once—now it's dust and muddle and shutters falling off in tall streets.

ONE WHO HAS DROPPED TWENTY-THREE ME-tres in the Bollène lock on the Rhône could be expected to arrive at Fonsérannes with a wry smile. Between all six of them the Fonsérannes locks don't rise fourteen metres. But I was nervous. There would be a queue of hirers and I had no experience of a waterways queue in a foreign land. The French culture does not contain the queue, and Germans are not always at their best in situations involving precedence. Hire-boaters have had only ten minutes' tuition and their plastic trays contain families even unto the fourth generation, united against the world, all with loud voices and boathooks. The locks on the Midi are a funny rounded shape and the lock-keepers fill them too quickly and won't help with the ropes. And the six locks of the Fonsérannes flight were a staircase, and I don't understand staircase locks.

Alien cultures, hostile crowds, machinery, death by water—this could be a bad day.

We got to Fonsérannes early and were the first in line. The sun was shining and Goodness me on the towpath there was Den. Had a bit of a do last night, he said. German beer—need a walk. Here, give me your rope. We went into the first chamber with two German families. Behind us two Englishmen were wrestling on the towpath over their place in the queue.

I would like to explain how the staircase locks of

Fonsérannes work but I really have little idea. We were riding a waterfall upwards, aided by a shutting and opening of gates, and a girl lock-keeper with a loud voice and a hard face. I had not before seen gates open while your lock chamber was filling, or sailed up into a new chamber against a current. The hirers, who had generations of crew to take ropes, and did not have sixty feet and sixteen tons to handle, did well enough. They shouted a lot at each other and sometimes they shouted at me, but I didn't understand them.

Monica threw our ropes up from the bow, and I threw them up from the stern. Den, who seemed to know what was happening, caught the ropes and passed them round a bollard and dropped them back for us to hold. As we crashed and blundered up the cataract I found I could tie a knot halfway along a thirty-foot rope by waving it and shouting, without letting go of the end.

Alongside the Fonsérannes staircase there is an inclined plane that takes you up in a tank on rails so you don't have to go through the locks. Get that inclined plane working again, you lads at the Voies Navigables de France, or you have seen the last of me at Fonsérannes.

UNDER THE TABLE IN THE PIZZERIA AT Colombiers, in the shadow, there was an expression, like Alice's Cheshire cat. But it was not a grin. Whippets can grin, and yawn and doze, but their normal expression is as one betrayed—My last walk was very short and you won't let me kill the cat next door and I am not getting enough attention and I have not had a piece of cheese or a pork scratching for days and it's a bloody disgrace. Such an expression had assembled itself under the table round the stricken eyes of a whippet. A female whippet, the same colour as Jim, slender, beautiful. Jim was pleased to see her, only too pleased, and when the shouting had died it took us five minutes to stand the tables and chairs back where they ought to be.

Here in Languedoc there has always been much wine, said the *patronne*, but it was just *vin de table*. Now we have the *vins de pays*. Monica and I had a pizza and a bottle of red Vin de Pays d'Oc. The pizza had six-inch anchovies, and the wine was like the sound of trumpets.

There are many English here, said the *patronne*–they are always buying houses. You can eat outside in January, February, March. There are storms but they do not last. I love your boat–it is a moment of England. And your Jim, he is a male, he is strong, he is magnificent.

THE CANAL POUND ABOVE THE STAIRCASE WAS fifty-four kilometres long. Through the plane trees vineyards green enough for any salad, and long fields and brown ridges and low chalky cliffs and cypresses and bamboo and palms and red-roofed houses and blue mountains. The start of the Canal du Midi had been dowdy–But Miss Jones, you're beautiful!

Jim and I got off for a walk. The vines came up to the canal. I expected the grapes to be bitter but the black grapes of the Minervois are full of the warm south.

The fortified church at Capestang sailed into view–its clock forty-four metres above the vineyards. The church militant, the church bang on time, the church well able to look after itself thank you, and just see the size of this. The canal drifted along its contour and the church came nearer and we were gaining on it and passed it but watch out here it comes again. The vines turned grey and the plane trees turned black and the fortified church lit up in fury at being left behind and we tied up to some roots and went to sleep.

When I woke I looked out at the trees. My shoulder was stiff from the Etang de Thau and I had drunk deep on beauty and on *vin de pays*. I wanted to be really cold and have a holiday. But how can I have a holiday—I am over-holidayed, overfed, overdrunk, overheated, and over here.

I rolled out of bed and let Jim on to the towpath. Then I went to the gas locker and took out the kit for the pump-out machine. Despite our success with the old hooligan from Leighton Buzzard, we had not tamed the pump-out machine. My nerves had been shaken by the pump-out machine, my brain had been rattled by the pump-out machine. Like the South Goodwin light vessel, it was always with us, waiting its chance. It had held us up for ten days in Belgium because of a crossed thread. It had sent Monica over the side in Watten, hanging from the grab-rail, her little face pathetic, and I had to pull her up by her wrists like a trapeze artiste.

The problem is getting your balance to screw the hose into the gunwale. Unless you have a firm footing the hose keeps trying to pull you into the cut and the threads cross and your wrist goes and you want to break down in tears. So you have to find a firm and level quay just the right height. Such quays are rare and there are usually boats moored already, with crews enjoying the fresh air. Should we stop here, if we go on will we find another quay in time? It took an hour to pump out and usually something went wrong and we had to do it every week and we hated pump-out day.

Here at Capestang we were in the country and the boat had hit bottom a yard from a soft verge so in principle it could not be pumped out. But I had a plan. I laid my equipment on the bank—pump, handle, stout vacuum tube, transparent bit of pipe that lets you see what's going on, long brown outlet hose, kitchen paper, WD-40 spray and first-aid box. Then I pulled out the big one.

I lifted the gangplank off the top of the boat and put one end on the bank and the other on the gunwale. I put one foot on the plank and the other on the gunwale. From this secure footing I leaned down, and with the touch of an eye surgeon screwed the transparent bit into the orifice and the stout hose into the transparent bit.

It all went together first time and I stepped back on to the bank. I pulled on the handle and the pump primed and sent the sewage along the pipe and deep into the cut. I pumped thirty times and stopped before I was tired and walked along to check that all was well on the output side, and then pumped thirty times again. I felt Olympian. I jammed the hose in the cut alongside the boat so it could not leap out and hiss at me and pumped fresh water through the system and washed all the kit and put it back in the gas locker.

Jim had returned, and stood close by me. He had rolled in something left on the towpath by a creature not in the best of health.

Monica woke up. I would have done it with you, she said. I overslept. It was the *vin de pays*. You always said you could never do a pump-out without me. You used to need me but now you're all independent, being a martyr.

Monnie, I said, this was a private defiance, *un défi personnel*. Forgive me darling, but I have learned so much. You would think that success with a pump-out came from screwing everything up and pumping like hell. But if you do that it bites you in the bum. If you screw things tight they jam up like they did in Belgium and if you pump too hard you get tired or die.

It's like business or sport—the principles are just the same.

To prevail in life psychological preparation is required, a winner's attitude, new ideas, a good night's sleep, the right materials, delicacy of touch, rest periods, personal cleanliness, and scrupulous attention to detail.

You should write a book, said Monica, *The Secret of Success—The plane trees rustled and the birds sang and I said to myself Goodness me I am indeed a proper marvel, as I stand here in Languedoc on a bendy platform, pulling on a little handle, pumping shit into the cut.*

THE CANAL DU MIDI HAD SAVED ITS BEST—cathedrals of plane trees more grand than Fradley, aisles thronged with light. Long views over fields and woods to the Pyrenees, rocky cuts hanging with bushes, and always the sun, and the hot wind a torrent pushing us from the south as sideways we pressed to our goal.

Jim walked along the roof and licked my face, and lay down in his bed by the lifebelt and pushed his muzzle straight up and worked his cheeks to pass the air into his nose so he could tell what was going on and what had been going on and what was going to happen next.

What are we going to do when we get there? asked Monica. Why did we want to go to Carcassonne anyway?—I have forgotten. Because it has a nice-sounding name, I said, but I had better ring the port. It would be a shame if there were no room.

The *capitaine* at the port was two ladies, Sylvie and Stéphanie. They've got lovely voices, I said to Monica, very sexy and breathless. Sylvie is coming out to meet us. She's probably fifteen stone, said Monica, and fought with De Gaulle.

We passed through the Saint Jean lock and moored up and

there appeared in the bushes above me lacquered red hair, a pretty face, a halter top, a tailored skirt, legs to stir the raiment of a stone saint, and flip-flops decorated with precious stones. I am Sylvie, your *capitaine*, she said, the *capitaine* of the port of Carcassonne, and she slid down the bank and nearly into the cut.

Sylvie helped us tie the six-foot English flag across the window on the one side, and the French flag on the other side, and the lines of bunting along the roof to the backside.

The wind tugged at the flags and I steered the boat looking through the flapping lines. I put on my Breton sailor's cap, and we pushed slantwise across the wind through the tunnel of planes and the wobbling sun.

I COULD SEE BUILDINGS THROUGH THE TREES, and beyond them walls and towers. It ain't over till it's over, I thought, and sometimes it's not over then, but it's nearly over now. At the lock the queue of hirers parted like the Red Sea and a gamine in jeans came running, and shook all our hands and shook Jim's hand—I am Stéphanie.

We held on tight in the surf and came out into the big basin in the middle of modern Carcassonne and moored in front of the *capitaine*'s cabin. There were little notices taped to posts, saying, *Welcome to Carcassonne, Phyllis May.* It was five to four on 8 September. We were five minutes early.

Sylvie jumped off with a rope and people waved from the quay. There were friends from Stone who had moved to France, and their relations, and friends from Stone who were on holiday, and the couple from the next boat, and a chap who had come to service the showers in the *capitainerie* and one or two gongoozlers.

Monica and I hugged and kissed and we hugged Jim and

one of Monica's lady friends started to cry. A little girl gave Monica some flowers and people took a lot of photographs. We made it, we said—we have been so lucky.

We all went down into the boat and Jim jumped everyone and licked them and brought out the frog of plush and people patted him and asked if he was a good boat dog and why was he so thin and can you really see through him? Monica fetched the pork scratchings she had brought from Stone and Jim sat up and then he lay down and then he lay on his back and waved his legs in the air and then he stood up again—Is there anything in particular you want me to sing? Owen rang and congratulated us and explained he was down the café with Ianto, and Valmai had run off with the car.

Captain Sylvie presented Monica and me each with a canvas briefcase with brochures about Carcassonne and a T-shirt and a child's baseball hat with the device of the city and a blue and red pen shaped like a rocket and a compliments slip from the mayor, offering his devoted and cordial sentiments. Stéphanie ran out and came back with pink plastic soap dishes, shaped like elephants, with the device of Carcassonne in their bellies, and gave one to each of the three little girls in the party.

The corks from Grandfather Gosset's champagne bounced off the ceiling and we talked about Stone and about France and the men got stuck into the beer. On the hi-fi Chet Baker was singing of love. Monica and I showed Cousin Ken's pictures from Dead Man's Wharf with the rotting pier in front and told stories about the Sea Cat and the Rhône and the Etang de Thau. Our visitors went through the galley and the cabin and the engine-room and marvelled at the engine and climbed out on to the pontoon and came in again at the front door.

We used the champagne glasses, and the wine glasses, and

the mustard glasses, and the tankards off their hooks, and got halfway into the china mugs. The bunting flapped at the windows and the sunlight yellowed and faded.

TOMORROW WE'LL GO TO THE MEDIEVAL walled town, said Monica—it's the sort of place you are supposed to visit. But Carcassonne has already given us the marvellous voyage—the green Thames, the Avon full of ink, the great bridges, the light in the sea, the Channel, Paris like a silver bowl, royal Burgundy, even the Rhône, the destroyer. It has given us the Camargue with the lakes and the flamingos, and the vines of the Midi. It has given us adventure, and friends, and some worst of times that were the best of times.

It's like the poem by Cavafy the Greek chap, I said. The one about Ulysses, whom I so closely resemble—

> *Keep Ithaka always in your mind,*
> *Arriving there is what you're destined for.*
> *But don't hurry the journey at all.*
> *Better if it lasts for years,*
> *So you're old by the time you reach the island,*
> *Wealthy with what you've gained on the way,*
> *Not expecting Ithaka to make you rich.*
>
> *Ithaka gave you the marvellous journey.*
> *Without her you wouldn't have set out.*
> *She has nothing left to give you now.*

On the quay Jim was trying to push his entire body inside a bag of pork scratchings. Didn't Ulysses have a dog? asked Monica. Ulysses had a very fine dog, I said, called Argus. Ulysses didn't take him to Troy because Argus was too young. Argus was a hunting dog–hares and deer. He was good, not like Jim–he used to catch things. But when Ulysses came back to Ithaka in disguise after twenty years Argus was lying in a corner covered in fleas because he was old and no one cared about him any more. Argus was the only one to recognize Ulysses. He wagged his tail and said Hello and fawned on Ulysses and dropped dead. I thought that was really respectful–I can't see Jim doing that, eh Jim, our narrow dog to Carcassonne?

Jim stood up. He looked at Monica and he looked at me. He stretched, grinned, and farted.

French in Fifteen Minutes
by Terry Darlington

The only way to learn to speak French is to go somewhere where you have to speak the language or starve and do without sex.

But you can make it through the day with the aid of a simple rule, and eighteen phrases, and two useful tips. Fifteen minutes and you are on the road.

THE SIMPLE RULE

English works the other way round to French. The Englishman has been brought up to feel remorse at being born and causing inconvenience to others, while the Frenchman sees no reason to apologize.

Come and see my new car—the Englishman's voice descends slowly, as if advising of the death of a distant relative. The Frenchman says— *Venez voir ma nouvelle voiture!* landing with a cry on the last syllable, as if he had designed and built his *nouvelle voiture* with his own hands, and had just heard that the state had honoured him for doing so.

Say the word *pullover*, which exists in both languages. The Englishman starts high and falls away, but the Frenchman rises triumphantly—*Pull-o-VAIR*, as if his head were emerging from a tight woollie. So the simple rule is—

English falls, French rises.

Do not be afraid to move your hands and body around with the new rhythm. At times of high excitement your action should be similar to a man standing beneath a tree catching plums.

THE EIGHTEEN PHRASES

Ça, alors—That, then. But stronger—I'm damned. In both languages the speaker places the stress at the wrong end of the sentence, showing to what extent he feels the natural order has been threatened.

C'est déjà quelque chose—That's already something. We would say—That's a good start, but the French is more positive—Something has been accomplished. This is one of the phrases you should use all the time—it moves matters on, doesn't mean very much, and will not cause offence.

C'est magnifique, mais ce n'est pas la guerre—It is magnificent, but it is not war. Purse your lips, look at the object or concept brought to your attention, shake your head, and say *C'est magnifique, mais ce n'est pas . . .* and then add the object, such as *La Tour Eiffel*, or *Johnny Hallyday*.

C'est possible—It is possible (and I will do it for you). In English It is possible means—It is possible (and I will not do it for you).

Chinoiserie—Chinese stuff—messing about. Can be used to defend yourself against French bureaucracy. *Pourquoi cette* *chinoiserie?* But remember the public sector in France is strong, has a literal mind, and believes in its mission.

Comme MacArthur, je reviendrai–Like MacArthur, I shall return. Careful with this one, because MacArthur is pronounced Macca-tour, with the accent heavy on the last syllable, and if you do not accent it strongly enough they will call you back and ask what the hell you are talking about.

Espèce de–Sort of. If you are going to abuse someone in French start with this. It gives you a moment to choose your words and warns the other party that you are about to become offensive, so the proper dignities can be observed. The normal term of abuse is *Espèce d'idiot*, but *Espèce d'imbécile* is also widely applicable.

Il exagère–He exaggerates. Lean strongly on the last syllable and draw it out and the sense comes through–he is overdoing it and what is more he is a prat.

Impeccable–the nearest we have in English is the obsolete 'first-rate'. Just say *Impeccable, impeccable*, quietly every five seconds, and smile, with a few simple gestures. The land and all that is in it will be yours.

Je vous en prie–I beg you to. You're welcome–but softer, more polite. We have a near translation in English, but only for men–My dear chap. The French say *Je vous en prie* all the time. You can use it continuously, alternating with *impeccable*.

Merci–Thank you. As a boy in Lille I did not realize that it also means No thank you, and nearly starved in the midst of plenty.

Messieurs 'dames–Ladies and gentlemen. When entering a room say this and then shake the hand of everyone in sight. Also when leaving. It is not always possible to observe the letter of this convention, for example in a crowded super-market, but you must do your best.

Narrowboat anglais avalant–English narrowboat coming downstream. Useful if you find yourself in a narrowboat on a big river and have a VHF radio and want to say something into it. Upstream is *montant*, or perhaps it is the other way round.

Où sont les neiges d'antan?–Where are the snows of yester-year? The most beautiful line in French poetry. In conversa-tion you can replace *neiges* with *voitures*, or *chanteurs* or anything you like really. Unlike the British, the French know their poetry. If you can quote it they will react strongly in your favour, offering you hospitality or in extreme cases al-lowing you to sleep with their daughters.

Quand vous serez bien vieille, le soir, à la chandelle–When you are old, by evening candlelight. The second most beauti-ful line in French poetry. In 1975 I took a team of runners in relay from the Eiffel Tower back to Stone, and we had a drink in my favourite Paris bar, run by the beautiful Monique. Mick Powell, our best runner, said this to Monique and she asked him into the room behind the bar, where she gave him a surprise.

Un petit vin de la région–A modest wine from round here. On a research job in France I was keen to impress my beau-tiful assistant, and casually used this phrase. *Mais monsieur,* replied the waiter–*nous sommes à Calais–il n'y a pas de vins de la région*–so please note they don't make wine round Calais.

Vous n'avez pas de ... ?–You haven't got ... ? *Vous n'avez pas de moules frites? Vous n'avez pas de carte postale de Johnny Hallyday?* Say this and the French will rise to their feet, *Mais si, monsieur!* and rush to the kitchen or the postcard rack to show that you have misjudged them.

THE TWO USEFUL TIPS

When you set out to try your luck never start speaking with an English phrase in your head. If you are stuck say *Impeccable, impeccable, je vous en prie, je vous en prie,* and twist your hands nervously from the wrists. The French will offer a phrase to start you off and then you are away.

If you want to be understood the vowel sounds are very important, and so is the rhythm of course, but don't feel you have to pronounce every consonant. A confident French person will slur and soften the consonants and talk in a deep tone, as if in the last stages of sexual exhaustion.

Quotations, References, Echoes

Most of the sources below stayed in the memory because they gave pleasure. A reader with nothing worthwhile to do could seek entertainment by matching them to the text. –T.D.

Epigraph
Waugh, *Brideshead Revisited*

Chapter One: Moon River–Stone to Westminster
Warner, "Speedy Gonzales" • Croce, "Bad, Bad Leroy Brown" • Williams, "Bony Moronie" • Tennyson, "Ulysses" • Eliot, "The Waste Land" • Mancini, "Moon River" • Melville, *Moby-Dick* • Unknown, "The Wanderer" • Merill/Larue, "Ma Petite Folie" • St Luke, Ch. 2 • Kennel Club, *Whippet Breed Standard* • Pope, *The Dunciad* • TV series, *The Lone Ranger* • St Matthew, Ch. 6 • Hopkins, "Pied Beauty" • II Samuel, Ch. 1 • Ziegler, Nixon government statement • De Nerval, "El Desdichado" • Tennyson, *Idylls of the King* • Malory, *Morte d'Arthur* • Shakespeare, *Henry IV* • Sir Hugh Fish, conservationist • General Mills, Jolly Green

Giant • Shakespeare, *The Tempest* • Traditional, "What Shall We Do with the Drunken Sailor" • Unknown, *Beowulf*

Chapter Two: The Flies, the Flies–The Thames to the Severn

Spenser, "Prothalamion" • Philippians, Ch. 4 • Yeats, "Long-legged Fly" • Kipling, "If" • Marvell, "The Garden" • Shakespeare, *Julius Caesar* • Pott, "The Strife Is O'er" • Fitzgerald, *The Rubáiyát of Omar Khayyám* • Capehart/ Cochran, "Summertime Blues" • Shakespeare, *Hamlet, Macbeth* • Arnold, "A Closer Walk with Thee" • Elizabeth Barrett Browning, *Sonnets from the Portuguese, No. 43* • Shakespeare, *Hamlet* • Wordsworth, "Resolution and Independence" • Shelley, "Ozymandias" • Eliot, "The Waste Land" • Gloucester Harbour Trustees, *Small Boat Passage of the Severn Estuary* • Newman, "Praise to the Holiest" • Tennyson, *Idylls of the King,* "Crossing the Bar", *In Memoriam A.H.H.* • Roddenberry, *Star Trek* • Shakespeare, *A Midsummer Night's Dream* • Pott, "The Strife Is O'er" • Keats, "Ode on a Grecian Urn" • Tennyson, *Idylls of the King* • Flecker, *The Golden Journey to Samarkand* • Thorpe, letter to Norman Scott

Chapter Three: Dead Man's Wharf–Stone to Southwark

Chaucer, *The Canterbury Tales* • Ransom, *The Archaeology of Canals* • Newman, "Praise to the Holiest" • Ideal World, *Help at Home* catalogue • Cohen, "First We Take Manhattan" • Spenser, *The Faerie Queen* • Kipling, "If" • Eliot, "The Waste Land" • Conan Doyle, *The Sign of Four* • Bolton, *Race Against Time* • Howard, *Slipstream* • Drabble, *Angus Wilson* • Duke of Edinburgh, state visit to China • Yeats, "Long-legged Fly" • Chaucer, *The Canterbury Tales*

Chapter Four: The Sea Cat–England to France
Maupassant, "Le Horla" • Tennyson, *Idylls of the King* •
Bosquet, on the Charge of the Light Brigade • Milton,
Comus • The *Sun*, headline • Tennyson, *The Princess* •
Newman, "Lead, Kindly Light" • Hawkins, Elizabethan
naval commander/star of film *The Cruel Sea* • Forrester, *Mr
Midshipman Hornblower* • Bader, Cunningham, WWII fighter
aces • Bannister, first mile under 4 minutes, 1954 •
Moorcroft, 6 seconds off 5000-metre record, 1982 • TV se-
ries, *The Lone Ranger* • Jagger, Richards, "Jumpin' Jack
Flash" • Keats, "On First Looking into Chapman's
Homer" • Football song, "Here We Go" • Ferry disaster,
1987, 194 passengers drowned • McCullers, *The Ballad of the
Sad Café* • Trenet, "La Mer" • Berlin, "Blue Skies" • Paul,
"Plaisir d'Amour" • Thomas, "When, Like a Running
Grave"

**Chapter Five: Mindful of Honour–Calais to
Armentières**
Wordsworth, "I Wandered Lonely as a Cloud" • Auden,
"The Shield of Achilles" • Cain, *The Young Guns* • Scott, *Top
Gun* • St John, Ch. 1 • Friedman, book title • Siegal and
Shuster, *Superman* • Curtiz, *Casablanca* • Churchill, speech,
10.11.42 • Curtiz, *Casablanca* • Hart, *History of the Second
World War* • Guderian, *Panzer Leader* • De Nerval, "El
Desdichado" • De Gaulle, speech, 18.06.40 • Delaplace,
*Activités Aériennes dans le Ciel de Watten et Eperlecques
1939–45* • Town of Braydunes, French Infantry Memorial •
Dufay, *La Vie dans l'Audomarois sous l'Occupation* • Aragon,
"Ballade de celui qui chanta dans les supplices" • Larkin,
"Cut Grass" • Rowland/Carlton, "Mademoiselle from
Armenteers"

Chapter Six: The Dark Tower–Courtrai to Waulsort

Unknown, "The Wanderer" • Frost, "Tree at My Window" • Milton, *Comus* • Williams, *Hughie Long* • Browning, "Childe Roland to the Dark Tower Came" • Wells, *The War of the Worlds* • Archimedes, *Synagoge* • Pope, *The Dunciad* • Tennyson, *The Princess* • *Daily/Sunday Sport*, front page • Spenser, *The Faerie Queen* • Internal Audit Service, the European Union, report, April 2003 • Yeats, "The Lake Isle of Innisfree" • Lamartine, "La Vigne et la Maison"

Chapter Seven: The Drunken Boat–Charleville-Mézières to Paris

Rimbaud, "Le Bateau Ivre" • Hopper, *Nighthawks* • Moustaki/Monnot, "Milord" • Campbell, "Prince Harry Hotspur" • Simenon, *Le Charretier de la Providence* • Du Maurier, *The Birds* • Unknown, "The Wanderer" • Milton, *Paradise Lost* • Marlowe, *Doctor Faustus* • Arnold, "The Scholar-Gypsy" • Rimbaud, "Faim" • Westworld, "Sonic Boom Boy" • Brooke, "The Old Vicarage, Grantchester" • Rimbaud, "Le Bateau Ivre" • Shakespeare, *Macbeth* • Gibbon, *Memoirs of My Life* • Fitzgerald, *The Rubáiyát of Omar Khayyám* • Chandler, *Farewell My Lovely* • Verlaine, "Mon Rêve Familier" • Shakespeare, sonnet • Berger, translation of traditional fado • Baudelaire, "L'Albatros" • Spenser, *The Faerie Queen* • Rimbaud, "Le Bateau Ivre"

Chapter Eight: A Silver Bowl–Paris and the Seine

Prévert, "Je Suis Comme Je Suis" • Wordsworth, "Lines Written on Westminster Bridge" • Carné, *Hotêl du Nord* • Nation, *Doctor Who* • Apollinaire, "Le Bestiaire" • Apollinaire, "Le Dromadaire" • Sartre, *Les Chemins de la Liberté* • Herrick, "Delight in Disorder" • Waugh, *Scoop* •

Bosquet, on the Charge of the Light Brigade • Unknown, *Beowulf* • Porter, "At Long Last Love" • Fleming/Hamilton, *Goldfinger* • Milne, "Vespers" • Bosquet, on the Charge of the Light Brigade • Tennyson, *Idylls of the King*, "The Lady of Shalott"

Chapter Nine: Jack the Disemboweller–The River Yonne

Charles d'Orléans, "Rondeau" • Watkins, *The War Game* • Fitzgerald/Nugent, *The Great Gatsby* • Petit, *Le Sennonais Libéré*, 23.04.04 • Marvell, "To His Coy Mistress" • Cornwell, *Jack l'Eventreur* (trans. Jean Esch) • Keats, "Ode to a Nightingale" • Norbert Dentressangle, road haulier • Wheatley/Fisher, *The Devil Rides Out*

Chapter Ten: Their Several Greens–The Burgundy Canal

Calilli, Lookofsky, Sansone, "Walk Away Renée" • Shakespeare, *Hamlet* • Simon, *Fluvial* magazine, April 2004 • Anka, "My Way" • Shakespeare, *Macbeth* • Wallace, O'Hogan, "Old Father Thames" • Redford, *Quiz Show* • Frakes, *Star Trek: First Contact* • Carné, *Le Jour Se Lève* • Cocteau, *Orphée* • Chabrol, *Les Cousins* • Jammes, "Prière pour aller au paradis avec les ânes" • Boorman, *Deliverance* • Wynette, "D.I.V.O.R.C.E." • Berger, letter to T.D. • Marlowe, *Doctor Faustus* • Tennyson, *Idylls of the King* • Milton, *Comus* • Rimbaud, "Le Bateau Ivre" • Townshend, "Pinball Wizard"

Chapter Eleven: Battles in the Clouds–The Saône

Marlowe, *Doctor Faustus* • Cornford, "The Coast, Norfolk" • Gautier, "Symphonie en Blanc Majeur" • Charles d'Orléans, "Rondeau" • Pompadour, saying • Wordsworth, inside of

King's College Chapel, Cambridge • Mancini, "Moon River" • Marshall, "Rose Garden" • Cohn, "Je Trahirai Demain" (attributed) • Morgan, *An Uncertain Hour*

Chapter Twelve: The Destroyer of Worlds–The Rhône

Bagehot, *The English Constitution* • Stevenson, *Dr Jekyll and Mr Hyde* • Maupassant, "Le Horla" • Milton, *Comus* • Croft and Perry, *Dad's Army* • St Matthew, Ch. 6 • Oppenheimer, on atomic bomb • Berlin, "Let's Face the Music and Dance" • Debussy, Prélude No. 10 • Malory, *Morte d'Arthur* • Anon, "Sur le Pont d'Avignon" • Oppenheimer, on atomic bomb

Chapter Thirteen: The Wine-dark Sea–Languedoc-Roussillon

Dumont/Vaucaire, "Je Ne Regrette Rien" • Anka, "My Way" • Tennyson, *Idylls of the King* • Rimbaud, "Le Bateau Ivre" • Valéry, "Le Cimetière Marin" • Homer, *The Odyssey* • Shakespeare, *Macbeth* • *Book of Common Prayer*, Psalm 23 • Berry, "Johnny B. Goode" • Otis, "Willie and the Hand Jive" • Weintraub, *Peel Me a Grape* • Smith, description of heaven • Keats, "Ode to a Nightingale" • Trinder, comment on American GIs (attributed) • Blackwell/Hammer, "Great Balls of Fire" • Yogi Berra, comment on National League pennant race • Dickens, *A Tale of Two Cities* • Cavafy, "Ithaka" • Homer, *The Odyssey*

Permissions

Extracts from *The Kennel Club Whippet Breed Standard* used by kind permission of The Kennel Club.

Extract from "If" from *The Definitive Edition of Rudyard Kipling's Verse* published by A. P. Watt Limited, used by kind permission of A. P. Watt Limited on behalf of The National Trust for Places of Historic Interest or Natural Beauty.

Extract from *Safety Guidance for Small Boat Passage of the Severn Estuary* used by kind permission of Gloucester Harbour Trustees.

Extract from *1940–1944, la Vie dans l'Audomarois sous l'Occupation* by Raymond Dufay, published by l'Imprimerie de l'Indépendant in 1990 and translated by Terry Darlington, used by kind permission of Mme. Dufay.

Extract from "Ballade de celui qui chanta dans les supplices" from *La Diane Française* by Louis Aragon, published by Éditions Seghers in 1945 and translated by Terry Darlington,

About the Author

Following the publication of *Narrow Dog to Carcassonne*, Terry Darlington, his wife, Monica, and their whippet Jim planned to sail the *Phyllis May* down the Intracoastal Waterway from Virginia to Florida–an adventure which, should they survive it, will be the subject of their next book, *Narrow Dog to Indian River*, coming from Delta in 2009.

For news on their travels, visit their website at www.narrowdog.com.